WITHDRAWN

Stafford Library
Columbia College
1001 Rogers Street
Columbia, Missouri 65216

Judgment and Justification in the Nineteenth-Century Novel of Adultery

**Recent Titles in
Contributions to the Study of World Literature**

Camelot in the Nineteenth Century: Arthurian Characters in the Poems of Tennyson, Arnold, Morris, and Swinburne
Laura Cooner Lambdin and Robert Thomas Lambdin

Writing the Body in D.H. Lawrence: Essays on Language, Representation, and Sexuality
Paul Poplawski, editor

Postcolonial and Queer Theories: Intersections and Essays
John C. Hawley, editor

The Novels of Samuel Selvon: A Critical Study
Roydon Salick

Essays on the Fiction of A.S. Byatt: Imagining the Real
Alexa Alfer and Michael J. Noble, editors

Victorian Writers and the Image of Empire: The Rose-Colored Vision
Laurence Kitzan

Immigrant Narratives in Contemporary France
Susan Ireland and Patrice J. Proulx, editors

Aristocracies of Fiction: The Idea of Aristocracy in Late-Nineteenth-Century and Early Twentieth-Century Literary Culture
Len Platt

Salman Rushdie's Postcolonial Metaphors: Migration, Translation, Hybridity, Blasphemy, and Globalization
Jaina C. Sanga

Imagining Africa: Landscape in H. Rider Haggard's African Romances
Lindy Stiebel

Seduction and Death in Muriel Spark's Fiction
Fotini E. Apostolou

Unorthodox Views: Reflections on Reality, Truth, and Meaning in Current Social, Cultural, and Critical Discourse
James L. Battersby

Judgment and Justification in the Nineteenth-Century Novel of Adultery

Maria R. Rippon

Contributions to the Study of World Literature, Number 112

Greenwood Press
Westport, Connecticut • London

Library of Congress Cataloging-in-Publication Data

Rippon, Maria R.
    Judgment and justification in the nineteenth-century novel of adultery / Maria R. Rippon.
       p. cm.—(Contributions to the study of world literature, ISSN 0738–9345 ; no. 112)
    Includes bibliographical references and index.
    ISBN 0–313–32164–7 (alk. paper)
    1. Fiction—19th century—History and criticism. 2. Adultery in literature.
I. Title. II. Series.
PN3352.A38R56 2002
809.3′9353—dc21   2001050129

British Library Cataloguing in Publication Data is available.

Copyright © 2002 by Maria R. Rippon

All rights reserved. No portion of this book may be reproduced, by any process or technique, without the express written consent of the publisher.

Library of Congress Catalog Card Number: 2001050129
ISBN: 0–313–32164–7
ISSN: 0738–9345

First published in 2002

Greenwood Press, 88 Post Road West, Westport, CT 06881
An imprint of Greenwood Publishing Group, Inc.
www.greenwood.com

Printed in the United States of America

∞

The paper used in this book complies with the Permanent Paper Standard issued by the National Information Standards Organization (Z39.48–1984).

10 9 8 7 6 5 4 3 2 1

Copyright Acknowledgments

The author and publisher gratefully acknowledge permission for use of the following material:

Excerpts from *Anna Karenin* by Tolstoy, translated by Rosemary Edmonds (Penguin Classics, 1954) copyright © Rosemary Edmonds, 1954. Reproduced by permission of Penguin Books Ltd.

Excerpts from *Effi Briest* by Theodor Fontaine, translated by Douglas Parmeé (Penguin Classics, 1967) copyright © Douglas Parmeé, 1967. Reproduced by permission of Penguin Books Ltd.

For Brett, a truly ideal husband

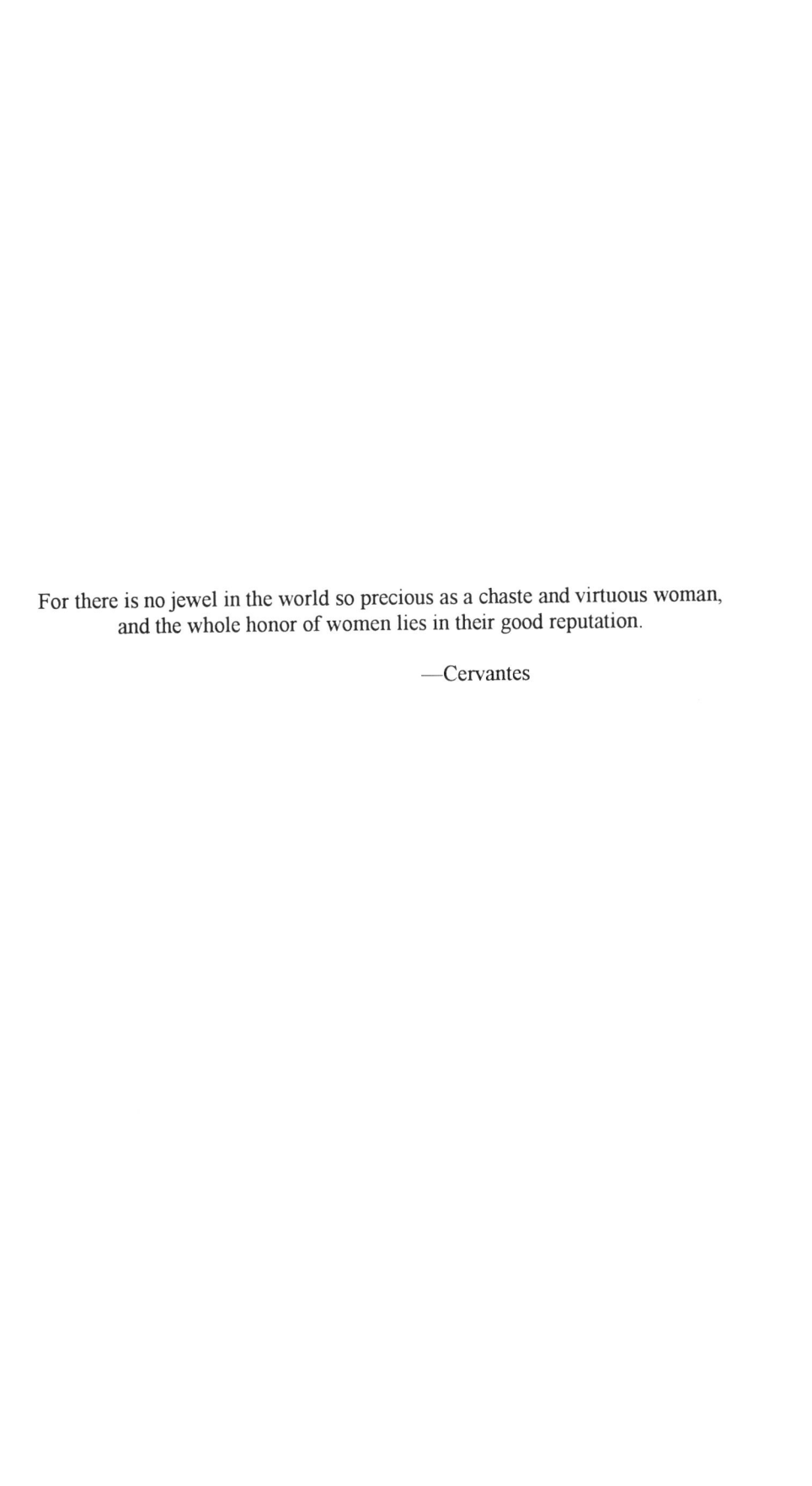

For there is no jewel in the world so precious as a chaste and virtuous woman, and the whole honor of women lies in their good reputation.

—Cervantes

Contents

Introduction	xi
1 Rite of Initiation	1
2 Stained-Glass Windows	21
3 Tower of Babel	57
4 Judgment Day	81
Conclusion	131
Bibliography	137
Index	143

Introduction

Marriage has been a frequent topic of literature. As a social institution, its roots are entangled with the mystery of society itself. It is the conventional conclusion to comedies, and it continues to be the dream and purpose of many fictional and not so fictional young women of the common era. Its breakdown—that is, adultery—became topical in realist novels of the nineteenth century, though certainly, adultery is as old as marriage itself. The tales of Tristan and Isolte and Lancelot and Guinevere are powerful icons of passionate love with no counterpart in a happily married couple. Indeed, the "classic" love triangle "is a figure at once tense and indispensable: it calls for a resolution that the skilled storyteller first withholds and at length grants."[1] Tony Tanner in his *Adultery in the Novel* asserts, for instance, "Adultery as a phenomenon is in evidence from the earliest times . . . and indeed we might suggest that it is the unstable triangularity of adultery rather than the static symmetry of marriage, that is the generative form of Western literature as we know it" (12). Happiness, death, the "perfect union" are all "nonnarratable," as far as D. A. Miller is concerned, by which he means that they cannot generate a story (5), or, to paraphrase Tolstoy, all happy marriages are alike; unhappy marriages are unhappy each in its own way. The instability of an unhappy marriage and an affair, what Gay calls "the unstable triangularity of adultery," is precisely the narratable material of the nineteenth-century novel of adultery. In the following pages we see how Flaubert, Queirós, Tolstoy, Clarín, Fontane, and Chopin resolve and bring to closure, return to a state of "nonnarratable quiescence," the "narratable disequilibrium"[2] of the classic love triangle, which in some cases has become rectangular. Love is often cherished by readers and authors alike, but adulterous love, from a societal viewpoint, must always be punished since it threatens the very institutions upon which society functions and grows. Very often, the conflict arises in these novels between wives who crave novelty, excitement, and undying passion and husbands who live by the code of conduct prescribed by their societies to the detriment of their seemingly happy marriages.

The earliest composition is Flaubert's *Madame Bovary* (1857); the latest, Chopin's *The Awakening* (1899). Although the female protagonists in the novel of adultery move in very different social circles as a result of their differing social strata, they share common limitations: education, marriage, and frustrated desire. Women in the nineteenth century had few life options: they could marry, enter a convent, remain a dependent on the family for life, or, in extremely rare cases, pursue an ignoble career in the arts—the option with the greatest freedom, though the least respect and protection, marginalized as they were from society proper. Marriage offered the most reputable social status, was often a welcome escape from an unbearable home situation, and offered women protection in exchange for their obedience. Fontane's Effi Briest is alone in her idyllic home life at Hohen-Cremmen, but then she is also the most youthful and childlike and marries prematurely, as her parents surmise in the end. She craves a different kind of freedom, like Edna Pontellier, who wants to be free to be herself—in Effi's case, to be a child of Nature.

In addition to gender, a woman's opportunities were further limited by class and geography. Middle-class women, for example, would not have had the financial resources or societal connections to prepare for, and sustain themselves in, the cosmopolitan life of coming-out balls and soirees. Their chances, thus, of meeting and marrying a gentleman and thereby raising their status would have been slight. Luísa of Queirós' *O primo Basílio* and Emma Bovary of Flaubert's *Madame Bovary* are bourgeois—a term that in the nineteenth century came to be used interchangeably with the middle class[3]—whereas Ana Ozores in Clarín's *La Regenta*, Anna Karenin[4] in Tolstoy's *Anna Karenin*, Effi Briest of Fontane's eponymous novel, and Edna Pontellier in Chopin's *The Awakening* are all of the upper classes. Regardless of the adulteress' class, Friedrich Nietzsche's theory of *ressentiment* ethics and the subsequent work of philosophers and sociologists such as Max Scheler, Sven Ranulf, and Maria Ossowska account for many of the judgments made by the secondary characters in these novels.

Friedrich Nietzsche, as he began to explore the origins of society's moral judgments of good and evil, developed an ethics that he associated with the bourgeoisie and that he labeled "*ressentiment* ethics." Nietzsche equates this moral system with "slave morality," which he describes as the inverted evaluation of the good for the species, promulgated by the weak at the expense of the strong in order to weaken the latter. He writes is his *Genealogy of Morals* (1887), "Whereas all noble morality grows out of oneself, slave morality immediately says No to what comes from outside, to what is different to what is not oneself" (section 10). Thus, our adulteresses suffer the *ressentiment* of their societies since they are envied and subsequently punished for their differences, for their failure to abide by the codes of the herd, of society proper. Typically, *ressentiment* ethics can be found among the bourgeois class since the morality, as Nietzsche describes it, is "the instinct of the mediocre against the exceptional,"[5] and yet even our aristocratic adulteresses feel the sting of *ressentiment* from other aristocrats since these latter envy their seemingly natural nobility. The middle class is neither exceptionally rich nor exceptionally poor; it is *mediocre* in the true sense of the word and is ever anxious to distance itself from the prole-

Introduction

tariat and emulate the wealthy, though outwardly professing disdain for the latter's way of life precisely because it is unattainable.

This herd instinct really exists at all levels; each class forms its own herd, and all of humanity becomes a herd for the moralities of religion, science, and philosophy. Every herd defends itself "on both sides, against those who have degenerated from it (criminals, etc.) and those who tower above it."[6] Anna Karenin and Ana Ozores, in particular, bear the brunt of their society's *ressentiment*, both for "towering above" their respective societies by refusing to associate with society proper and then for "degenerating from" society's code of conduct by either openly flaunting the adultery (Anna Karenin) or allowing the affair to become known and cause the death of one's husband (Ana Ozores). Ironically, with the upper classes, the deviating from the herd comes not with the act of infidelity and deception but with the adulteresses' refusal or inability to keep that act a secret. Edna Pontellier, also of the upper class, is defiant in her rejection of her husband's bounty but not so open about her love for Robert Lebrun or her indiscretions with Arobin. She flaunts certain conventions but not all.

Max Scheler, in his phenomenological approach to ethics, builds upon Nietzsche's formulation of *ressentiment* ethics, but whereas Nietzsche saw such an ethic behind Christian *and* bourgeois moralities, Scheler defends the Christian and isolates the phenomenon of *ressentiment* ethics to the bourgeois morality. In his *Ressentiment* Scheler notes that feelings of impotence are naturally to be found in women since they are the weaker sex and must compete with one another for men's favor based upon physical qualities that they are powerless to alter (61). According to Scheler, *ressentiment* explains the "strong feminine tendency to indulge in detractive gossip"; it is a woman's only way to vent her anger, hatred, and/or envy of a more superior specimen. In the novel of adultery both men and women, clergy and laity engage in gossiping and murmuring about "the affairs" of deviants. This tendency to gossip is particularly pronounced in the provincial European novels, such as *Madame Bovary*, *La Regenta*, and *O primo Basílio*.

Scheler also briefly touches upon the *ressentiment* of priests in the aforementioned work, which has some bearing on our discussion here. Priests, according to Scheler, must present the appearance of peace and harmony at all times, even though they are far from experiencing the same, and so they are even more impotent than a woman to exact revenge or vent anger, hatred, or envy since they must be above such emotions and represent "the image and principle of 'peacefulness'" (66). Don Fermín in Clarín's[7] *La Regenta* is emblematic of Scheler's description here. Fermín feels love for Ana and envy toward Don Álvaro, yet he is powerless to avenge himself since he must portray the image of control and peacefulness to his flock. He cannot exact the revenge that he so desires for what he perceives to be Ana's betrayal and for Don Álvaro's seduction of her except by proxy, by inducing Don Víctor, who feels no hatred or anger, to avenge himself on Don Álvaro. Later, Don Fermín is able to express his *ressentiment* and wreak his own revenge on Ana by exercising the only power that he has as a priest: by refusing to pardon her and take her back into the fold after she has strayed.

Svend Ranulf, a Swedish sociologist of the twentieth century, continues to explain bourgeois morality as a manifestation of *ressentiment* ethics in action, as did Nietzsche and Scheler before him. In his *Moral Indignation and Middle Class Psychology* (1964), he identifies a correlation between the level of what he calls the "moral indignation" of a society, which he describes as a rather pronounced disposition to punish, and the strength of the middle class. He decides that behind the apparent disinterested desire to punish among the middle classes is really envy of the greater liberty afforded the upper classes by their wealth. Since the bourgeoisie was forced to exercise self-control in order to escape the poorhouse, it made self-control a virtue and its opposite, the spendthrift, self-indulgent behavior of the upper classes, a vice. Thus, the economic limitations of the lower middle class made thriftiness and utilitarianism virtues out of necessity. The bourgeoisie was more concerned than the laboring class with appearances and often cherished the hope of joining the upper classes by carefully saving and amassing wealth, while the working classes were too far removed from the top to develop a reactionary ethics. The proletariat would more likely take their cue from the lower middle classes; however, the agricultural laboring class seems to have had a slightly more lax moral standard than the industrial since in its isolation it enjoyed more freedom from prying eyes and often resorted to common-law marriages.

Ranulf identifies some of the predominant virtues and vices of the bourgeoisie, throughout time and across religious and national boundaries: "Practical and calculating circumspection, prudence, order, economy, regularity of work—these are the bourgeois virtues. . . . The most degrading vices are those which cause disturbance in the world of business and in the enjoyment of vested property: improbity, theft, fraud, and abuse of confidence" (23). If we recall that wives were considered the property of their husbands in the nineteenth century, with no civil rights of their own, we will see that adultery was really a "disturbance . . . in the enjoyment of [the] vested property" of the husband through an "abuse of confidence." Because the bourgeoisie was so pragmatic (spiritless, some might say), it could not understand a longing for passion and love since love has no value in a utilitarian society where value is placed not on what something or someone is but rather what that something or someone can *do*.

Although more limited in scope, Ossowska makes use of Ranulf's research and concurs that the bourgeois morality in the mid-nineteenth to mid-twentieth centuries was, indeed, an example of *ressentiment* ethics: "[T]ypical of bourgeois morality . . . is the tendency toward keeping a malicious eye on what other people are doing, a tendency to be shocked or scandalized by their behavior, even when this in no way impinges upon the interest of those who resent it" (215). Hence, the bourgeoisie tended to become indignant over behavior that in no way affected it. It is "disinterested" in that its interests are not altered by the deviant behavior it seeks to punish, but it is nevertheless upset by anyone who acts in a manner different from that of the herd, and the moral indignation increases in proportion to the herd's desire to be doing the same activity as the deviant. Such moral indignation is expressed in the nineteenth-century novel of adultery in the rejection of the adulteresses after the exposure of their affairs—

Introduction

they literally cannot be received by society proper—and in the murmuring of the townspeople. In *La Regenta*, moral indignation culminates in the figure of the *magistral*, who can barely contain an impulse to assassinate the repentant sinner.

Before delving into the novels any further, we must first establish our terminology. It is particularly important with these nineteenth-century novels of adultery that we distinguish who *sees* from who *tells*, else we find ourselves equating the judgments of the narrator with those of the adulteress, which is not at all accurate. The narrators in these novels often see either *with* their female protagonists (with their eyes) or *into* their heads, and yet their judgments remain distinct from those of most all the characters, including the protagonists. I am indebted to Dorrit Cohn's *Transparent Minds: Narrative Modes for Presenting Consciousness in Fiction* (1978), wherein she proposes three possible modes of narration: psychonarration, quoted monologue, and narrated monologue, and Gerard Genette for his *Narrative Discourse: An Essay in Method* (1980), wherein he introduces his concept of focalization and furnishes narratologists with a common language.

Dorrit Cohn analyzes narrators' distance from the stories that they tell and identifies three modes of narration: psychonarration, quoted monologue, and narrated monologue. According to Cohn, "psycho-narration" "identifies both the subject-matter and the activity it denotes" (11). It is the most distant of the three modes since the narrator uses his words to interpret the character's consciousness for us. In quoted monologue we most clearly have the discourse of a character, but the reality effect suffers thereby since we do not usually voice our mental soliloquies or ever formulate them with the clarity and sophistication with which they are rendered in the textual medium. Cohn does note that the technique of quoted monologue did not become refined until the mid-nineteenth century; thus, she does not consider the dramatic soliloquies of the eighteenth-century novel to be examples of quoted monologue. Dramatic soliloquies were often preceded by a lengthy justification for the character's outburst; however, by the time of the realist novel, there was no need to give an elaborate introduction of the interior voice to justify its seeming manifestation in speech: "Realist novelists," writes Cohn, "take the inner voice entirely for granted" (60). There is no longer any need for a lengthy introduction as we see in the eighteenth-century novel.

Cohn is careful to distinguish between the technique of stream of consciousness and quoted monologue since the presentation and effect of the two are so radically diverse. Thus, Cohn deliberately avoids the term "interior monologue," a logical juxtaposition for the technique that she labels "quoted monologue," since "interior monologue" is a term used by Dujardin to refer to the technique of stream of consciousness. Her answer is to add "quoted" and drop the "interior" as being redundant—hence, we have "quoted monologue" to describe "the reference to the thinking self in the first person, and to the narrated moment . . . in the present tense" (13). Characters' thoughts are rendered exactly as they are purportedly thinking them and simultaneously to their thinking them.

"Narrated monologue" is Cohn's term for free indirect speech, only Cohn does not recognize the possibility that the author's discourse might be conflated within a character's mental discourse. According to Cohn, narrated monologue is "like psycho-narration [in that] it maintains the third-person reference and the tense of narration, but like the quoted monologue it reproduces verbatim the character's own mental language" (14). Cohn claims that the effect of narrated monologue is to leave the relationship between words and thoughts "latent" and to cast "a particularly penumbral light on the figural consciousness, suspending it on the threshold of verbalization that cannot be achieved by direct quotation" (103). Thus, this technique of narration says something about an author's philosophy of the relationship between thought and language. The author does not attempt to directly iterate the speech of a character with narrated monologue, for thought cannot always be expressed clearly or even, at times, at all. Narrated monologue, furthermore, can grant the narrative a certain "temporal fluidity," "revealing a fictional mind suspended in an instant present, between a remembered past and an anticipated future" (126). In the nineteenth-century novel, narrated monologue most closely approximates the effect of stream of consciousness. It has its temporal fluidity, though it is more structured and suggests that the content might not match the form, and vice versa.

If we think for a moment of Henry James' distinction between showing and telling, then we might say that narrated monologue dramatizes the temporal fluidity, whereas psychonarration tells about it. What thoughts transpire in the mind of a character are made transparent in the narration; they are dramatized, for the immediacy of seeing how the world impacts a character's psyche adds drama to an otherwise pictorial representation of character. Psychonarration, since it is most distant from the showing of a character's consciousness, has, as Cohn declares, an "almost unlimited temporal flexibility." Thus, Flaubert uses psychonarration to "survey" a "psychic syndrome over a period of time" (Cohn 36). He uses the iterative tense, for example, to emphasize the habitual nature of life in Tostes and to summarize this time for the reader. The effect is to convey the monotony of Emma's life without, at the same time, boring the reader.

Each mode of narration implies a certain distance between the narrator and the narrated, and each has a context, the importance of which cannot be overstated. A title, such as "Mr." or "Mrs.," or an adjective, such as "poor," or a possessive pronoun, such as "our," can be very telling of a narrator's attitude toward the character about whom he is speaking or through whose mind or into whose mind he is gazing. Gerald Prince labels the terms that identify a narrator's position in the text either spatiotemporally or attitudinally "deictic" and "modal," respectively. Deictic terms would include words such as "now," "here," "today," and so on, and modal ones, "perhaps," "unfortunately," "poor," and so on. Together they are signs of a narrator's "knowledge of worlds other than that of the narrated" (Prince 10). Particularly in Flaubert's *Madame Bovary*, Queirós' *O primo Basílio*, and Fontane's *Effi Briest*, we must rely upon deictic and modal terms to signal the presence of the narrating voice since it rarely intrudes directly in the narration.

Cohn's terms structure our analysis of the voice in each text. For focalization we must rely upon the terminology of Gerard Genette. Genette makes an important distinction between who *sees* in a narrative (the focalization) and who *tells* the story (the narrator(s)/implied author). Genette has rejected the term "point of view" in discussing the perspective of a narrative since whether the narrator speaks in the first person or the third, it is still the same person who sees. Wayne Booth also notes that simply classifying novels as "first person point of view" does not do justice to the remarkably diverse "first-person" narratives that exist, such as Cervantes' *Don Quixote*, Sterne's *Tristram Shandy*, George Eliot's *Middlemarch*, and Henry James' *The Ambassadors*, to name but a few of the many "first-person" novels that would be lumped together in such a system of classification.

Booth suggests that rather than speak of "persons," we should ask ourselves whether the narrator is "dramatized" or "undramatized" and if he is "self-conscious" or not about his role in the text. An undramatized narrator may be collapsed into the category of the implied author, but he may also remain distinct, depending upon whether the reader is aware of the story's passing through the consciousness of a teller. If there is no such awareness, then we are dealing with an implied author, according to Booth's terminology; if there is even the slightest awareness, then we have a dramatized narrator (151). Flaubert may, at first glance, seem to employ an undramatized narrator in *Madame Bovary*, but, as Booth notes, "even the most reticent narrator has been dramatized as soon as he refers to himself as 'I'" (or in Flaubert's case, "we").

Genette reserves the terms "voice" and "narrator" for the speaker of a text and "focalizer" for the one who sees in a text and creates the mood—and, for our purposes, the judgment. Genette's three types of focalization are zero focalization, internal focalization (which may be fixed, variable, or multiple), and external focalization. Zero focalization is something like our traditional "third-person, omniscient point of view." The focalizer is not attached to a single consciousness and sees and knows more than any single character or collective of all the characters. Internal focalization is derived from the "third-person, limited (or restricted) point of view." Here the one who sees is a single character (fixed), or a number of characters in succession (variable), or a number of characters on the same event (multiple), as in epistolary novels. External focalization is like an "objective point of view." The one who sees tells the tale without ever entering into the minds of the characters. All is told from without. It is important to note, as Genette does, that an author rarely commits himself to a single focalization throughout the entire novel. Very often the focalization fluctuates. In *Madame Bovary* Flaubert begins with external focalization, switches to variable (first through Charles, then through Emma, where the focalization remains through most of the novel), and occasionally draws back to external focalization for the presentation of Yonville, the carriage scene in Rouen, and, of course, the conclusion of the novel after Emma's death.

In all six novels our adulteresses are first presented through the male gaze. In Flaubert, it is Charles who first sees Emma; in Queirós, it is Jorge who first sees; in Chopin, it is Mr. Pontellier who watches his wife and Robert Lebrun slowly approach from the beach; in Tolstoy, we first see Anna through Vronsky's eyes at the train station; in *La Regenta*, we first see Ana Ozores through Don Fermín's eyepiece; and in *Effi Briest* the narrator (a male gaze) describes the enchanting Effi, dressed in a childish smock with a sailor's collar, talking and embroidering in the garden with her mother and periodically pausing for calisthenics. The women are always described externally first, through the masculine gaze, before we read their thoughts or see through their eyes.

All of these realist novels of adultery, representative of different national traditions, share certain similarities, which allow us to foreground distinct treatments of the subject of adultery based on national character, philosophical grounding, and/or class differences: all six novels deal with adulter*esses* who have faithful husbands whom they do not love, who believe that they have found happiness in their extramarital affairs, and who either die or suffer degradation due to their affair(s). Of utmost importance in this study is the focalization—who sees: is the focalization such that the protagonists in these novels are being punished by death or released from an unsavory life? Is the dishonor that Anna Karenin, Ana Ozores, Luísa Mendonça, and Effi Briest endure a simultaneous indictment of their respective societies, which are responsible for the mental torment that the protagonists suffer? Do the adulteresses' deaths and degradations elicit the reader's sympathy or judgment? Are the implied authors themselves ambivalent? If the narrators or implied authors (or both) do not judge them, then who does, and are the judgments implicit or explicit, reliable or unreliable? Finally, what is behind the judgments—*ressentiment*, Christian morality, humanitarianism? Although we begin with the sociological data of women, class, and education in the nineteenth century in France, Spain and Portugal, Russia, Germany, and America,[8] the focus of this study is neither historical nor sociological; it is literary, narratological, and philosophical. This study does not aim to reach any conclusions about marriage, the family, male–female relations, or adultery in general. It does stand as an analysis of six realist novels of adultery, and the extent to which generalizations can be made should be limited to other novels of adultery of this same period. In all, I have been most concerned with focalization, with "who sees," with who tells, and with the philosophy that informs the judgments made in each text. Adultery is not shown in these six novels to be a woman's issue or an expression of freedom. On the contrary, the protagonists are shown to be as trapped in their adulterous affairs as they are in their marriages and as Edna Pontellier in *The Awakening* is within herself.

Naturally, there is no shortage of monographs and articles about any one of these six novels of adultery studied here. There are even numerous articles and a few books that compare some of these very same novels. There is not, however, to my knowledge, any one book that brings these six novels together in a comparative study or one that takes a narratological and philosophical approach to them. Judith Armstrong in *The Novel of Adultery* (1976) omits the Iberian Peninsula and Germany in her discussion of the nineteenth-century novel of adultery and tarries over examples drawn especially from Hardy after first correctly observing that England, due to the greater liberty that women enjoyed, did not have a strong tradition of novels of adultery in the nineteenth century. Moreover, Armstrong deals with adulterous husbands while I focus solely on adulterous wives. Biruté Ciplijauskaité in *La mujer insatisfecha* (1984) delivers a remarkably astute, comparative analysis of *Madame Bovary, La Regenta, Anna Karenin,* and *Effi Briest*, but she does not include Queirós' *O primo Basílio* or Chopin's *The Awakening*. She notes that the four novels of adultery that she has chosen are from the male point of view—that is, they are written by men, and without digressing into point of view versus focalization, I would concur that the tone and resolutions are rather traditional and not reflective of the women's movement in the nineteenth century. Not only does the addition of Chopin to my study permit a contrast among novels in the Western tradition, representative of various national literatures, but as the sole female author in the study, we can also note Chopin's unique preoccupation with the self-realization of her protagonist. Ciplijauskaité also includes additional studies in her monograph on the nineteenth-century realist novel of adultery—near brushes with adultery in *The Portrait of a Lady* and *A Doll's House* and two Spanish novels, *Fortunata y Jacinta* and *La Gaviota*, which, as Ciplijauskaité acknowledges, are not really novels of adultery. She is concerned in her chapter on the philosophy in each novel of adultery to determine whether the overarching philosophy of each novel is in favor, or against, the woman. My approach is not confined to the woman question alone, as I am interested in probing the ideas of the age and the philosophy of the authors on more than a single question. Tony Tanner's seminal work *Adultery in the Novel: Contract and Transgression* (1979), as Ciplijauskaité notes in her introduction, is not limited to a single epoch, focuses on Rousseau, Goethe, and Flaubert, and relies heavily upon the theories of Freud, Lacan, and Derrida. Finally, the most recent monograph on the novel of adultery is Alison Sinclair's *The Deceived Husbands* (1993), wherein she takes Melanie Klein's theory of "object relations" as the basis for her psychoanalytic approach to texts that span from the Middle Ages to the twentieth century. As with Tanner's book, Sinclair's does not focus primarily on a specific time period and, as her title suggests, is more concerned with placing the "deceived husbands" into the categories of the cuckold, "man of honor," or "man of distinction." Her purpose is not to study the character of the adulteresses or the nature of adultery.

    The preponderance of realist novels in the latter half of the nineteenth century that deal with adultery bears out Peter Gay's blanket statement (which makes no distinction between romantic and realist texts) that "[n]ineteenth-century novelists explored all the themes that mattered: money, class, politics . . . . But their governing preoccupation always remained love."[9] Whereas the romantics were peddlers of the ideal, with all its "accoutrements," the realists scathingly attacked the institution of marriage as a socioeconomic contract, the hypocrisy of societies laden with *ressentiment*, the ideal of undying passion—all to cure the societal ill of adultery. Some set out to expose the lovers; others, the adulteresses; and still others, adultery itself. These six novels gathered here all expose adultery as much as they debunk romantic notions of love—neither of which should be taken as an unequivocal argument for the sanctity of the institution of marriage as it was arranged (quite literally in most countries) in the nineteenth century. The type of loveless marriages that are arranged or foolishly entered into in these novels fails to meet the needs of women who expect love and passion and who long for the perfect union. Their husbands fall far short of the mark: they are fawning or inattentive bores or overly ambitious men of principles; nevertheless, a pervasive theme of these novels of adultery is that adultery is not the resolution to the flawed institution of marriage. As the illusion of adultery dissipates, as the novelty wears off, so does the attraction, and adultery proves to be as monotonous as marriage. These realist authors of the nineteenth century take up the theme of love, as did their romantic predecessors, but love is a romantic ideal, and adultery is a very real societal ill.

The degree of emotional attachment between the wife and the lover in the nineteenth-century novel of adultery corresponds to the value that the narrator or implied author concedes the wife. The lovers are all typically donjuanesque types (at least in spirit), but the more admirable the women's qualities, the more genuinely smitten are the lovers. In *La Regenta, Madame Bovary,* and *The Awakening* the classic love triangle is modified to include the figure of the friend/confidante who also aspires to be a lover. Ana Ozores and Anna Karenin appear more noble and admirable because they are women of high society in their respective milieu who are not striving to attain a higher social status. They set the standards rather than imitate them (as do Luísa and Emma). Ana's reputation for purity is renowned, and Anna's grace and passion for life impress all around her. Effi Briest, while not noble in bearing, is cast in a positive light due to her youth, inexperience, and affinity to Nature. Emma, like Anna, seems to captivate many of the men in her milieu, but her character is deeply flawed by her pretensions, materialism, and self-absorption—only the last of which mars the beauty of Anna Karenin.

We begin with a brief, historical account of the status of women in each of the pertinent countries and with the voices and modes of representing consciousness and focalization in each of the six novels. In general, women in the mid- to late nineteenth century had the identity of their husbands, fathers, or legal guardians and could not sue for any reason, enter into a contract (other than marriage), inherit property, or profit from any business as part of their inheritance. They were never educated as well as their male counterparts, if they were educated at all. Usually, their education would consist of those subjects deemed pertinent to their social sphere: domestic chores, performative arts, and religion. Marriages were often arranged, and in these cases it was expected that the husband would find happiness with a lover and that the wife would be understanding and ever-faithful, as the honor of the husband would reside in her. The strength of the middle classes, as we shall see, was not uniform from country to country, nor did "progress" refer to enlightened views on the equality of men and women.

NOTES

1. Peter Gay, *The Tender Passion*, 182.
2. The terms are D. A. Miller's. See page 109 of his *Narrative and Its Discontents*.
3. Pilbeam, *The Middle Classes in Europe*, 3.
4. I am following Rosemary Edmonds' practice of eliminating the final "a" in Karenin since it is not customary in English to use a feminine form of names. See her introductory note to the 1978 Penguin edition of *Anna Karenin*.
5. *Will to Power*, section 274.
6. Ibid., section 285.

Introduction   xxi

      7. Leopoldo Alas wrote under the name of Clarín, which is the name adopted by literary critics and used here.

      8. While recognizing that "America" is a term that encompasses all the countries in North, South, and Central America, I use it here to reflect the common usage of equating the United States with America, particularly in the nineteenth century, and because "American" makes a much better adjective than the U. S. does. It is not my intention to perpetuate an insular, imperialistic perception of the Western Hemisphere.

      9. *The Tender Passion*, 135.

1

Rite of Initiation

CLASS, EDUCATION, AND CIVIL RIGHTS

France

The importance of the middle class in France cannot be overestimated; after all, the very term "bourgeoisie" is a French one. Indeed, this term encompassed such a motley group of people in the nineteenth century that historians divide the French middle class into *"la grande bourgeoisie"* and *"la petite bourgeoisie"*— the "upper" and "lower" middle classes. The *petite bourgeoisie* is the class in which Ossowska identifies the *ressentiment* ethics described by Ranulf, and it is to this class that Emma Bovary belongs, the class known for its disinterested punishment of crimes and its rigid moral standards.

Aside from England, France was the first to really engage in the "woman question." The French Revolution was seminal for its questioning of authority (man's over woman's, for instance)—the roots of the suffragette movement can be traced back to the eighteenth century as a result—however, the creation of the French Empire under Napoleon, along with the promulgation of the Napoleonic Code in 1816, "was a fatal moment for women's interests" (Stanton 238). Under this code a man could divorce his wife for adultery, and she could serve anywhere from three months to two years in prison, but a husband would not be imprisoned for the same crime, only fined if his concubine were brought under the same roof as his wife (Stanton 254). Not until 1893 were women granted certain civil rights, and divorce, once legalized in 1792, was prohibited by the Napoleonic Code until 1884.

Women were often educated in convent schools during the time in which Flaubert lived and wrote, much as the fictional Emma Bovary is. It was, according to Balzac, an aristocratic custom before the Revolution that was imitated by lesser families to permit their daughters to mingle with daughters of gentlemen and thus learn how to act. Balzac describes the boarding school in his

Physiology of Marriage thus: "The most terrible laziness prevails, and the cloisters kindle the imagination" (73). Flaubert's characterization of Emma Bovary bears out the truth of Balzac's assertion. Emma's imagination develops during her years in the convent school, while she seems to learn little about household management, the performative arts, or religious duties.

If the relations could afford to do so, a young girl would live in the convent for some years, much like a cloistered nun, learning nothing of the world, until her release in her early teens, when she would return to her father's house (another cloister, really) until a marriage could be arranged for her. This is the pattern of Emma Bovary's life, a member of the *petite bourgeoisie*, who seizes the opportunity to associate with more wealthy members of society proper at the convent and later at La Vaubyessard out of her insatiable desire to take a place in high society.

Spain and Portugal

Spain and Portugal, though not to the extent of Russia, remained behind the times compared to the rest of Europe in the nineteenth century because of their geographic isolation on the Iberian Peninsula; thus, literary, social, political, and economic change came very slowly to these countries. For instance, the middle class in Spain was considerably smaller and less active than those in France and England, and regionalism, which had been overcome in France at the end of the eighteenth century, continued in Spain into the twentieth. Thus, Jean Bécarud can point to the Restoration of the Bourbon monarchy in 1874 as the beginning of the era of provincialism (11). Education lagged, and freedom of worship was not granted until as late as 1869. While the Industrial Revolution had begun in England as early as 1800, "[a]s late as the 1870's there was very little in the way of a genuine Spanish bourgeoisie of the entrepreneurial variety" (Bécarud 21). With little industrialization and a very modest middle class, Spain remained a country of regional provinces dominated by the church and aristocracy.

Since Spain had a very small middle class in the latter half of the nineteenth century, it should not be surprising that Clarín, like Tolstoy before him, chose a member of the upper classes for his protagonist. Ana Ozores has a humble beginning in the sense that she is orphaned and raised by aunts; nevertheless, she is able to marry well and takes her place in the very best (albeit provincial) society, though she often refuses to associate with "society proper." "Society proper" during the Restoration revolved around those who represented the new regime—the *Vegallana* in *La Regenta*—while those who opposed the Restoration of Alfonso XII (likewise, aristocrats) and those antagonistic to the church (those who were sincerely religious and thus despised the hypocrisy of the social institution) were displaced—the *Carraspique* in Clarín's novel.

It is interesting that in both *Anna Karenin* and *La Regenta* the protagonists are of the upper classes: the "*alta burguesía*"[1] in Ana Ozores' case and the aristocracy proper in Anna Karenin's, classes renowned for their peccadilloes, and yet both adulteresses are ostracized for their affairs—a paradox in classes not known for their rigid moral standards. Why were not Anna and Ana afforded the same leniency as other society women? It should first be noted that it has always been more acceptable for a man to commit adultery than a woman. Provided he did not house his mistress under the same roof as his wife, a man was not censured for his indiscretions. Moreover, in countries where marriages were arranged, such as in Spain, Portugal, France, and Italy, society was willing to overlook mistresses and lovers provided the affair was carried on discreetly.[2] Thus, since England conceded greater freedom to its daughters in the choosing of a mate at this time, adultery was strongly censured, which may go a long way toward explaining why there is no archetype of adultery in the British Isles: it was either not as common, not as great a societal ill, not as appealing to the imagination of better-educated young women, or simply not attractive to authors who could not make the story assume tragic proportions where the women had more freedom to choose a suitable mate and prided themselves on their sense rather than their sensibility. Whatever the reason, though there are numerous tales of seduction and scintillating brushes with adultery and even instances of adultery, no British adulteress assumes the status of an archetype as her continental counterparts do, nor does any British novel stand out as a novel *of* adultery.

Due to its location on the Iberian Peninsula, Portugal, like Spain, remained geographically isolated from the industrialization of much of Northwest Europe. Portugal, although it did not have Spain's problem with regionalism in the nineteenth century, developed even more slowly than its neighbor on the Iberian Peninsula (Payne 531). Between the years 1821 and 1890, the middle classes (both upper and lower) grew just slightly, from 12% to approximately 15%; similarly, the laboring class decreased proportionately over the course of those years. Unlike Spain at this time, the government of Portugal was transferred peacefully from one party to the next. Nevertheless, Portugal's time of peace was not devoted to the education of better citizens: "Proportionately less was spent on education [in Portugal] than in any other European state save the Ottoman empire" (Payne 546). Hence, we should not be surprised that Luísa's education in *O primo Basílio* is never described: it must have been exceedingly rudimentary.

Although the middle class was relatively insignificant in Portugal in the nineteenth century, Queirós, unlike Clarín, does choose a middle-class woman for his protagonist in *O primo Basílio*. Luísa's husband, Jorge, is one of the new, technologically competent bourgeoisie. He and Luísa live in greater luxury than Emma Bovary does in the provinces of France; however, Lisbon in the nineteenth century was not the cosmopolitan center that it arguably is today. Though the capital and commercial center of Portugal, Lisbon was nevertheless outwardly provincial due to the overall lack of progress and innovation in Portugal as a whole—a fact that Cousin Basílio drives home to Luísa by his incessant criticism of her bourgeois ways. So, though seemingly of a higher social status than Emma Bovary, Luísa Mendonça is made to feel as "common" as the bourgeoisie in France and England at this time, and her class may be considered comparable to that of Emma Bovary, the protagonist to whom she is most closely allied; Paris was for them the epicenter of both fashion and goodbreeding.

Russia

Russian society in the nineteenth century was some 200 years behind European society at that time. The economy was still based on the feudal system of agriculture until the freeing of the serfs in 1860 under Alexander I. There were little to no industrialization and, as a result, a very small middle class. Peter the Great's Table of Ranks, which continued until the 1860s, divided Russia into a tiny privileged minority who did not have to pay taxes, serve in the military, or be subject to the penalty of capital punishment and a vast majority who were taxed, required to serve in the military, and could be put to death. The 1860s did see the rise of the *intelligentsia*, a class particular to Russia, who were "minor officials, clergy, some teachers, doctors, and the new and growing body of technically trained men" needed to run the *zemstvos*, local governing councils created in the wake of the emancipation of the serfs (Pilbeam 20). These local councils form the backdrop for many a heated soiree in *Anna Karenin*; however, the intelligentsia does not figure significantly in the novel, which dwells primarily on the lives of two aristocratic couples.

As backward as Russia may seem in its government and economic system in the nineteenth century, Pilbeam claims that Russians "always seem to have been more willing to educate girls than other European societies" (206). Thus, our appreciation of Anna Karenin's intellect is no mistake. Unfortunately for her, her greater education must have made her position all the more unbearable, for despite her education, a Russian woman had less freedom than her European counterparts in the selection of a husband: "Still, speaking broadly, middle-class English, and even more, American girls were far less inhibited from selecting their husbands, or cajoling their parents, than their German or French, let alone their Russian counterparts."[3] Although we know nothing of Anna's thoughts at the time she agrees to marry Karenin, we do know that the marriage was arranged by an aunt of Anna and that Anna married without loving Karenin.

Germany

Effi Briest is set in Prussia and Berlin of the Second Reich under Kaiser Wilhelm II. Unification had taken place in 1871, following the Prussian-Austrian War of 1866 and the Franco-Prussian War of 1870, and in March 1890, the young emperor Wilhelm II forced Chancellor Bismark to resign. The Junkers, landed aristocrats who were extremely conservative and defended "a Calderonian concept of honor,"[4] exercised a great deal of influence over the local administrations, thus preserving the influence of the nobility in the Second Reich not only in the courts but in society at large. In keeping with the attitudes of the nineteenth-century European bourgeoisie in general, the middle class in Germany sought to emulate the Junker class and its aristocratic values. It is in this context that David Blackbourn concedes that it is fair to talk about the "feudalization of the bourgeoisie" (228), as so many historians do with regard to the German middle class. Most lived "in a preindustrial world of state service, artisanal production, and small enterprise" (Sheehan 25). Any chance for the middle class to rise up and dominate the German states as it came to dominate France and Great Britain was squelched with the revolutions of 1848, as was any progress on the woman question.

Any gains made by a feeble women's movement in the eighteenth century in Germany came to a halt with the reactionary period following the revolution of 1848. The lack of civil rights, the subjugation of women to their fathers, brothers, and husbands, and an education in domesticity (if women received any education at all) were typical of other countries in Europe governed by the Napoleonic Code, as we have seen. "What was unique," according to Gordon A. Craig, "was that the subordination of women was more stubborn and protracted [in Bismarckian Germany] than in the advanced Western countries" (147). Here as elsewhere, women sought escape from undesirable home lives and the vacuity of materialistic culture through reading and attending the opera.

What is perhaps most particular to Germany is a national character of obedience[5]—perhaps traceable to the Thirty Years' War, undoubtedly present in the Third Reich. This obedience encourages Effi to accept the match that her mother has made for her, this obedience drives Innstetten to fulfill his duty to an outdated, Prussian military code, and this obedience enables Effi to forgive her husband and resign herself to death.

America

If the French had a reputation for being promiscuous, the product of a certain candidness about sex, American women were seen as fast and loose because they were better educated, enjoyed greater liberty in choosing their mates, and were more militant in their quest for equality before the law. One has only to read Henry James to see how American girls were perceived by Europeans: American girls are brash, outspoken, unrefined, and devoid of grace and charm—all due to their paltry cultural tradition in this upstart nation. Because of its new wealth and social mobility, its lack of aristocracy and the equality of all before the law, America has, at times, been hailed as a classless society, but this is as false now as it has always been. The society that Kate Chopin describes in *The Awakening* is highly stratified, along the lines of its European model, as the Creoles in New Orleans strove to preserve the customs of their French ancestors: "That community about which she [Chopin] wrote was one in which respectable women took wine with their dinner and brandy after it, smoked cigarettes, played Chopin sonatas, and listened to the men tell risqué stories" (Ziff 297). It is more like the French aristocracy at La Vaubyessard in *Madame Bovary* than it is like the American *nuveau riche* of Fitzgerald's *The Great Gatsby* or the women suffragettes in Henry James' *The Bostonians*. Edna Pontellier in *The Awakening*, though American, is nevertheless comparable to Anna Karenin and Ana Ozores in her aristocratic lifestyle and position at the top of her social scale in Creole society. She is unlike her continental counterparts, however, in that she is the creation of a female writer and the product of a half century of advances in the education of women. She alone of the six adulteresses attempts to live without men, and she alone is more concerned with her identity and place in the universe than any other wife in the novel of adultery.

Before discussing the explicit or implicit views of the narrators, it behooves us to first identify the voices that the authors have chosen for the telling of their tales and the ways in which they represent the psyches of their protagonists. The narrators are all dramatized, though ever so slightly, typically with the first-person, plural subject pronoun (in English, "we"). They are not, for the most part, intrusive, though an occasional exclamation escapes their lips, and an irresistible desire to demonstrate authority manifests itself in the creation and subsequent filling of story gaps. Even the most subtle of narrators can be detected in their use of temporal and modal terms, and it is these terms and the occasional authoritative intrusion that we use to determine the philosophy at work behind each of the narratives.

VOICES AND MODES OF REPRESENTING CONSCIOUSNESS

The very opening lines of our six novels establish the tone and voice of these narratives. The opening line of *La Regenta* leaves little doubt as to the implied author's attitude toward Vetusta: "*La heroica ciudad dormía la siesta*" (The heroic city was taking a nap) (15). The irony in this opening sentence sets the tone for the rest of the novel. Just as we question how heroic a city could be that sleeps, so we later question how "noble" and "loyal" is a city that turns its back on one of its own penitent members in her time of greatest need. Tolstoy opens with a generalization (the first of many): "All happy families are alike but an unhappy family is unhappy after its own fashion." He goes on to describe the misfortunes of the two couples, Anna and Vronsky and Levin and Kitty, in the authoritative manner intimated by the tone of this opening. Queirós and Chopin immediately create a mood of monotony in their novels (also evoked in *La Regenta* by the droning of the church bells and in Flaubert's *Madame Bovary* with the use of the iterative tense). In Queirós the monotony is created by the season (a sultry midday in July), by the inactivity of the protagonists (they are lingering over the remains of lunch, reading leisurely), and through the monotonous buzzing of the flies over the table. The summer at the Grand Isle in *The Awakening* has the same effect as July in Lisbon, for the sound of the parrot, who keeps repeating "over and over" the same phrase, like the droning of the flies in *O primo Basílio* or the clanging of the church bells in *La Regenta*, creates the feeling of sameness and ennui. In *Madame Bovary* Flaubert positions the narrator as a witness to the events that transpire by his use of "We" to open the novel. The narrator is a classmate of Charles Bovary, a class that is sleeping and awakened by the entrance of this new, very provincial, and slow-witted young boy. The details that follow in the opening pages about Charles' dress, hat, and bovine habits set the derisive tone that characterizes the narrator's attitude toward all things provincial. Fontane opens *Effi Briest* with a rather detailed description of the Briests' house in Hohen-Cremmen, a fitting commencement since one of the prevailing themes of this novel is the effect of heredity and whether nature or nurture is to blame for Effi's character—really "*too* big a subject," as Effi's father says.

All the narrators and implied authors are heterodiegetic, meaning they are not characters who act in the stories that they tell, and are dramatized to varying degrees. In all, we really hear only one voice. Our authors do not employ a series of narrators or multiple layers of narration; moreover, the single narrators we have are only minimally dramatized. However, precisely because these narrators are univocal, authoritarian, and reliable, we are able to see through the eyes of many of the characters. None of our authors confine themselves to a single consciousness, as James and later Lubbock advocated, nor do they restrict themselves to a single method of focalization for the course of the novel.

Madame Bovary

Flaubert's narrator is dramatized with his use of "*nous*" in the opening, thereby making him an anonymous schoolfellow of Charles Bovary, a very wise schoolfellow at that since he is capable of supplying us with an analepsis into Charles' upbringing by his very "thrifty" parents (an attribute that immediately marks them as bourgeois). After Part One the "*nous*" disappears, and the narrative assumes the characteristics of zero-degree narration and iterative mood and fluctuates from picture to scene. The "*nous*" does not surface again until Emma's burial and there it, again, dramatizes the narrator as a witness by placing him at the cemetery with the others. He says that the sound of the coffin's striking the stone "*nous semble être le retentissement de l'éternite*" (seemed to us to be the ringing of eternity) (356). There is a certain closure in reintroducing the "*nous*" at the end of the novel, a feeling that is reinforced by the temporal consonance in the end between story time and narrative time. After Charles' death, the narrator summarizes events to the present day. Thus, the verb tense changes from the past tense, to the present perfect, to the present and ends with Homais' "just" receiving the Legion of Honor.

These fluctuations of voice in *Madame Bovary* reveal Flaubert's documented distaste for provincial life. The voice shifts from "*nous*" in the first part of the novel to "*on*" in the opening of the second, which describes the locale of Yonville. The reader is no longer in collusion with the narrator, but neither is the narrator a member of this village by his use of the impersonal subject pronoun. The way that the town spreads out along the river, for instance, "*on l'aperçoit de loin*" (one could see from afar), and if "one" followed a certain road to the right, "one" would end up at the cemetery (106). Moreover, the narrator directly refers to the act of narration with the impersonal "*on*": "*Depuis les événements que l'on va raconter, rien, en effect, n'a changé à Yonville*" (After the events that one is about to relate, nothing, in effect, has changed in Yonville) (108). The pronoun is often translated as "we" since this sounds more appropriate in English, and yet it is interesting to note that Flaubert does not use "*nous*" here as he does in Parts One and Three. The irony in the narrator's voice distances him from the inhabitants of Yonville. It is one thing to be a perceptive young boy in Charles Bovary's class (one can always develop into something worthwhile); it is quite another to be a member of the stagnant community of Yonville, where all leads to the cemetery. There would be no place for the narrator, as he is dramatized in *Madame Bovary*, within the society of Yonville or Tostes, for that matter. The ironic distancing calls for a member outside and above the provincial bourgeoisie.

Though not as intrusive as the narrators of *Anna Karenin*, *La Regenta*, and *The Awakening*, the narrator of *Madame Bovary* does intrude into the story aside from the first-person, plural subject pronoun. For instance, in the third part of *Madame Bovary*, when Emma is outraged that Leon has missed their tryst, she is able to detach herself from the affair by denigrating her lover, and the narrator notes the effect that this has not just on Emma but on everyone: "*Il ne faut pas toucher aux idoles: la dorure en reste aux mains*" (It is better not to touch our idols: the gilt comes off in our hands) (304). Such impersonal generalizations are rare in Flaubert, and yet they do exist, as does an uncharacteristic contradiction of a character's assertion. When Homais lists his membership in "several" learned societies as one of his qualifications for the Legion of Honor, the narrator declares in a parenthetical aside, "(*il l'etait d'une seule*)" (he was a member of only one) (364).

We must consider the connotations of the descriptive language in Flaubert as well as the denotations. Emma never asks herself if she loves her husband since, in her mind, if you have to ask, it must not be love, for she believes love should come "*tout à coup, avec grands éclats et des fulgurations—ouragan des cieux qui tombe sur la vie, la bouleverse, arrache les volontés comme des feuilles et emporte à l'abîme le coeur entier*" (all at once, with great thunderclaps and flashes of lightning—a hurricane from the sky that descends upon life and turns it upside down, overwhelming the will like leaves and carrying the whole heart into the abyss) (133). The narrator immediately undercuts her romantic reverie by adding that Emma did not know that the rain formed puddles on the flat roofs of houses whose drainpipes were clogged. In other words, the narrator suggests that the passion that Emma longs to experience will have no outlet and so will collect in stagnant pools inside her that will destroy her. She is, ironically, swept into an abyss, but Emma's abyss is not the anticipated one of self-abnegation through exhilarating passion; on the contrary, Emma's abyss is loss of self in despair.

O primo Basílio

There is never any mention of "we" in Eça de Queirós' *O primo Basílio*, and yet the implied author is manifest in modal and deictic terms and in his commentary on the thoughts of his characters. Queirós is most like Flaubert in his predilection for narrated monologue to represent the thoughts of his characters. He, like Flaubert, rarely signals a character's discourse with quotation marks or the phrase "he thought." He moves almost seamlessly in and out of his characters' minds, and we readers are left with the difficult task of trying to sort out implied author's judgments from characters'. The following passage demonstrates Queirós' technique. Although it appears to be strictly expository narration, it ends with narrated monologue that seems to mimetically represent Luísa's thoughts, just as she is having them: "*Havia doze dias que Jorge tinha partido e, apesar do calor e da poeira, Luísa vestia-se para ir a casa de Leopoldina. Se Jorge soubesse, não havia de gostar, não! Mas estava tão farta de* estar só! Aborrecia-se tanto!" (It had been twelve days since Jorge had left and, in spite of the heat and the dust, Luísa got dressed for Leopoldina's house. *If Jorge knew, he would not like it, no! But she was so fed up with being alone! She was getting so bored!*) (59; emphasis added). We move inside Luísa's head without any indication from the narrator that we are doing so and with the uncertainty of whether the discourse is, in the final analysis, the narrator's or Luísa's. Though indirect, since the implied author maintains third-person grammatical pronouns in order to refer to Luísa, the effect of the discourse is nevertheless more intimate for the uncertainty.

Effi Briest

Fontane, like Flaubert, has recourse to letter writing to reveal character, but, unlike Flaubert, the voice of his narrator is more present in the story. There is, first of all, a greater concern with time in *Effi Briest*. Thematically, Fontane asks his readers to consider when and if an act of adultery might be forgiven. Unlike our other five novels of adultery, the adultery in this case does not take center stage, does not in fact take place onstage, and Effi's indiscretion is discovered six years after the fact, during which time she has been completely faithful and fully cognizant of her responsibility and guilt. Throughout the novel it is the narrator who tells us the date (3 October, 2 December, "the middle of November," "the middle of June") and even the time of day ("This conversation took place at about eleven o'clock. At twelve . . .") and tells us abruptly of the passage of time: "Yes, Effi took the question of inheritance lightly, as charming young women do; but after a very long time—they had already been in the new post more than six years . . . " (204). It is almost an aside, an afterthought, yet the amount of time that has passed becomes important in Innstetten's and Wüllersdorf's subsequent conversation about Innstetten's options after discovering the affair and in our judgment of those concerned.

Fontane is not as intrusive as Tolstoy but more so than Flaubert and Queirós. He tends to maintain his distance from his characters, rarely allowing the narrator's and character's voices to reach consonance. He uses far more psychonarration and quoted monologue to represent consciousness, especially Effi's. For instance, as Effi heads for the pastor's the first afternoon to announce her engagement, "she said to herself: 'I think Hulda is going to be annoyed. I've got in before her after all—she always was stuck-up and pleased with herself'" (26). A much longer passage of quoted monologue occurs when Innstetten leaves Effi alone for the first time in the seemingly haunted house in Kessin. The lines of quoted monologue that follow are in italics: "'*If I do that, I'll become completely maudlin; I'd better read.*' She started looking for a book. The first one that she discovered was a thick red travel guide, out-of-date, perhaps even dating from the time when Innstetten was a lieutenant. '*Yes, let me read some of this, there's nothing more tranquilizing than this sort of book; the only trouble is the maps; but I'll avoid that dreadfully small print*'" (70; emphasis added). Fontane uses single quotation marks here as elsewhere to convey the thoughts of Effi exactly as she is thinking them without any interpretation or mediation from the narrator.

The occasions of narrated monologue in Fontane's *Effi Briest* are kept to a minimum and are often a line or two in a passage of psychonarration. Innstetten's suspicions are dramatically represented in narrated monologue, for example, in the following, in italics: "Innstetten blenched. *What did that mean?* Something that had repeatedly, if fleetingly, passed through his mind for some weeks, now reappeared" (168; emphasis added). While Effi fabricates her excuse for such effusive thanks on hearing that they were to be reassigned to Berlin,

Innstetten [had] kept his eyes fixed on her and followed every word. *What could be the meaning of the words. . . . And what she had just said before. . . . What was all this about? What had caused it?* And he felt his vague suspicion stirring again and becoming stronger. But he had lived long enough to know that every sign is deceptive and that our jealousy, even with its hundred eyes, can still often mislead us even more than our blind trust. *Things might be as she had said: and if that was so, why shouldn't she exclaim: "Thank God!"* (169; emphasis added)

The passages of narrated monologue are never very long, usually interspersed among psychonarration, and are not frequent in *Effi Briest*. In this last passage, the technique of narrated monologue is well chosen to add drama to the scene since outwardly Innstetten feigns understanding while inwardly he is beset by doubts.

    The narrator in *Effi Briest* does intrude occasionally with editorial comments. There are times, for instance, when the narrator directly and unequivocally gives his assessment of a character. Our introduction to Hulda Niemeyer, the pastor's daughter, includes the following in the voice of the narrator: "More ladylike than the other two, she was also more boring and conceited, a lymphatic blonde with rather protruding, stupid eyes" (17). When Frau von Briest says to herself, while she and her daughter are shopping for the trousseau in Berlin, that Effi is not pretentious and that she lives in her dreams and imagination, the narrator adds, "All this was true enough, but only half the truth. Effi did not care a great deal whether she possessed a larger or smaller quantity of everyday things, but . . . if . . . she had really set her heart on something, this thing had always to be quite outstanding. And in this she *was* pretentious" (29).

    The narrator similarly judges Innstetten and Crampas. Innstetten's propensity for Wagner, we are told, has led some to conclude that the music settled his nerves and others that he was anti-Semitic, and the narrator adds, "Both parties were probably right" (99). He tells us that "Effi was quite right" that the von Innstettens and the Crampases would not develop a close relationship and that Crampas is a man who could help a friend one minute and deceive him five minutes later: "He would do both these things with all the good will in the world" (101,127). These intrusions by the narrator eventually graduate to a few rhetorical questions near the end of the novel and the mention of a "we" that demands the collusion of his readers.

    Though intrusive, Fontane's narrator is nevertheless subtle; thus, it is uncharacteristic of the narrator to show himself so transparently in rhetorical queries, which he makes to anticipate the reader's surprise that Roswitha is with

Effi after the latter's renunciation by her family and society: "Was Roswitha with Effi, then? Was she in Kröniggrätzsstrasse instead of Keithstrasse? Indeed she was and had been for a very long time. . . . Indeed, three days before Effi had moved in, Roswitha had come to see her beloved mistress and it had been a great day for both of them, so much so that *we* must go back and report how it had happened" (236–237; emphasis added). The narrator, who, in the first place, is the author of our amazement, asks for our continued collaboration to fill the gap that he has created.

La Regenta

Clarín tends to render his characters' thoughts either indirectly in psychonarration or directly in quoted monologue; thus, we do not have the difficulty created by narrated monologue (free indirect discourse) in Flaubert and Queirós, in separating the implied author's thoughts from the character's. The characters' thoughts in *La Regenta* are often either set in quotation marks or reported with indicators like "he thought" or "she wondered." For example, the following passage moves from psychonarration, to an introduced quoted monologue, to psychonarration, to an unintroduced quoted monologue:

Aborrecía ahora las cavilaciones. Sin embargo, sin investigar las causas de ello sintió durante todo aquel día una alegría de niña satisfecha en sus gustos más vivos, y aún más intenso fue su placer al despertar a la mañana siguiente con este pensamiento: 'Voy al Vivero a hacer vida de aldeana, a correr, respirar, engordar . . . , alegrar la vida . . .' y como un acompañimiento musical que encantaba toda aquella perspectiva, Ana sentía una indecisa esperanza que era un sabor con perfumes. . . . 'Aquel Benítez la estaba rejuveneciendo.' (744)

She hated the bickering now. However, without investigating its causes, she felt during that whole day the happiness of a child satisfied in its most vivid pleasures, and even more intense was her pleasure on awakening the following morning with this thought: 'I'm going to Vivero to play the role of a country woman, to run, to breathe, to put on weight . . . , to enjoy life . . . ' and like a musical accompaniment that was charming all about her, Ana felt an indecisive hope that was a taste with scents. . . . 'That Benítez was rejuvenating her.'

Clarín does employ narrated monologue occasionally, as well, but the instances are much fewer—his tendency being to represent his characters' thoughts in a more direct manner. His implied author is, consequently, far more visible in the novel as an authoritative voice than Flaubert's in *Madame Bovary* or Queirós' in *O primo Basílio*.

Clarín's narrator does not hesitate to tell us more about a character than the character knows about him or herself. Thus, when Ana receives Mesía's letter from Madrid at the end of the novel, the narrator tells us about thoughts that Ana was not to have until much later: "*no pudo por entonces pensar en la pequeñez de aquel espíritu miserable que albergaba el cuerpo gallardo que ella había creído amar de veras. . . . No, en esto no pensó la Regenta hasta mucho más tarde*" (at the time she failed to think about the smallness of that miserable spirit sheltered in his gallant body, which she had believed she truly loved. . . .

No, the Regent's wife did not think about that until much later) (860). Ana's physician Benítez cautions her against such mental torments, for the mental activity of memory, self-accusation, and regret is more than her physical body can bear and amounts to her gradual suicide. When her physical health improves, there will be time enough to confront the reality of Mesía's deception and the hypocrisy of the world around her.

Clarín's narrator, like all of those previously discussed with the exception of Queirós, also makes use of the first-person plural subject pronoun—in one instance, to express his disgust for the "barbarous" custom of dueling that Vetusta has inherited from the Middle Ages and, in the second, to anticipate our meeting Frígilis in a later chapter: *"En su traje pulcro y negro se veía algo que Frígilis, personaje darwinista que encontraremos más adelante, llamaba la adaptación de la sotana."* (In his [Don Saturnino's] neat, black suit one saw something that Frígilis, a Darwinist character whom *we will encounter* later, called the adaptation of the cassock) (Clarín 37; emphasis added). These are, perhaps, the only uses of the first-person, plural pronoun in the dense tome, so we should not exaggerate their importance, but they do constitute, however slightly, a dramatized narrator. In fact, Clarín's narrator is far more dramatized than either Flaubert's or Queirós'—though more for the modal terms that he employs than for the construction of a narrating voice.

Anna Karenin

Tolstoy and Chopin create even more authoritative voices than Clarín in their novels of adultery since neither the implied author nor narrator makes extensive use of irony; thus, their commentaries, while still ambiguous at times, especially in the case of Chopin, are more straightforward and univocal than Clarín's, Flaubert's, Queirós', or Fontane's. Tolstoy, like Clarín, favors psychonarration and quoted monologue over narrated monologue; his use of the latter is extremely rare. A character's thoughts are either clearly in the discourse of the implied author, who knows more about the characters than they do about themselves (psychonarration), or the words in the characters' minds are represented directly, in quotation marks, exactly as the characters think them (quoted monologue). Even more authoritative than the words or thoughts of the characters themselves, rendered exactly as they are thinking/saying them, are the words of Tolstoy's implied author.

Thus, in addition to the opening generalization, we learn that the only answer to Oblonsky's rhetorical musings about how he should resolve his family crisis is "life's usual answer to the most complex and insoluble questions . . . live from day to day; in other words, forget" (16). To make Anna's discomposure at the sight of Vronsky at her brother's all the more significant, we are told, "There was nothing out of the ordinary or odd in a man calling on a friend at half-past nine to find out about a dinner they were arranging and refusing to come in"(90)—thus calling attention to the event at the same time that he pretends to downplay its importance. To explain how Anna, Karenin, and Vronsky can continue so long in their triangular love affair without any attempt to resolve the instability, Chapter 23 of Part Seven begins thus: "Before anything can be embarked upon in married life, there must necessarily be either absolute antagonism between husband and wife or loving agreement. When relations are uncertain, neither one thing nor the other, no move can be made" (771). The implied author in *Anna Karenin* not only tells the story but editorializes throughout.

Aside from these overt intrusions on the part of the implied author, we have more unobtrusive ones, which nevertheless remind us of a world outside the narrative. The implied author appeals to his readers' knowledge of the world and human nature to corroborate what he is saying, as well as gives his readers a dose of his own worldliness. For example, when Dolly does not hear Anna's entrance in Part One of *Anna Karenin*, even though she has been anxiously listening for her arrival, we read: "She was watching the clock, on the look-out for Anna every minute, but, *as often happens*, missed the moment when her visitor arrived and did not hear the bell" (80–81; emphasis added). When Kitty falls in love with Anna when she first meets her, we are led to believe that this, too, is not uncommon; Kitty "felt herself not only under Anna's sway but in love with her, *as young girls do fall in love* with married women older than themselves" (85; emphasis added). Finally, when we see Anna at Princess Betsy's, enjoying her secret knowledge of the princess' affair, while pretending to be amazed that the princess is not welcome in certain circles, we discover that the game of a hidden secret "had a great fascination for Anna, *as it had for all women*" (319; emphasis added). Once again we witness the implied author's propensity for sweeping generalizations; it is not just many or most women who love intrigue—they *all* relish it, even when it may be unnecessary, as it is here where all present are aware of the princess' affairs.

Tolstoy's implied author is such a strong presence in *Anna Karenin* because he does not let the characters' speech or mental discourse go unchallenged. He is able to tell us when a character is willfully blind to the truth and when he is conscious of telling a lie. More often than not it is Karenin's mental discourse that is controverted by the implied author. After giving us psychonarration that "Karenin believed . . . that in no previous year had he so much official business as this year," the narrator informs us that Karenin "*was not conscious* of the fact that this year he invented work for himself, that this was one of the ways of keeping closed the compartment where lay his feelings" (219; emphasis added). Karenin is similarly not aware that "above all" he wanted to punish Anna—"this he did not admit to himself" (304). On the other hand, Karenin *is* aware that "he could not exert any moral influence over his wife, that such an attempt at reformation could lead to nothing but lies" and that, though he makes his decision not to seek a divorce or separation from Anna without regard to the requirements of religion, he uses religion to give him "complete satisfaction and a measure of comfort" (304–305). The implied author does not let his readers be misled for a single moment by Karenin's self-deception and outward appearance. He reports Karenin's silent musings in quoted monologue but immediately contradicts them: "[T]his was not true: he [Karenin] had never sympathized with misfortunes of that kind but had always plumed himself the more whenever he heard of wives betraying their husbands" (302). The implied author always has the final say in *Anna Karenin*.

As we shall see momentarily with the narrator in Chopin's *The Awakening*, despite the commanding presence of the implied author in *Anna Karenin*, there are occasions when he pretends not to know why things happen and can offer only an "either . . . or" or a "might" to explain events. Tolstoy does this when his implied author cannot tell us why the guard is run over at the train station when Anna and Vronsky first meet: he was "either drunk or too much muffled up against the bitter frost" (78). The natural disposition of the reader must then take over, inducing him or her to take a cynical or optimistic interpretation of events; either one is possible. Drinking to excess and the bitter cold are both very common occurrences in the guard's world. Second, Dolly's children immediately take to Anna, whether they sense their mother's attachment for this aunt or are charmed themselves, the implied author cannot say (86). Finally, Vronsky's code of principles, which dictates, among other things, that "one must not lie to a man but might to a woman" and that "one must never cheat anyone but one may a husband" "*might* be irrational and not good," according to the implied author (327; emphasis added). Since the implied author proves none too reticent to judge elsewhere, we might best understand this line as ironic understatement. Vronsky's code of conduct is clearly inconsistent as it is loosely based on self-serving principles of dandyism and acceptable forms of behavior in Vronsky's social circle.

The Awakening

Kate Chopin's narrator in *The Awakening*, though intrusive and authoritarian like Tolstoy's and similarly able to tell us more about the characters than they know about themselves, is more distant, confining herself to psychonarration almost completely, except for moments of narrated monologue when Edna Pontellier becomes more self-aware. Psychonarration is the technique, you will remember, that creates the most distance since the characters' thoughts are mediated by and through the implied author's/narrator's discourse, and narrated monologue (or free indirect discourse) is the consonance of authorial discourse with that of a character's thought (the least mediated). Thus, it is suitable that as Edna Pontellier awakens, Chopin does allow moments of narrated monologue, which suggests that as Edna becomes more aware of herself, her needs, and her place in the world, her thoughts become more verbal—that is, they hover on the point of expressibility in narrated monologue. Previous to her awakening, the narrator interprets Edna's thoughts for the reader, thoughts that Edna herself could not verbalize, and tells us what her protagonist is *not* thinking or is not aware that she is thinking (as do the narrator and implied author in Clarín and Tolstoy).

When Edna cries after being upbraided by her husband for her lack of maternal concern, the narrator tells us that Edna "could not have told why she was crying" and that "[s]uch experiences as the foregoing [her crying] were not uncommon in her married life" (9). Like Tolstoy's implied author, Chopin's narrator does not hesitate to pass judgment on a character. She says of Arobin, for instance, that his manner "was so genuine it often deceived even himself" (77). Arobin's sincerity or insincerity is something that does not even concern Edna:

"Edna did not care to think whether it was genuine or not" (77). Consciously or unconsciously, Edna prefers her blindness, but this is not something that Edna could ever verbalize about herself; the narrator tells us more than the character can; consequently, the narrator is more reliable than the characters, and her words resound with greater authority.

Chopin's narrator is the closest to her protagonist of the six novels under discussion here: temporally, physically, emotionally, and morally. She never wears the mask of a member of the milieu that surrounds her protagonist. Her voice seems to come from the very psyche and soul of Edna Pontellier. The latter's marriage to Léonce Pontellier has not been full of life-changing experiences—even childbirth is a vague memory that she recalls with dread after witnessing Madame Ratignolle's experience with it; thus, the narrator conveys expository information about Edna's life through "iterative narrative" (when the narrator narrates at one time what happened "n" times[6]), as when she describes a habit that continues into the present—such as Mr. Pontellier's sending a box from New Orleans when he goes to the city on business. We are told that "Mrs. Pontellier *was always* very generous with the contents of such a box; she *was quite used to* receiving them when away from home. The *patés* and fruit *were brought* . . . the bonbons *were passed around*" (9; emphasis added). Edna's children have also developed a routine over the years. If one of them fell, he "was not apt" to run to his mother; rather, he "would more likely pick himself up . . . and go on playing" (9). This use of the iterative tense communicates a feeling of stasis to the reader. Life is unchanging; years can be summed up in just a few sentences (as we saw with Flaubert's description of Tostes). It is against this backdrop of boredom, conveyed in the very grammar of the text, that the life-changing events of the novel are dramatized.

Despite the narrator's obvious knowledge of Edna, there are times, as we saw with Tolstoy, perhaps to increase *l'effet du reel* (the reality effect), that the narrator feigns uncertainty. She knows more about Edna than Edna herself could ever verbalize, and yet, when describing possible influences on Edna that summer when she loses her mantle of reserve, the narrator suddenly hesitates before deciding upon Adèle Ratignolle: "There may have been—there must have been—influences, both subtle and apparent . . . but the most obvious was the influence of Adèle Ratignolle" (15). Again, the narrator can only speculate that perhaps the contrast in the two women's personalities "*might* furnish a link" (15; emphasis added). She then goes on to rhetorically query, "Who can tell what metals the gods use in forging the subtle bond which we call sympathy, which we might as well call love?" (15). Her rhetorical questioning of the reader and use of the first-person, plural pronoun demands our understanding and acknowledgment of the inadequacy of conventional language to describe true emotions.

The narrator of *The Awakening* moves closer to the story that she is telling, both temporally and emotionally, from the start to the conclusion, which we discern through her modal terms. In the end, it is no longer "that morning" but "the morning," and we move closer to Edna through more instances of narrated monologue. We never know how distant the narrator is from the time of the story, but this is clearly not an example of "zero degree narration," where the story is past tense but followed without any apparent disparity between the time of the story and the time of the narrating. The end of the novel does not have the same feeling of contemporaneity that Flaubert's *Madame Bovary* does in bringing us to the present day with its conclusion; however, Chopin's narrative becomes more focalized through Edna; therefore, there is a corresponding disregard for the outer world of space and time.

FOCALIZATION

We should note at the outset that there is a difference between seeing *with* the eyes of a character and seeing *into* the mind of a character. Fontane, Clarín, Tolstoy, and Chopin are much more apt to look *into* the minds of the characters than they are to see *with* the character. Flaubert and Queirós, on the other hand, as might be expected from their tendency to use narrated monologue, let us see with the character to a greater extent, though we still do not have anything like a rigorously internal focalization since the protagonists are often referred to in the third person, and their vision often receives ironic commentary from the narrators or implied authors. As Genette writes, "[T]he very principle of this narrative mode [internal focalization] implies in all strictness that the focal character never be described or even referred to from the outside, and that his thoughts or perceptions never be analyzed objectively by the narrator" (192). This, of course, is not at all the case with our six realist novels of adultery. As we have already seen in our discussion of voice and narrative modes, our narrators often comment upon what the characters see and refer to them in the third person even in narrated monologue.

Flaubert and Queirós dance between internal and external focalization. As we read *Madame Bovary*, we start off with internal focalization through Charles' classmates for our introduction to the pathetic misfit Charles, the focalization then becomes internal to Charles for our introduction to Emma. Thus, it is through the masculine gaze that we first see Emma. We then see Charles through Emma's eyes and continue to see with Emma for most of the remainder of the novel (until Emma's death). I say "most" because there are moments of zero and external focalization interspersed between internal, and as Lilian R. Furst notes in her *Fictions of Romantic Irony*, "Sometimes the point of view[7] of several different characters is adopted successively within a few pages, and occasionally that of several characters at once" (76). In order to provide the narratee with a description of first Charles' and then Emma's upbringing, our narrator resorts to zero focalization, the mode of the traditional omniscient narrator. It is through external focalization that we first see Yonville and witness the carriage scene in Rouen in Part Three. In general, however, we might say that the vision of Emma dominates the novel, and yet we must remember that Emma's vision is often immediately commented upon by the narrator and complemented by the vision of the men who surround her, which is not strictly internal focalization, as was mentioned earlier.

Queirós opens *O primo Basílio* with external focalization for our first glimpse of Jorge and Luísa, and it, too, becomes internal, variable focalization in the style of Flaubert for the remainder of the novel. The implied author refers to the characters in the third person and similarly subtly comments upon their vision. Unlike Flaubert, however, Queirós varies his focalization to a greater degree. Instead of whole sections seen through the eyes of a single character, Queirós allows us to see more frequently through the eyes of multiple characters in a scene. More often than not we see with Luísa, yet we also see with Basílio and Juliana in the same scenes as we see with our protagonist. Jorge does not become a primary focalizer until he returns from his business trip in the last third of the novel. We see with him, then, as he learns of his wife's infidelity and watches her die.

O primo Basílio is unique in that our last sights are through the eyes of the lover, through Basílio, and it is his name that graces the title page. In no other novel of adultery discussed here is the ending focalized through the lover. The implied author, who does have the last line in telling us that Basílio and Reinaldo go to play chess in the *Taverna Inglesa*, refuses to comment on Basílio's closing speech, wherein Basílio has compared Luísa to a stumbling block ("*um trombolho*"), expressed his disdain for her bourgeois lifestyle, and ended by wishing he had brought his French mistress with him since Luísa has so inopportunely died. Queirós allows the diction of this speech and its flippant tone to convey Basílio's brutality in so coldly and disrespectfully accepting the news of his cousin's death. Even the most obtuse readers must appreciate Cousin Basílio's insensitivity without the implied author's subsequent commentary.

In Chopin's case, the focalization is, once again, not fixed, but it does tend to be more consistently internal with Edna. We never know what Robert Lebrun really thinks of Edna until his words reveal his love for her in Chapter 26. We see into the minds of Arobin and Mr. Pontellier but not often *with* them. When we do see with Mr. Pontellier in the opening of the novel, his vision provides Chopin with the means to introduce the setting and some of the residents of the Grand Isle. After these preliminary chapters, Mr. Pontellier's vision does not figure in the novel. Nevertheless, it is interesting to note that even in a novel written by a woman, we start with a man's perception of the protagonist; we do not begin with a woman's focalization. Chopin and thus her protagonist cannot envision a new and viable self because they are still, to a certain extent, seeing with the eyes of tradition.

After the first few chapters of *The Awakening*, we do not see with Mr. Pontellier again. The focalization vacillates between zero and internal, fixed. Before Edna has completely awakened to her physical and emotional needs, we see through the narrator's eyes. We may have the impression that we are seeing with Edna since we read so many passages of psychonarration, but we are really seeing with the narrator. Edna cannot convey much about herself or her world, particularly in the beginning of the novel; hence, we are given a more intuitive, perceptive focalizer at the start. After the summer on the Grand Isle, instances of narrated monologue become more frequent, and we do tend to see more with Edna, but these instances are very often followed within the same paragraph by an intrusive narrator.

In Tolstoy, we do occasionally see with characters, but the predominant focalization of this text is zero. Tolstoy's implied author is more apt to *tell* us about a character's psyche than to *show* us the internal workings of the mind.

There are whole chapters devoted to a character's thoughts, like Chapter 13 of Part Three, which seems to be focalized through Karenin; however, the implied author mediates all his thoughts. He dips into Karenin's mind, but he does not allow us to see with Karenin's eyes. There are times when we do see *with* a character, such as our first sight of Anna through Vronsky's eyes; however, the norm in Tolstoy is that we either see through the implied author's eyes or witness a scene mimetically through character dialogue, with zero focalization. The instances of internal focalization are not sustained for long, but they are as variable as there are living creatures in the novel. There is even a brief chapter devoted to the perception of Laska, Levin's hunting dog.

Clarín's *La Regenta* follows a pattern similar to that established in *O primo Basílio* except that it contains much more zero focalization since the narrative is rife with authorial analepsis. Each time a character is introduced, we are treated to a lengthy description of his or her antecedents. The novel does begin in external focalization for our first glimpse of Vetusta and the church at its center; however, we very quickly move to internal focalization through Don Fermín to complete our description of the town, as he surveys it through his eyepiece. Indeed, when the focalization is internal, it is typically internal to either Ana or Don Fermín. To see through their eyes conveys to the reader their common frustration in not being able to live as they wish, that they must be voyeurs instead of active participants in life. Don Fermín's looking through the eyepiece in the opening of the novel serves as a metaphor for his psychosis. He must be a voyeur all his life, taking pleasure in watching others, since to live and love as the laity do is taboo for a man of the cloth, such as himself.

Much of the focalization of *Effi Briest* is external or zero. Aside from the epistles and quoted monologue, we do not often see into or with the characters in Fontane's novel. The few instances of narrated monologue provide us with sporadic glimpses into the workings of the characters' minds; it is then that we can see with the characters, and the focalization is variable. We see with Innstetten, with Effi, and with Gieshübler. The novel opens with external focalization—much like the historical novels of Scott, for example, of whom Fontane was a great admirer. Effi and her mother are described as "the mother" and "the daughter" and then "the daughter whom her friends called Effi" (16). Since we are able to see into so many of the characters' minds at will, however, the focalization must be labeled zero for much of the remainder of the narrative, aside from the instances of narrated monologue, as this is the focalization akin to a traditional third-person, omniscient point of view.

We now turn to our adulteresses—how they see themselves, their world, and those in it; how they are seen by the others; and how the narrators/implied authors tell about them. We will see what has conditioned them and created discontent and longing, what choices they make as they try to live out their fantasies within their restricted societies, and whether they are happy with the outcomes. Finally, we will witness their gradual disillusionment, their "staining" by society, and their (self-)castigation.

NOTES

1. The classification is Ciplijauskaité's.
2. Priscilla Robertson notes that adultery was more tolerated in countries where the marriages were arranged in *An Experience of Women*, 237.
3. Gay, *The Tender Passion*, 100.
4. Ciplijauskaité, 15.
5. See Gordon A. Craig's chapter "Historical Perspectives" in *The Germans* for a more in-depth discussion of the German national character and its genesis.
6. Genette, *Narrative Discourse*, 116.
7. Furst uses "point of view" here as Genette uses "focalization."

2

Stained-Glass Windows

> [T]he body seemed contained in a miraculous glass cabinet through which no sound could penetrate, and the mind, freed from any contact with fact . . . was at liberty to settle down upon whatever meditation was in harmony with the moment.
> —Virginia Woolf, *A Room of One's Own*

> I thought how unpleasant it is to be locked out; and I thought how it is worse perhaps to be locked in.
> —Virginia Woolf, *A Room of One's Own*

The image of a woman who either sees or is seen from a window is a leitmotif of literature and film expressing women's entrapment in the home, in domesticity, and relegates her to an object of desire for the male gaze.[1] Women are spectators of life, as Emma Bovary is in Tostes and Yonville and Effi Briest is in Kessin, where Effi's sole amusement is to watch people from her window in the governor's house. Emma's practice of similarly relieving her boredom by hanging out of her window was quite common, according to the narrator, for windows in the provinces replaced the theater and promenades.[2] As our protagonists look out on the world, we readers look into their minds. Having such a window creates psychological realism, whose impact is further increased by showing the logic of cause and effect at work in the relation between the women's past and present, conveyed through analepses to the women's education and upbringing. Knowing their pasts can help excuse, or at least explain, their seduction and infidelity since these writers apply the positivist laws of cause and effect to the mind as well as the world. We understand the motivation of each adulteress to have the affair(s) and the extent to which she is a product of her milieu, the biological determinism of heredity, and a victim of circumstance. One longs for a child and affection. Many are bored, and a few are deceived by the illusory happiness found in fictional accounts. All are trapped in unhappy marriages.

Several authors have used the image of colored glass to suggest truth obscured by subjective relativism. Heinrich Kleist's introduction to Kantian philosophy made him question our access to Truth since it may be that we see the world through green glasses, a metaphor for the way in which our knowledge of the noumenal world—Truth—is mediated and tainted by our perception of the phenomenal world.[3] Fitzgerald's narrator Nick Carraway describes a billboard for Dr. T. J. Eckleburg, whose great blue eyes look down upon the world through "enormous yellow spectacles," a symbol of the romantic readiness that Nick so admires in Gatsby (23). Flaubert wrote an episode for *Madame Bovary*, which he later excised, wherein Emma looks through a multicolored glass window in a gazebo while walking about the grounds at La Vaubyessard after the ball. Emma sees beauty where a pragmatist, looking through the clear glass of reality, would not. R. J. Sherrington suggests that Flaubert deleted the "coloured glass" episode from the final version of *Madame Bovary* since not once would it have occurred to Emma to look through the clear glass (which she does in the excised episode after looking through the blue, yellow, green, and red); moreover, it was as if Flaubert "were openly negating his heroine's way of looking at things," which ran counter to the methodology of this meticulous stylist (123).

Luísa in O primo Basílio, Edna in The Awakening, Ana Ozores in La Regenta, and Effi Briest see with Emma Bovary's rosy lenses to the extent that they all have romantic notions about love and marriage; however, aside from Luísa, they do not all share Emma's attraction to wealth and material goods, nor do their lenses distort the image of their husbands as much as Emma's do hers, and Effi, in particular, is very much aware of the danger that Major von Crampas poses and labors under no misconceptions about his sincerity and the nature of his suit. Anna Karenin is the most levelheaded of the six: she reprimands herself for daydreaming about Vronsky when he is away and imagining him in the arms of another and does not derive the same pleasure from reading novels that others do since she knows the effect that they have of creating longings within her that cannot be satisfied, given the nature of her milieu.

"Stained-glass windows" is a metaphor not only for the colored glass of romanticism through which many of our adulteresses look but for the stigma attached to our reflectors. They do not wear Hester Prynne's scarlet "A," but the judgment of their society or husbands is damning enough, and the degradation is every bit as palpable to them as the "A" is to Hester Prynne. In the cases of Anna Karenin, Emma Bovary, and Edna Pontellier, the stain is deepened by their neglect of their offspring and their suicide. Ana Ozores and Luísa Mendonça do not have children; consequently, they do not struggle with the competing claims of offspring and the love that they feel for their lovers. Although Effi Briest has a daughter, Annie's upbringing with Innstetten does more to stain her husband and exculpate Effi than it serves to further condemn the adulteress. Fontane's treatment of adultery is unique in more ways than this, as we shall see. Luísa and Effi both die in the end of illnesses wrought from either anxiety or loneliness (psychosomatic diseases, we might say). Ana Ozores, alone of the six, lives on to face a fate worse than death—public ignominy and ostracization.

WOMEN AND CHILDREN FIRST

Women were bound by religious dogma and teachings, societal norms, and, most immediately, the will of the father, brother, or husband—all of which reinforced one another. Among a middle-class woman's responsibilities would have been the care of the children. Aristocratic women commonly employed nursemaids and governesses, but not the bourgeoisie. Even more than the tie of matrimony, women of the nineteenth century were bound by their children—if not as the sole care providers, then because of the affection (once assumed to be a biological given) that they felt for their offspring. As the young peasant woman at the inn where Dolly Oblonsky changes horses in *Anna Karenin* laments, "They [children] tie you hand and foot," and Dolly thinks, "It was cynical but there was some truth in what the girl had said" (637). Dolly is the epitome of the ideal mother in Tolstoy, and even she acknowledges that children are binding. They require self-sacrifice, something that Edna Pontellier in *The Awakening* is unwilling to give, although she questions her decision in the end. Anna Karenin is the most maternal of the four heroines with offspring, yet her feelings for her son undergo a change once she meets Vronsky. While she continues to love Seriozha, she chooses not to have any more children after Ani, not even with Vronsky, and feels torn between her love for Seriozha and her love for Vronsky, which are clearly incompatible. Effi enjoys the company of her daughter for the distraction that it provides her and bitterly rails against her husband for turning her daughter against her; nevertheless, the loss of her child does not consume her as much as the loss of her home does (her childhood home at Hohen-Cremmen). She simply does not define herself in the role of a mother and so can live her final days at her parents' estate quite happily. Edna does not love her boys enough to want them around, but neither does she ever abuse them verbally or physically, as Emma does Berthe. Emma, a seemingly unnatural mother who loathes her daughter because she is female and goes beyond neglect to physical abuse in her treatment of her, is the complete antithesis of Dolly Oblonsky. None of our adulteresses are maternal figures (though Anna Karenin might once have been, and Ana Ozores would like so much to be); they want undying passion, freedom, amusement, and the power of self-determination, and children only further tie them to their homes.

Emma's tendency to romanticize her surroundings proceeds from the novels that she reads and from her education in the convent. Ironically, religion, as we will see with Ana Ozores in *La Regenta*, feeds her imagination and provides fodder for her dreams of undying passion and love; consequently, Emma turns to the church between lovers to fill her need for transcendental passion. She is not engaged intellectually by the theology of the church; rather, she is moved by the emotions that the religious icons evoke and the atmosphere of mysticism. She loves the church not for the God whose servant it is but for its images, its smells, the passion of which its accidentals speak: *"Au lieu de suivre la misse, elle regardait dans son livre les vignettes pieuses bordées d'azur, et elle aimait la brebis malade, le sacré coeur percé de flèches aiguës, ou le pauvre Jèsus qui tombe en marchant sur sa croix"* (Instead of following the Mass, she looked at the blue-bordered religious pictures in her book; she loved the sick sheep, the Sacred Heart pierced by sharp arrows, or poor Jesus who falls in carrying his cross) (70). Emma does not meditate upon the mysteries that these beautiful pictures are meant to represent. She mistakes the accidentals for the essential. She hears the language of the church in speaking of Jesus as its bridegroom, and this *"lui soulevaient au fond de l'âme des douceurs inattendues"* (stirs up previously unknown sweetness in the depths of her soul) (71). This metaphor to explain the enduring, loving covenant between the divinity and his people induces Emma to think of the love that she anticipates with *her* bridegroom. Thus, it is with pleasure that Emma first throws herself into the role of the dutiful, accomplished wife of Charles and actively works to make their marriage conform to the paradigmatic relationships of passionate love about which she has read in her romances and, ironically enough, gleaned from the trappings of the church.

When Emma's attempts to make Charles respond in the conventional form of a husband and lover fail, and when she feels that her accomplishments in the arts cannot be appreciated by him or anyone else in Yonville, she abandons herself to the monotony of life in the provinces, which predisposes her to the seductive language and behavior of Rodolphe. Since the role of the loving, accomplished wife is unable to produce a life exactly like what was represented in her romances, Emma abandons the role shortly after she and Charles are married and passes the time holding the fire tongs in the fire and watching the rain fall. She no longer practices the piano, for *"ne pourrait jamais, en robe de velours à manches courtes, sur un piano d'Erard, dans un concert, battant de ses doigts légers les touches d'ivoire, sentir, comme un brise, circuler autor d'elle un mumure d'extase, [ce] n'etait pas la peine de s'ennuyer à etudier"* (never being able to play an Erard piano in concert, in a velour, short-sleeved dress, lightly striking the ivory keys with her fingers, and feeling, like a breeze about her, the murmur of ecstasy, [it] was not worth the pain of wearying herself with studying) (97). It is not enough that Emma be an important person in Yonville; Emma wants the life of the heroine in a romance, down to the very last detail. She cannot imagine a dream for herself that is not ready-made between the covers of a novel.

As a schoolgirl Emma dreams of going to Paris and living an aristocratic life, a dream shown to be rather tawdry by Emma's grasping materialism and slavish devotion to fashion. Emma never actively pursues this dream, but it is important that the modern reader keep in mind her limitations. Taking a trip to Paris for a middle-class woman was not as easy as popping into a stagecoach, especially not for a single woman, especially not for a woman unaccompanied; further, Emma's marriage to Charles is really through force of circumstance. What chance did Emma have to live an aristocratic life? Whom else could she have married? As a farmer's daughter there was little hope of her marrying into the aristocracy due to her poverty and the lack of social mobility in a stratified society. The bourgeois women who were marrying above their station in life at this time were enabled to do so by the decadence of the aristocracy, which left many of its heirs penniless. In the interest of maintaining their failing estates, many of these decadent nobles were forced to marry middle-class women who, though beneath their station, brought the necessary capital to shore up the estates.

Emma, however, has neither capital nor titles; moreover, living in the country as she does precludes her from meeting many men—certainly no one of the aristocracy. There were, of course, marriages for love in the nineteenth century (Ana Ozores' father in *La Regenta* marries a seamstress), but Emma has little or no opportunity to attract a gentleman. Unlike Becky Sharpe in Thackeray's *Vanity Fair*, who manages to insert herself in the Sedley family and marry her "dear" friend Amelia's brother, Emma is not shrewd enough or blessed with the same opportunities that Becky Sharpe has in living in a vital center such as London. Emma's station in life limits her to domesticity, which she naturally rejects since household duties are rarely glorified in the fiction that she reads to escape from the monotony of the bourgeois home.

Léon provides temporary relief from the monotony of Emma's existence; however, it is Rodolphe who unwittingly equips Emma with the wherewithal to conduct her own affairs and thus never be bored. Emma feels with Rodolphe as though she has become a part of some great collective of fictional adulterous women, whom she has always envied and admired; in reality, as the narrator shows us, she has been duped into thinking this by a man who knows how women think and is well aware of the dreams that they cherish. In the excitement following her first sexual encounter with Rodolphe, Emma thinks: "*Elle devenait elle-même comme une partie veritable de ces imaginations et réalisait la longue rêverie de sa jeunesse, en se considérant dans ce type d'amoureuse qu'elle avait tant envié*" (She herself was becoming a real part of that imaginary world and fulfilling her life-long dream, in considering herself in the line of those amorous women that she had always envied so much) (191). Emma believes that her dream is fulfilled, that she is now savoring all "*ces joies de l'amour . . . dans quelque chose de merveilleu où tout serait passion, extase, délire*" (these joys of love . . . in which marvelous realm all would be passion, ecstasy, and delirium) (191). It will take a second affair before Emma comes to see that adultery can be as monotonous as marriage. She never has time to tire of Rodolphe, who orchestrates the entire affair from start to finish, but as the aggressor in her affair with Léon, Emma wearies of the game, the dreadful sameness of it all, and must resort to more and more extravagant means of stimulation. Her dream is ephemeral and can exist only in a few fleeting moments, in the newness of an affair; thus, it is an unattainable dream, for Emma dreams of a lifelong attachment to a lover, and as all these novels show, this is impossible: the affair is exciting only as long as it is new, and desire, once satisfied, is spent.

Emma's materialism and self-interest are present in the analepsis to her education in the convent, for even as an adolescent, "*Il fallait qu'elle pût retirer des choses une sorte de profit personnel; et elle rejetait comme inutile tout ce qui ne contribuait pas à la consommation immédiate de son coeur—étant de tempérament plus sentimentale qu'artiste, cherchant des émotions et non des paysages*" (It was necessary that Emma be able to extract some kind of personal benefit from things, and she rejected as useless anything which did not contribute to the immediate gratification of her heart—being of a more sentimental than artistic temperament and seeking emotions, not landscapes) (71). In playing the part of the dutiful wife to Charles after they are first married, Emma derives neither "personal benefit" nor "immediate gratification" and so she abandons the role. She sees nothing extraordinary in Charles' love since she is incapable "*de comprendre ce qu'elle n'éprouvait pas, comme de croire 'a tout ce qui ne se manifestait point par de formes convenues*" (of understanding what she has not experienced, as of believing in anything that did not manifest itself in conventional forms) (78). She has never been able to see beyond the conventional; nevertheless, structurally speaking, the ball at La Vaubyessard marks the beginning of Emma's intolerance for her surroundings because of the indelible impression that it leaves upon her psyche.

The ball, unlike adultery, is all that Emma imagines and more—but only in her imagination. She learns to waltz with a handsome viscount, witnesses the arrangement of a tryst, and watches the duke and former lover of Marie Antoinette dribble his soup down his chin—this last has often been held up as the model of Flaubert's ironic undercutting of his protagonist's point of view. Emma can only see that this duke was once the former lover of Marie Antoinette and is enormously impressed; she cannot see that regardless of his status or claim to fame, he has become a doddering old man who cannot eat his soup gracefully. For Emma, nothing is the same after the ball. Her heart is like her satin slippers, which are stained by the wax from the dance floor: "*[A]u frottement de la richesse, il s'était placé dessus quelque chose qui ne s'effacerait pas . . . [Q]uelques détails s'en allérent, mais le regret lui resta*" ([F]rom rubbing up against the wealth, something was placed on her that would never be erased . . . [S]ome of the details faded with time but the longing remained) (90). With this longing eating away at her, Emma feels the gap between her life and the life of the guests at La Vaubyessard all the more acutely.

In her attempt to try to make her life more like that of the guests at the ball, Emma capriciously buys all sorts of luxuries, such as a subscription to two women's magazines, large vases for the mantelpiece, a silver-gilt thimble, and an ivory sewing box; she buys "*un buvard, une papeterie, un porte-plume et des enveloppes*" (blotting paper, stationery, a penholder, and envelopes), even though the narrator tells us that she had no one to whom she could write (94). After Léon leaves Yonville, and she is depressed once again, she feels justified in capriciously buying a Gothic *prie-dieu*, lemons with which to bleach her fingernails, a blue cashmere dress, and the "finest" scarf in Monsieur Lheureux's shop, all of which the merchant is more than happy to supply since Lheureux, like Rodolphe, is intent on seducing Emma—in this case not with the promise of everlasting love, but rather with the pleasures that money can buy.

Rodolphe's seduction of Emma is, in fact, facilitated by Emma's love for material goods. Emma is impressed by Rodolphe, for instance, when she first goes riding with him because he wears expensive clothes and surrounds himself with luxuries. Rodolphe is well aware of her impressionability and so deliberately wears "*longue bottes molles . . . son grand habit de velours et sa culotte de tricot blanc*" (long soft boots . . . his long velvet coat and white tricot breeches) to cultivate this deficiency in Emma's character to his own ends (186).

Emma's materialism is more pronounced than that of any of the other heroines and becomes linked to her sexual appetite. The more immersed she becomes in her affairs, the more she spends: "*Alors, les appétits de la chair, les convoitises d'argent et les mélancolies de la passion, tout se confondit dans une même souffrance;—et au lieu d'en détourner sa pensée, elle l'y attachait davantage, s'excitant 'a la douleur et en cherchant partout les occasions*" (Her carnal desires, her longing for money and the melancholy of unfulfilled passion all merged into a single suffering, and instead of trying to divert her thoughts, she concentrated more and more of her attention on it, stirring up the pain and always looking for a chance to suffer) (140). Emma *enjoys* her suffering; she relishes the seeming impossibility of ever finding true love, but her materialism keeps her from ever experiencing the kind of transcendental love for which she longs because she is too fixated on the external trappings to ever intuit more essential characteristics of love. The narrator tells that "*[e]lle confondait, dans son désir, les sensualités du luxe avec les joies du coeur, l'élégance des habitudes et les délicatesses du sentiment*" ([s]he was confusing, in her desire, pleasures of luxury with the joys of the heart, the elegance of customs with refined feelings) (93). Thus, Emma cannot see that Rodolphe's flattery is empty clichés because to her this is the language of love. To her, love is expressed is a formulaic manner: with letters, locks of hair, moonlight rendezvous, and expensive presents. She cannot understand love if it is not expressed in this conventional manner, and such behavior is inseparable in Emma's mind from "*grands châteaux qui sont pleins de loisirs, d'un boudoir à stores de soie, avec un tapis bien épais, des jardiniéres remplies, un lit monté sur une estrade, ni du scintillement des pierres précieuses et des aiguillettes de la livrée*" (great castles that are full of luxuries, from a boudoir with silk curtains, with a very thick carpet, from full window boxes, a bed mounted on a platform, or the glittering of precious stones and the aiguellettes of liveried servants) (93). Only such settings as these, imagined in great, luxurious detail in Emma's mind, could foster love.

Emma does not struggle, as Anna Karenin does, with the pain that she is causing her husband and child. She does, in passing, wish that Charles beat her "*pour pouvoir plus justement le détester, s'en venger*" (in order to feel more justified in hating him and taking vengeance on him), but this psychonarration occurs in Chapter 5 of Part Two, not long after Emma begins feeling adulterous desires (141). Later, not only does she not suffer mental anguish, as does Anna Karenin over the pain that she is causing her husband and child and her own loss of virtue, but Emma actually *repents* of her past virtue: "*Elle se repentait, comme d'un crime, de sa vertu passée, et ce qui en restait encore s'écroulait sous les coups furieux de son orgueil. Elle se délectait dans toutes les ironies mauvaises de l'adultére triumphant*" (She repented of her past virtue as of a crime, and what was still left of it was now collapsing under the furious onslaught of her pride. She *reveled* in all the malicious ironies of triumphant adultery) (213; emphasis added). Emma can engage in romantic fantasies about running off with Rodolphe, but Anna Karenin runs off with her lover de facto, and she finds nothing romantic about the cold reality of adultery and the isolation from society that results from the transgression of societal norms and laws.

Both Emma Bovary and Effi Briest give birth to daughters, and although Effi is not at all disappointed in her little girl, the disappointment is expressed in the words of the doctor, who says, "A pity it's a girl" (110). Emma, all too familiar with the frustrated existence of a bourgeois woman, looks for an escape in having a son who can give some measure of freedom to his mother, but instead, Berthe is born, an event that causes Emma to think, "[*U*]*ne femme est empêchée continuellement. Inerte et flexible à la fois, elle a contre elle les mollesses de la chair avec les dépendances de la loi . . . il y a toujours quelque désir qui entraîne, quelque convenance qui retient*" (A woman is thwarted continually. Inert and flexible at the same time, she has against her the weakness of the flesh and her subordination to the law . . . there is always some desire that carries her forward, some convention that holds her back) (122–123). Any sympathy that we might feel for Emma because of her very real imprisonment by her milieu, however, is diminished by her treatment of her daughter, which places Emma's character in an unfavorable light, for Berthe's sole offense is involuntary—*she* is not a *he*. Thus, Emma perpetuates the devaluation of her sex.

Emma keeps Berthe at the wet nurse's except for the occasional visit to the house for the sake of appearances. On one such occasion, when Berthe approaches her mother, Emma repeatedly tells her to leave her alone, and when the toddler does not, actually shoves her away, causing Berthe to cut her cheek on one of the ornaments on the dresser. The narrating voice elicits the reader's sympathies for the child with the following description of Berthe, which has the effect of subverting the character of Emma, who sees this same scene with very different eyes: "*De grosses larmes s'arrêtaient au coin de ses paupiéres à demi-closes, qui laissaient voir entre les cils deux prunelles pâles, enfoncées; le sparadrap, collé sur sa joue, en tirait obliquement la peau tendue*" (Big tears had gathered at the corners of her half-closed eyelids, allowing one to see the pale, deep-set pupils between the two eyelashes; the plaster, stuck to her cheek, was diagonally pulling at the tender skin attached to it) (148). The tears, the paleness of the child, the tender skin being pulled by the plaster are all details meant to tug at the sentimental reader's heartstrings. Ironically, in this instance, Emma, through whose eyes readers may think that they are visualizing the foregoing, remains unmoved and reveals a pragmatic assessment of her offspring in quoted monologue: "*C'est une chose étrange . . . comme cette enfant est laide!*" (It's amazing how ugly that child is!) (148). Rarely do we have such dissonance in Flaubert between the focalization of the narrating voice and the focalization of one of the characters, but this incident clearly differentiates the perspectives of the narrator and Emma, leaving Emma in an unflattering light.

Emma does not die a graceful, romantic death. She poisons herself and even vomits black bile as the townspeople are preparing to bury her. There is little to admire in the way that she lived her life (or in the way that she died), much to criticize, much that is mocked surreptitiously by the narrating voice, and very little with which to sympathize. Yes, she is the product of her milieu. Yes, she is limited by her gender and her social class, but she is also devoted to fashion, slavishly imitative of the aristocracy, and blind to the unconditional love of the truly pathetic Charles and Berthe's need for the same. She can surely serve as an admonition to young girls of the perils of reading too many romances and of a sentimental education. If after reading *Madame Bovary* the reader still finds adultery attractive, then the reader also sees through colored glass and is deaf to the narrating voice.

Anna Karenin is infinitely more noble in characterization than Emma Bovary. She is of the uppermost class in Petersburg society, married to a high-ranking official at the ministry, beautiful, intelligent, graceful, and a devoted mother—at least some of the time. One of the most ennobling features of Anna's portrayal is that she does struggle with her culpability and with her love for her son Seriozha and her lover Vronsky. She has never dreamed of having an affair and repents of her infidelity the moment it is a fait accompli. The conflict between her love for Vronsky and her will-to-live and feelings of shame, degradation, and jealousy overwhelms Anna, and it is she who ends the affair by her suicide, not Vronsky, who has not quite surfeited his senses. Though self-centered and petty at the end, Anna's struggle to resist temptation and her sincere compunction once she stumbles, her noble beginning and her broken ending endow her character with such tragic proportions that few, if any, protagonists of the novel of adultery could compare.

Despite Anna's transformation from mother to mistress and her degeneration into a jealous harpy who must take morphine to sleep at night, she remains a nobler figure than either Emma or Luísa. Her death would not seem so tragic if she were not a noble figure in the beginning—the fall of nobility is, in itself, a tragedy. Anna "belonged to the best society" and has friends in all three groups of the top circle of Petersburg society. She is welcomed and admired by all, but this, in itself, is not enough to distinguish her from Emma and Luísa, for these women also instill admiration and even love in those around them. What distinguishes Anna are her social class and her disregard for Petersburg and its fashions. Anna lives in Petersburg and sets the fashions for women like Emma and Luísa to follow. She does not have to dream of a luxurious life; she lives it.

Emma and Luísa have doting husbands but none of the enchanting social life that Anna so little appreciates. Anna, on the other hand, has money and moves in the uppermost circles of society but does not value these things and instead craves the chance to feel alive, free of the stifling norms of society. Her passion for Vronsky is not fed by the trappings of wealth. Vronsky does not attract her because he is cosmopolitan. He attracts her because his "hero-worship" intoxicates her and nourishes her will-to-live. He does not offer her an elevated position in society; on the contrary, Anna considers him an "officer lad" and actually loses her respectable status in her social circles by cohabiting with him. No woman but Dolly visits her in Moscow, and Anna fears even appearing in society after her experience at the theater in Petersburg. Whereas Emma and Luísa dream of attending the theater in a great metropolis like Paris, Anna's affair with Vronksy bars her from such pursuits. She does continue to entertain handsomely in the country, but her guests are people who are willing to risk their good reputations or, more likely, those who have no such reputation to risk. She has exchanged her high society for a bohemian one; thus, she, too, descends into materialism in the end, but it is not the wealth that attracts her. It is the freedom and the *living*.

Many people immediately fall in love with Anna. Before being upstaged by Anna at the ball, for instance, Levin's wife, Kitty, had also fallen in love with her. For the most part, these two couples (Vronsky and Anna, Levin and Kitty), around whom the entire novel is built like a contrapuntal fugue, do not intersect, but as Kitty watches Anna enter the ball, we read: "Kitty had been seeing Anna every day and was in love with her," and the passage ends with this zero focalization of Anna: "It was Anna alone, simple, natural, elegant, and at the same time gay and animated, whom one saw" (93). What may at first seem like a change in focalization in this passage is really the difference between psychonarration and an intrusive implied author. Even Kitty's impressions of Anna's elegance, set off by the simplicity of her dress as a picture is by its frame, are focalized through the implied author since it is he who sees *into* Kitty's mind for the lines of psychonarration. The implied author would seem to be as taken with Anna, as are so many of the characters.

Anna is more than just beautiful. She is intelligent, graceful, natural, and sincere. Levin, often interpreted as a thinly concealed characterization of Tolstoy himself, notes "her beauty, her intelligence, her cultivated mind, together with her directness and sincerity" as she greets him during her exile from society with "the manners of a woman of high society, always self-possessed and natural" (733, 729). Her naturalness is part of her sincerity. She does not try to hide her difficult situation from Levin, just as she did not try to hide her affair from her husband: "Anything is better than lying and deceit," she says (315). Even without them, Anna is powerless to prevent the pollution of her natural nobility in the course of her affair and cohabitation with her lover.

Unlike the other adulteresses, Anna is able to read "serious" literature as well as novels, such as the technical journals of interest to Vronsky—so well, in fact, that he actually seeks her opinion first in these matters and is "amazed at her knowledge and her memory" (674). She is more mature than her counterparts in the novel of adultery and so does not romanticize adultery in the way that the others do, which adds to the impression of her intelligence. She does not, for instance, dream of taking a lover, nor does she enjoy vicarious pleasures through reading novels since identifying with the lives and adventures of fictional characters only serves to remind her of how limited her own life is. She shares Emma and Edna's habit of idealizing the absent image of her lover; however, she is quick to note the difference between her mental image of Vronsky and the flesh-and-blood Vronsky before her, thus demonstrating a clearer vision of herself and the people around her.

Anna reads as a pastime, but she is very much aware of the disparity between fiction and reality and the impossible desires that fiction can create: "Anna read attentively but there was no pleasure in reading, no pleasure in entering other people's lives and adventures. She was too eager to live herself. . . . But there was no possibility of doing anything, so she forced herself to read" (115). Reading about others' exciting lives, even though they are fictional, is frustrating to Anna since it emphasizes her own limitations; however, the very fact that she recognizes her limitations, recognizes that her life cannot imitate the fictional lives of novels attests to her pragmatism and lends her affair with Vronsky more than a touch of sincerity since Anna does not expect life to imitate art.

Emma Bovary is more attracted to Léon in his absence than when she is with him, and Edna Pontellier feels closer to Robert Lebrun in Mexico than she does when he returns, but neither woman draws any conclusions from these passing fancies. Anna *compares* her mental image of Vronsky with the one before her (when she sees Vronsky again): "She was studying his face, making up for the time she had not seen him, comparing, as she did every time they met, the picture of him in her imagination (incomparably superior, impossible in reality) with him as he actually was" (382). She is well aware that her mental picture of him will never match the reality of him, and she loves him despite his imperfections and despite her own desire not to.

Thus, since Anna is more realistic in her expectations from life, she struggles against her feelings for Vronsky and occasionally feels compunction for Karenin, as when she likens her abandonment of Karenin to that of a drowning man shaking off another drowning man: "The thought of the wrong she had done her husband aroused in her a feeling akin to revulsion, like the feeling a drowning man might have who has shaken off another man clinging to him in the water. That other was drowned. It was wicked, of course, but it had been the only hope of saving oneself" (489). Karenin has been like a deadweight around Anna's neck, stifling all emotion and spontaneity in his slavish devotion to the proprieties. He is, after all, a very high civil servant and would not hold the position that he does if he did not, at least outwardly, conform to societal norms. Unfortunately for Anna, Karenin has internalized these norms at the expense of a higher, moral law. Anna's will-to-live may not coincide with moral laws either, but she is far too happy with Vronsky in the beginning to let her regrets trouble her overly. It is not long, however, before her happiness with Vronsky begins to fade, as she questions his commitment to her and simultaneously hates herself for depending upon him alone for her happiness.

Anna's struggle begins so much earlier and is more intense than that of any of the others because she cannot live with the deceit, and it is the sincerity of her struggle that ennobles her in the reader's eyes. Effi is similarly uncomfortable with the lying, the cover-up, but she admits to feeling no guilt for what she has done; the adultery itself does not shame her, though the fact that she feels no shame does. Anna and Effi are both unaware of the importance that societal approbation plays in their lives until they have lost it. They are free spirits, natural, sincere, graceful, disdainful of lying and deception, and yet both chart a course replete with the latter, which consume them with unhappiness and guilt. Anna is consumed by feelings of shame and guilt for abandoning all (especially Seriozha) in favor of personal happiness with Vronsky. The guilt arises after the adultery is a fait accompli, but Anna's internal struggle between her attraction to Vronsky, itself a manifestation of her will-to-live, and her sense of familial and societal obligations begins upon her first encounter with Vronsky at the train station.

Anna's chance meeting with Vronsky at the train station disturbs her almost immediately. When he comes over to the Oblonskys later that evening, Anna is conscious of "a strange sensation of pleasure mixed with apprehension" (90). When she tells Kitty, an impressionable young woman infatuated with Vronsky and anticipating an offer from him, of her conversation with his mother on the train and seeing him at the station, she leaves out the part about the 200 rubles that Vronsky gives the dead guard's wife: "For some strange reason she did not like thinking about them. She felt there had been something in the incident to do with her personally, that should not have been" (88). Her apprehension turns to shame after the ball when she realizes that her behavior has been noticed by others—most notably Kitty, who is offended by her making a conquest of Vronsky, not that there would be anything amiss about the adulation and pursuit of a married woman. Single, married, and widowed societal women had their conquests. What Kitty bemoans is what she perceives to be Anna's bad taste in making a conquest of *her* beau. Anna never intended to make a conquest of Vronsky; she was obeying her inner drive, her will-to-live, though in the tranquil reflection on the train ride home, with the will quieted, she feels ashamed of her behavior at the ball.

Others notice Anna's inner turmoil. Dolly notices it almost as soon as her children do. She judges Anna to be "in that troubled mood . . . which does not come without cause and generally cloaks discontent with oneself" (112). The children manifest their cognizance of the change in Anna by their lack of concern that she is leaving. When Anna first arrives at her brother's house, the children all vie for her attention, but when she leaves (after the encounter with Vronsky at the ball), the implied author notes, "Whether the children were fickle of whether their senses were acute and they felt that Anna was not at all the same now as she had been the day they had lost their hearts to her and that she was no longer interested in them . . . they abandoned . . . their affection for her, and were not in the least concerned that she was going away" (112). These children intuit Anna's degeneration before she herself is aware that her interests come to exclude all but Vronsky and herself—her "chief preoccupation" being herself, we are told (674).

Anna is distinct from our other heroines in that she experiences a feeling of humiliation immediately after she and Vronsky have sexual intercourse. Her initial feeling is not one of euphoria, as with Emma and Luísa; rather, "[S]he drooped her once proud, gay, but now shame-stricken head. . . . She felt so sinful, so guilty, that nothing was left to her but to humble herself and beg forgiveness" (165). She feels the need to beg forgiveness for what she has done, but she can confess only to Vronsky. She has turned away from divine wisdom in pursuing personal pleasure rather than the good of the general welfare. Vronsky is now her confessor, her lover, her husband, and her friend. She has no other ties to society and life, none to which she has any right.

Anna does feel a tie to Seriozha, her son, but she has no legal claim to him and is not even permitted to see him. Before leaving Karenin, Anna confesses to Vronsky that she does not see how she can divorce Karenin if he will not let her have Seriozha. Vronsky urges her that it is better to give up her child than to continue in her degrading position. "Degrading for whom?" she queries. "'For me there is one thing and one thing only—your love. If that's mine, I feel so uplifted, so strong, that nothing can be humiliating to me. I am so proud of my position, because . . . proud of being . . . proud . . . ' She could not say what she was proud of. Tears of shame and despair choked her" (339). Anna, like Effi and Ana Ozores, lives through the exposure of her affair. Even without the scarlet letter on her breast, she is a known adulteress who is even more limited in her role as mistress than she was as wife, ostracized by society, and ashamed for having exchanged her son for her lover.

Despite the impoverishment of Anna Karenin's character due to her affair with Vronsky, she was, at the outset, a very doting mother. She certainly thinks of her son Seriozha more often than Emma considers Berthe and is genuinely concerned for how she will appear in his eyes and whether or not she will be able to maintain custody of him in the event of a divorce. She is more maternal than Emma (it would be hard to be less); however, the sincerity of her maternal feelings is questionable since she contradicts her own avowal of attachment to her son with her attachment to Vronsky. She herself is aware of the price that she has paid for Vronsky's love in forfeiting her place as the respected wife of a civil servant and mother of his child and is not at all convinced that it has been worth it.

Although we see Anna looking for opportunities to speak of Seriozha and show his photograph when she is visiting the Oblonskys to resolve her brother's marital dispute, her maternal feelings are soon displaced by erotic ones. She claims in a quoted monologue that she would do anything to keep her son by her side—a resolution that she almost immediately contradicts in thinking, "If on hearing this news [that she has confessed everything to Karenin] he [Vronsky] were to say to her firmly, passionately, without a moment's hesitation: 'Throw up everything and come with me!' she would give up her son and go away with him" (338). As is often the case in Tolstoy, the voice of the implied author contradicts what the character is thinking. Anna may not admit it to herself, but the implied author can see into her mind and knows that she would give up her son for her lover, as she indeed does.

Anna is aware of the "partly sincere, though greatly exaggerated role of the mother living for her child, which she had assumed during the last few years" (311). Though insincere at times, the role should serve to remind her that her son once did give her life the meaning that Vronsky cannot. Until her fateful meeting with Vronsky, Seriozha sustained Anna in her marriage to the cold, punctilious, and self-righteous Karenin, for Anna transferred all the love that she did not feel for her husband to her son: "On her first-born, although he was the child of a man whom she did not love, had been concentrated all the love that had never found satisfaction" (567). Thus, ironically, Anna loves the product of her loveless marriage with Karenin and despises the "love child," Ani, whose father is Vronsky, for Seriozha is the offspring of a licit marriage whereas Ani is the product of an illicit affair, yet even her love for Seriozha is not enough to keep her in this life after her disillusionment with Vronsky.

Throughout her affair with Vronsky, Anna periodically places her hope of happiness on having her son with her when she fears that Vronsky will not live up to her expectations of him. When she is confident of Vronsky's love, this is enough to sustain her happiness, but when she doubts his response (i.e., to her telling Karenin of their affair), she pretends that Seriozha is all she needs. She loves them both "equally," or so she tells Dolly,[4] but when Vronsky fails her in the end (according to Anna's perception of events), the thought of her son does nothing to console her—perhaps because she knows she can no longer have anything to do with him. Moreover, she recognizes that she has lived without him and been happy as long as Vronsky continued to satisfy her; she reflects aloud, in quoted monologue, "Seriozha? . . . I thought, too, that I loved him and used to be moved by my own tenderness for him. Yet here I have lived without him. I exchanged him for another love, and did not complain so long as the other love satisfied me" (797). She comes to question the enduring power of love in the darkness of her despair and concludes that we are placed upon this earth for no other reason than to hate and torture one another.

In addition to flouting convention by refusing to play the game of secrecy with her lover, Anna is unique, as well, in choosing death before her affair with Vronsky has come to its natural conclusion. The other heroines consider suicide only once their affairs are exposed (or threatened to be so in the case of *O primo Basílio*). In the case of *Effi Briest*, Effi welcomes the chance to start anew with her husband in Berlin and end her affair with Crampas. She even resigns herself to her punishment once the affair is discovered—lonely certainly, but not ready to commit suicide. Anna actually wishes she had died in giving birth to Ani—before she and Vronsky have even gone abroad together, long before the discord, ennui, and feelings of confinement begin. She returns to the idea of death in remembering this incident and thinks aloud in quoted monologue, "The shame and disgrace I have brought on Alexei Alexandrovich, and on Seriozha, and my own awful shame—would all be wiped out by my death" (777). Thus, she commits suicide, as do Emma Bovary and Edna Pontellier, to escape from an unpleasant and unbearably desperate situation. Unlike Emma and Edna, however, Anna also hopes her death will avenge her suffering by precluding Vronsky's peace thereafter. Emma and Edna choose death for very selfish reasons, but their suicides are at least not primarily intended as a means of vengeance.

Effi Briest does not actively commit suicide in the end of Fontane's eponymous novel, but like Luísa in *O primo Basílio*, her consumptive demise might be interpreted as a psychosomatic illness by today's standards—in Effi's case, brought on by her loneliness in being excluded from society. Mary Louise Coffey notes in her *Feminine Resistance in the Nineteenth-Century Novel of Adultery* the metaphorical association in literature between the figure of the artist and a "sensitive soul" (76). Effi does not begin as an artist, nor does she seem very sensitive or intuitive at first glance: she is a child of nature, young, naive, and uninhibited by principles of any kind. She is an agnostic like her father, though she will later admit the importance that religion bears for a society as a whole, contrary to her individual opinion. She craves amusement and adventure, loathes deception, and professes an ambition over and above Innstetten's own. Notwithstanding these initial attributes, Effi develops her artistic side as she takes up painting after her divorce (exiled as she is from all social activity, even of the charitable kind) and practices her technique with a passion. She gains sensitivity through her ostracization and dies a "sensitive soul," unable to live divorced from all social ties.

Susan Sontag in her *Illness as Metaphor* describes the connotations of tuberculosis in the nineteenth century and cancer in the twentieth as metaphors for the effects of a repressive society on individuals. "Tuberculosis," she writes, "was understood as a disease that isolates one from the community"—a disease "that individualizes, that sets a person in relief against the environment" (37–38). Effi does suffer from the repression of society, from an inability to express her passions first, then from her forced isolation from the community. Her disease seems to result from the isolation and not the other way around, which was the normal course of events.

Romantics will often waste away from consumption (tuberculosis); they can be both listless and feverishly active as a result of their disease, and Effi is most like Emma, Luísa, and Ana Ozores in her susceptibility to romanticize. She demonstrates a proclivity for the exotic, for fairy tales, and for extrasensory phenomena. She expresses no interest in the preparations for the play to be performed on the eve of her wedding since she does not believe that it could be any better than the production of *Cinderella* that she, her mother, and her cousin have seen on their last night in Berlin. When asked by her mother what she would most desire for her wedding, Effi finally admits that she has her heart set on a Japanese bedroom screen, and she wants the bulb in the bedroom to give off a red light (once again, the image of colored glass appears as a metaphor for the protagonist's tendency to romanticize). Her mother succeeds in persuading her daughter of the dangers of incurring the disapproval of society in Kessin, "above all because we're women," but Effi finds it hard to relinquish the image of all bathed in a red glow: "But I confess that I had imagined it all lovely and poetic to see everything bathed in a red glow"—to which her mother responds, "You're just a child. Lovely and poetic indeed, that's just imaginings. Reality is different and it's often a good thing, instead of a red glow, to have it quite dark" (35).

Henry Garland in his study of Fontane's Berlin novels lays much of the blame for Effi's immaturity upon Frau von Briest, who continues to dress Effi as a child "because of her . . . unavowed vanity" (173). Frau von Briest does not want to acknowledge her own age, which she would have to do by preparing her daughter to take her place in society as a young woman. Emma, Luísa, and Ana Ozores are all older, more mature women. Effi is just 17 years old, sheltered like the former, but unlike these three women, she has been spoiled as the only child of wealth parents. Her tendency to live in her dreams and imaginings seems only natural in one who has led a free, easy life, unschooled in society's mores and without the need to abide by many principles. Stanley Radcliffe sees in the opening of *Effi Briest* an emphasis "on brightness and light, ease of living, openness, balance and naturalness" (49). The setting for our meeting with Effi is a "rural idyll," as Radcliffe describes it (50). As it turns out, Effi is not at home in any other environment. Kessin and Berlin do not provide her with the same freedom, the same beauty of nature, the same cocoon of love as does the idyllic Hohen-Cremmen.

Effi's youth is stressed throughout the novel. "Young" is, in fact, one of the narrator's preferred modal terms to describe Innstetten's wife, and Effi's youth is the final consideration that Frau von Briest gives at the novel's conclusion as to how she herself might be to blame for what has transpired: "and finally, what I accuse myself of, because I don't wish to remain blameless in this matter, whether she wasn't perhaps too young?" (267). When the novel opens on the charming scene of mother and daughter engaged in sewing and conversation (though Effi seems little interested in the former), we meet a schoolgirl who wears a linen smock, with a sailor boy's collar (not at all the garments of a young woman on the verge of marriage, more like a schoolgirl's pinafore), who periodically rises to do her calisthenics, who drowns the gooseberry skins with a mournful dirge, plays tag, and enjoys her swing. In all she evinces a "childlike amusement," something that she will not lose until her affair with Crampas turns her into a woman. In her marriage to Innstetten, like Ana Ozores' to Don Víctor, she remains a daughter as her husband (like Don Víctor) is a paternal figure much older than she, who so little fulfills his duties as a lover and acts as her educator.

Effi's youth is part of her attraction in the opening of the novel and very likely curbs our judgment of her, as we might be inclined to punish a minor less severely for a crime than we would an adult. She simply does not have the moral compass of principles to guide her. Thus, she is described by her mother as one who is "fond of letting herself drift. . . . She's not one for struggling or resisting" (198). The narrator affirms this assessement by intruding to help explain Effi's willingness to engage in an affair with Crampas when she seems to see him clearly for what he is: "But although she was capable of strong feelings, she was not a strong character, she lacked endurance and all her good impulses came to naught" (157). Effi repulses Crampas' initial advances, but after the chance ride together alone in the sleigh, she can struggle against her natural inclination for adventure no longer.

As with so many of our adulteresses under discussion here, Effi falls victim to the dapper, seductive figure because of boredom. Like Emma Bovary, Effi's sole entertainment in Kessin is to watch people from her bedroom window. Radcliffe notes that as the wife of the local *Landrat* (governor) there were only a handful of houses that she could respectably visit: "the clergyman, the doctor, the chemist, the harbormaster and the depressive Frau Crampas" (27). Her husband's career dictates their social life, and even Innstetten sees little in the *Landadel* (landed gentry) to recommend them: "Petty-minded, jealous, parochial and terrified of new ideas, they exhaust not only Effi but Innstetten too" (Radcliffe 27). Effi generalizes her impression of Kessin society to all of Pomerania, finding them all "strict and self-righteous" (83). Gieshübler, an outsider himself, is the only person with whom Effi feels she can talk, "the only real human being here," as Effi says (68). Annie is to be her "precious toy," but although Effi is not uninterested in her daughter and certainly does not resent her gender as Emma does, she is not amused by the role of mother and so relinquishes the care of her child to Roswitha.

The reaction of Frau von Briest to Effi's frequent references to Gieshübler makes Effi realize what her marriage lacked: "[S]he needed someone to adore her, stimulate her, show her small attentions. Innstetten was good and kind, but he was not a lover. He felt that he loved Effi, and his good conscience in this respect led him to neglect making any special effort to show it" (99). While Gieshübler gives her these small attentions (indeed, he is enamored of

Effi), neither is he the prince of her imaginings or a cure for her boredom. Like Emma after the ball at La Vaubyessard, Effi becomes more painfully aware of the monotony of her existence in Kessin after the New Year's ball, which had been "rather nice" and made life afterward seem even more dreadfully dull. The scene is set for the impact of Major Crampas; in fact, Effi narrates his arrival to her mother at the end of a letter written during the monotonous months following the ball, during which time Effi has actually come to miss the Chinaman's ghost—a sure sign of her loneliness and readiness for an affair. Once terrified of the ghost, Effi now longs for its company and so brings Roswitha into her service for companionship but also in the hopes of rousing the ghost, who is rumored to appear when a new person visits the house.

Effi's longing for love is more like a child's longing for the attention of its parents than a woman's longing for the eroticism of a lover. In contrast with other protagonists, most notably, Emma, Luísa, and Ana, Effi does not expect marriage to bring her everlasting love. She marries out of ambition, as she naively admits to her husband: "You can't believe how ambitious I am. I really only married you out of ambition" (81). In this, as in everything before the affair, Effi speaks with shocking candor. She prides herself on her truthfulness and despises her lying even more than her act of adultery. She feels guilty after the affair not for her infidelity but because the adultery has involved her in a web of deceit and artifice that goes against her nature.

Effi at first claims that she is looking for love, but as she herself admits to Innstetten in the aforementioned citation, she, in fact, marries out of societal considerations of status. This much she has absorbed from her mother. Her cousin Dagobert would suit her temperament infinitely better than Innstetten, the man of principles, but Effi dismisses the idea when her mother proposes it to test her daughter's feelings for Innstetten: Cousin Briest, says Effi, "is still half a boy! Geert is a man, a handsome man, someone I can cut a dash with, someone who is going to be somebody in life" (38). Effi claims love is most important to her in a marriage, but it is hard to see evidence of this in her life choices. She says to her mother in describing her model marriage, "Love comes first but immediately after that comes honour and glory and then comes amusement—yes, amusement, always something new, always something to make one laugh or cry. What I can't stand is boredom" (36–37). Once again we have a protagonist who craves novelty and who learns to do so through the act of reading.

Effi has not been honest with herself, for if she were, she would have given her priorities inversely: amusement, ambition, then love. When Effi's mother reports the aforementioned conversation to Briest, she reiterates Effi's professed predilection for love but explains to her husband that Effi

"is not the sort of girl who is really set on love, at least not on what is properly called love. She talks about it, of course, as if she believes in it and she even harps on it, but only because she has read somewhere or other that love is the noblest, the finest, the most splendid thing there is. . . ."
    "And what is there at the moment? What does she feel?" [queries Briest]
    "To my mind and according to what she herself says, too, there are two things: love of pleasure and ambition." (43)

Effi marries according to the will of her parents—the rule rather than the exception until well into the nineteenth century (Garland 173)—but she is not the traditional woman Frau von Briest is, who can be content with an ambitious marriage and the comforts of wealth and societal status. Effi remains nostalgic for Hohen-Cremmen since she continues to crave the attention and doting love she has received from her parents there and forfeited prematurely in marrying Innstetten. As Henry Garland explains it, the reason that Effi is so fixated upon her home in Hohen-Cremmen "is the consequence of an extremely happy childhood, followed by a too early marriage with far too great a difference in age, and the partly negligent and partly repressive attitude of the husband" (184). Either from her reading or her milieu (or both), Effi has naively conflated the idea of a noble love with "cutting a dash" with someone significant in society. This may seem attractive to a young girl just coming out in society, but Effi, like any immature, spoiled child, must be constantly amused. She is a child of nature, while Innstetten is a man of art. She loves adventure, risks, and impulsive behavior. Innstetten follows the code of society and is a man of principles. The idea of him proves to be far more enticing than the reality, which is that, precisely because Innstetten is a high civil servant, there are very few places in Kessin where he and Effi can "cut a dash." Thus, far from coming to love her husband, Effi fears this man of principles since she has none.

With Effi Briest, we once again have a young protagonist who exemplifies the dangers of unsupervised reading. As Effi matures (her affair with Crampas is said to make her into a woman), she is able to recognize the source of her dreams and ideas about love and marriage: "[O]ne's ideas are a funny thing. They don't only come from one's own personal experience but from what one has read somewhere or learnt quite by chance, as well" (141). Since Effi has led a very sheltered existence in the country prior to her marriage to Innstetten, her ideas cannot be said to proceed from personal experience. Like Emma Bovary, she goes from the convent of her family home to the prison of a marriage from which she longs to escape.

Effi is resigned in the end of the novel to her death and her culpability in the affair. She no longer blames Innstetten, and, in an act that redeems her character, she assumes all blame, knowing that her husband must be suffering pricks of conscience regarding his treatment of her. Edna Pontellier, in contrast, cannot resign herself to the sacrifices that she must make as a mother and so commits suicide rather than relinquish the sanctity of her awakened being.

Edna shares Emma Bovary's sentimentalism, but the focus of Edna's endeavors is on defining and liberating herself rather than attaining romantic dreams of grandeur and passion, and her defiance of her husband and convention begins almost immediately in the novel. We enter the story at the beginning of her metamorphosis, her awakening, and chart her development through the course of the novel. Whereas Flaubert, Queirós, Fontane, and Clarín dwell upon the monotony of life in the provinces and fixed ideas of love or children, Chopin posits a deeply troubled protagonist in the midst of all the distractions of a wealthy summer resort. It is Edna's self-discovery, and not the desire for distraction, that becomes the narratable material of *The Awakening*.

Edna bathes in the heat of the day, refuses to come indoors at her husband's bidding, stays away until nighttime with Robert Lebrun on the *Chênière Caminada*, abandons her Tuesdays at home, ignores old acquaintances, tramps off alone all day, and returns late at night. In short, she breaks out of her role as the obedient wife and sets out to make herself independent of her husband. She is, like Anna, Ana, and Effi before her, an artist. Anna Karenin and Ana Ozores are both writers, Effi takes up painting, and Edna Pontellier, aside from her tremendous appreciation for Mademoiselle Reisz's music, also sketches with a "natural aptitude" (Chopin 13). Edna becomes independent by distancing herself from her family and society but orphaned in the sense that she has no ideal that she can follow. Mademoiselle Reisz understands her flight from the restrictions of convention, but she herself is cut off from society. What Edna needs, like Effi, is to be herself, a new woman *within* society, for the individual cannot exist without society in *The Awakening* and *Effi Briest*.

Unlike Emma's sentimentalism, which stems from her education in the convent and her reading of romances, Edna's is elicited by music. Religion, to her, represents oppression and conformity. It is associated with her authoritarian father and a repressed childhood. Because of her repressed upbringing, Edna, like Ana Ozores in *La Regenta*, must have recourse to her imagination in order to express her pent-up desire for love and passion. Edna cherishes secret passions for various men: a cavalry officer, a neighbor's beau, and a renowned tragedian. When she decided to marry Léonce Pontellier, she believed that since she felt no passion for him, she was "closing the portals forever behind her upon the realm of romance and dreams" (19). She might have closed the portals temporarily but certainly not forever since her romantic dreams are reawakened by Robert Lebrun and fostered by the music of Mademoiselle Reisz, only to end in frustration and disillusionment.

The catalyst for Edna's renewed faith in the transports of passion is music, especially that of Mademoiselle Reisz. Previously, music would evoke certain mental images—"dangerous romancing," Karenin would say—but when Mademoiselle Reisz begins to play at the hall on the Grand Isle, "the very passions themselves were aroused in her [Edna's] soul, swaying it, lashing it, as the waves daily beat upon her splendid body" (27). These passions of "solitude, of hope, of longing, or of despair" are distinct from the experiences of the other adulteresses since they are not turned outward toward the lover, who often represents life and love. These passions torment Edna, "lashing" and "beat[ing]" her body with their onset. They do not stimulate; they depress, and yet just as Emma takes pleasure in her melancholic suffering, so, too, does Edna relish her solitude, her longing, and her despair, as when she reads Robert's letters to Mademoiselle Reisz with the latter's playing in the background. This music has the same effect on Edna that novels have on Emma and Luísa: a whetting of the appetite, a vicarious thrill, a longing for the "real thing." Unlike the flat figure of the wan lady of romance, who wastes away for love of her knight in shining armor, Emma, Luísa, and Edna seem to thrive on the pleasure that they derive from the very pathos of unrequited love. The longing for love and passion is so intense that the wives feel alive in experiencing the ache of desire rather than the customary torpor of monotony.

The heightened emotional state in which Edna finds herself, however, distorts the way that she sees the world around her. Emma Bovary's clouded vision makes her intolerant of Charles' manners and blinds her to both her husband's devotion and Rodolphe's powers of seduction. Edna, for her part, is seduced by the sea, for the voice of the sea seems to echo her own feelings of despair and solitude. As the authoritative voice of the narrator describes it, "The voice of the sea is seductive, never ceasing, whispering, clamoring, murmuring, inviting the soul to wander in abysses of solitude," and "[t]he touch of the sea is sensuous, enfolding the body in its soft, close embrace" (113). The latter citation, which follows discourse that could be Edna's thoughts in indirect discourse as she enters the water (following in italics), is striking for the change from the past to the present tense, indicating the presence of an external focalizer: "*The foamy wavelets curled up to her white feet, and coiled like serpents about her ankles.* She walked out. *The water was chill*, but she walked on. *The water was deep*, but she lifted her white body and reached out with a long, sweeping stroke. The touch of the sea is sensuous, enfolding the body in its soft, close embrace" (113). The emphasized text is the only *possible* lines of indirect discourse; the passage is much more consistent, however, if read as pure psychonarration with an intrusive narrator at the end.

The "wavelets" in the preceding passage "coiled like serpents" around Edna's ankles, and the sea enfolds Edna in its "soft, close embrace." The sea is seductive: it encourages Edna to come close and feel its encircling embrace, and it is deceptive, like the serpent who deceives Eve in the Garden of Eden. The voices that Edna hears in the garden outside her house are similarly seductive and deceptive, though also occasionally hopeless. The focalization is more internal in the following passage, when Edna is alone and brooding on a rainy day (as is her custom on such days) and listening to the voices without:

She went and stood at an open window and looked out upon the deep tangle of the garden below. All the mystery and witchery of the night seemed to have gathered there amid the perfumes and the dusky and tortuous outlines of flowers and foliage. She was seeking herself and finding herself in just such sweet, half-darkness which met her moods. But the voices were not soothing that came to her from the darkness and the sky above and the stars. They jeered and sounded mournful notes without promise, devoid even of hope. (53)

Edna finds herself in the "mystery and witchery of the night" because, like the night, which is dark and mysterious, Edna has been unable to plumb the depths of her own identity; she is merely aware of a sensation of bewitchment in the desires and longings that she now experiences. She "finds herself in just such sweet darkness which met her moods," yet the voices that she hears are not full of hope; they do not embrace her as the sea does. They seem to merely reflect her mood at the time, the pathetic fallacy of projecting her own thoughts onto nature, for when she listens to the voices at other times, Edna is "led on and deceived by fresh promises which her youth held out to her" (73). Thus, Edna is deceived by the continued promises of youth, seduced by the sea, and mocked by voices in the night devoid of promise and hope. Is there no voice of truth in this novel? In the end it is the voice of despair, the voices from the darkness, the night sky, and the sea—all symbols of infinity—that best matches Edna's mood and so convinces her to escape this life by suicide. Thus, *The Awakening* may be classified as a failed bildungsroman since Edna is unable to forge or find her identity, whether because she lacks the "courageous soul" necessary to disregard the claims of tradition and the biases of prejudice or because her milieu does not provide a suitable guide.

Mademoiselle Reisz and Madame Ratignolle try to give Edna direction, but she either *can*not or *will* not heed their advice or examples. Mademoiselle Reisz, for instance, tells Edna that if she would be an artist, she must "possess the courageous soul," the soul "that dares and defies" (63). She feels for Edna's wings on a subsequent visit and comments, "The bird that would soar above the level plain of tradition and prejudice must have strong wings. It is a sad spectacle to see the weaklings buried, exhausted, fluttering back to earth" (82). Is Edna, then, one of these weaklings? Her suicide, though an escape, is also a sign of triumph since Edna has overcome her fear of drowning and her inability to swim in order to end her pain of living. Mademoiselle Reisz, however, never advocates suicide; she is an eccentric, "imperious," "homely" woman who lives a life on the perimeter of society but who has the strength of character to do so. Edna has not her single-mindedness of purpose nor her taste for the eccentric, solitary life; moreover, Edna is too conflicted by competing desires to be independent and free, to find love with Robert Lebrun and to spare her children.

Madame Ratignolle succeeds in reminding Edna of her duty to her children, and yet Edna is nevertheless unwilling and/or incapable of assuming her friend's role as a "mother-woman." The narrator herself remarks after Mr. Pontellier's musings on Edna as a mother that "[i]n short, Mrs. Pontellier was not a mother-woman" (10)—an assessment borne out by Edna's belief that motherhood is a responsibility "which she had blindly assumed and for which Fate had not fitted her" (20). Although of very distinct temperaments, Edna admires both Madame Ratignolle and Mademoiselle Reisz. She admires the independence and artistic virtuosity of the artist and the beauty and candor of the mother-woman. Before coming to question the very norms of society, Edna admires Madame Ratignolle for being the quintessential woman, one of those who "esteemed it a holy privilege to efface themselves as individuals and grow wings as ministering angels" (10). This Creole is like a "bygone heroine of romance" or "the fair lady of our dreams" when Edna first makes her acquaintance on the Grand Isle, but Edna's envy soon turns to pity when she visits her friend in the city and witnesses her "blind contentment" with domesticity, which, in Edna's mind, is tantamount to forgoing life's delirium and anguish. Edna would rather have the anguish than the ennui.

Upon witnessing Madame Ratignolle's contentment as the domestic mother-woman, we may well wonder how such a type could have the effect of causing Edna to lose her "mantle of reserve," as the narrator suggests in the opening of the novel. Madame Ratignolle, however, is frank and physically demonstrative with her affection, which goes a long way toward explaining this phenomenon. My label of a "failed bildungsroman" for *The Awakening* is not meant to suggest that Edna's character is static throughout, only that her suicide puts an end to her incomplete metamorphosis. She never develops beyond the childlike stage of development. Her capricious flaunting of conventions is done without any preparedness for the future, as when she abandons her husband's house without a plan for confronting him when he returns. She is childlike in her self-centeredness: "But I don't want anything but my own way," she tells Dr. Mandelet, and though now aware of the price that must be paid to have her way—that is, the trampling of "the lives, the hearts, the prejudices of others"—she is unwilling to concede the fight; consequently, she saves herself from further reproach or self-sacrifice by committing suicide (110).

The outward manifestations of Edna's inner transformation from a piece of property to an independent woman are noted by Victor Lebrun and the doctor. Both notice that she seems more alive and consequently more beautiful—not unlike Anna Karenin, whose beauty is her vitality. Victor says, for example, that Edna looks "[r]avishing," and that "she doesn't seem like the same woman" (61). For Dr. Mandelet the change is more subtle, but it has transformed Edna from "the listless woman he had known into a being who, for the moment, seemed palpitant with the forces of life.... She reminded him of some beautiful, sleek animal waking up in the sun" (70). This image of an awakening in the sun reverberates in the final scene when Edna strips off her clothes and "for the first time in her life she stood naked in the open air, at the mercy of the sun" (113). She is like "a new-born creature," but she has also failed to find a way to assimilate her desired way of life with society's codes of behavior.

Edna's inner transformation, like Emma Bovary's, is manifested in an external manner. With Emma, her lust for sexual pleasure is matched by her lust for material goods. The link in Edna's case is not between sex and money but between sex and food—a neater parallel since both are more clearly appetites. Having experienced life in the jet set, Edna does not crave material possessions as much as the satisfaction of her physical appetites; consequently, her awakening to the needs of her body is matched by a corresponding hunger for food. The first instance of this occurs on the *Chênière Caminada* with Robert, after Edna has had her very long, sound sleep. She must take a rest at Madame Antoine's after being overcome by the "stifling atmosphere of the church"—more than just physically stifling for Edna. She notices as she takes off her clothes and bathes select parts of her body—symbolic of her rebirth—that she has "strong limbs" and sees "for the first time the fine, firm quality and texture of her flesh" (37). She awakes from her nap and tears into the bread beside her bed "with her strong, white teeth" (38). When Robert makes her dinner shortly thereafter, "He was childishly gratified to discover her appetite, and to see the relish with which she ate the food he had procured for her" (39). Edna has become aware of her body—her strength, her flesh, and her appetites. Her hunger for food is representative of her hunger for all sorts of pleasures.

The second instance of her hunger for food is after her day at the races and dinner with the Highcamps. Arobin escorts her home, and after he leaves, Edna is hungry again, for "the Highcamp dinner, though of excellent quality, lacked abundance" (75). Proof of Edna's self-indulgence (maybe even overindulgence) is the description of her double chin when Arobin runs his fingers along her face shortly before the farewell dinner: her "firm chin . . . was growing a little full and double" (82). Her consumption of food is emblematic of Edna's overall loss of restraint, even though she is aware of how society would judge her: "By all the codes which I am acquainted with, I am a devilishly wicked specimen of the sex. But some way I can't convince myself that I am. I must think about it" (82).

Effi Briest knowingly breaks the codes of nineteenth-century Prussian society; she knows how her adultery will be viewed by her husband and others in society, and yet she still cannot feel any compunction over it. She feels more guilt for the deception that she must employ to cover her crime than for the crime itself. Like Edna, she tries to make herself feel wicked, but she can muster no such feelings. Perhaps, if we read Effi's deathbed apology and assumption of guilt as heartfelt and not meant solely for the soothing of Innstetten's guilt, then Effi does convince herself that she has been wicked. Does Edna? She wants to; she wants to find a place in her society. That her struggle is unsuccessful is evident by her suicide. Effi, despite her confession of guilt, is no more successful. Her tuberculosis serves as a metaphor for her incapatability to live in such a repressive society.

Aside from Emma Bovary, who seems to enjoy the game of secrecy as much as the novelty of adultery, the other three protagonists whom we have discussed in this section are uncomfortable with the deceit involved in carrying on an affair. Anna chooses to reveal her affair to her husband and deal with the consequences rather than live with the deceit. Effi desperately grasps at the opportunity to leave the lies behind her and begin again in Berlin. Edna, though she is said to like money as well as most women, is anxious to "put away her husband's bounty in casting off her allegiance" (80). She moves out of his house and into her own little cottage.

In contrast to Anna Karenin, who struggles with her self-identity only after consummating her affair with Vronsky, Edna Pontellier struggles with self-definition before ever engaging in extramarital sex. She does not understand the desires that she comes to experience. She is caught between biological necessity and the romantic longing to experience "life's delirium" (56). In casting off the self that she wore for society, she "was becoming herself daily" and adding "to her strength and expansion as an individual" (57, 93). But it is ironic that if Edna is meant to be a champion of individualism, she should fall asleep while reading Emerson. Is there an implicit criticism in her being perhaps *overly* individualistic? She is a mother who refuses to sacrifice herself for her children—a new woman in this regard, very atypical of the era. She says, "I would give up the unessential; I would give my money, I would give my life for my children; but I wouldn't give myself" (48). If Edna feels no attachment to her husband and children, should she be obliged to obey man-made laws and respect her marriage and motherhood? Her suicide is an implicit acknowledgment that she, for one, could not disregard societal laws. Though she does not agree with them, she is either unwilling or unable to live a rebellious life that would trample upon the innocent lives of her children. She does not worry about Léonce overly, but she cannot disregard her children; neither is she willing to sacrifice her independence for them. Her only solution is the escape that suicide offers. Whether or not her suicide should be seen as the triumph of individualism or the tragedy of solitude is discussed in Chapter 4.

As was mentioned in the introduction to this chapter, it is interesting to note that, of the women discussed here, the mothers (with the exception of Effi Briest) are the ones who commit suicide. Ana Ozores and Luísa, as we shall see directly, do not commit suicide and do not have any children. Luísa's brain fever is almost certainly self-wrought, but this, at best, would constitute a passive suicide *à la Michael Henchard*, in Thomas Hardy's *The Mayor of Casterbridge*, who refuses to eat and so starves himself to death. Ana Ozores does not even attempt suicide, though her life of dishonor after the exposure of her affair with Mesía is a fate worse than death, making the suicides of the other protagonists described here more than understandable. And Effi's death of a tuberculosis-like disease demonstrates that her natural, individual joie de vivre cannot coexist with the repressive society that surrounds her. As Susan Sontag notes in *Illness as Metaphor*, "Disease metaphors are used to judge society not as out of balance but as repressive," and "[t]he disease that individualizes, that sets a person in relief against the environment, is tuberculosis" (73, 37). Effi is not torn between the demands of motherhood and self (she gives little thought to her alienated Annie once home at Hohen-Cremmen); she is beset by the irreconcilable differences between herself and a society that refuses to forgive her.

Why is it that the mothers so often choose suicide? No one prototype of motherhood fits the various protagonists. Effi, perhaps due to her youth, very quickly forgets her daughter once home again. Anna fights valiantly to be an ideal mother to her son Seriozha, all the while slowly realizing that she cannot be Vronsky's lover as well as Seriozha's mother, and she hates herself for the path that she chooses. Emma tries hard to disregard her role as mother since it is so very bourgeois, though she does make an ineffectual attempt to make amends for her neglect while on her deathbed. Edna, who lives a life about which Emma can only dream, is no happier for it. She prefers the freedom that she enjoys in the absence of her children to the brief mitigation of her solitude when she is with them. Edna has married into high society, but her husband does not please her any more than Charles pleases Emma, and high society proves to be just as boring as bourgeois; moreover, Edna has the sons whom Emma wishes she could have, but she loves them only slightly more than Emma loves Berthe.

Edna is the product of a half-century of progress in the education of women and the growing awareness of their inequitable subjection to men. Nevertheless, she, too, must struggle against unwanted motherhood, a myopic husband, and daunting tradition. Effi alone of these six adulteresses has a happy childhood and a loving mother, yet even her mother does not prepare her daughter well for society and marries her too young to her mother's former beau so as to live vicariously through her. Effi, the most childlike of them all, longs only for home, not for Mr. Right and not for children.

Our other protagonists do not even have affectionate mothers to serve as models for the reality of being a woman in their milieu. Such figures could have dispelled some of their misconceptions about love, marriage, and adultery.

As it is, all but Effi lose their mothers at an early age and grow up in cold, loveless environments or, at least in Emma's case, an unrefined, rural one, and yet despite their cold upbringing, it is with nostalgia that Anna and Edna think back to their childhoods. Even without the affection of a mother, their youths were full of innocence, dreams, and irresponsibility. These days are more dear to Anna Karenin and Edna Pontellier than the first blossoming of passion, for a passion's satiation is its death, and the woe left in its wake is unendurable.

The word "abyss" recurs frequently in these novels of adultery. It is as though the adulterous wife falls into an abyss of despair upon realizing that her dreams cannot become a reality. For Emma, the abyss is public disapproval, as when she claims that she would like to be open about her love for Léon (her first adulterous inclination) but decides that she would rather endure the hypocrisy than face the "*abîme*" (abyss). The abyss widens before her when she must return from Rodolphe's without the money; eating arsenic is Emma's way of avoiding the gaping chasm.

Karenin is said to similarly face an abyss, and the abyss that yawns before him can be said to yawn before all our protagonists: "The abyss was real life; the bridge, that artificial existence Karenin had been leading" (Tolstoy 159). The adulteresses build an artificial existence out of their romantic ideas of love and passion; Karenin deceives himself with a social construct of the happy, ideal family, which concedes a rather limited role to the dutiful husband. The abyss is the reality that they must all come to face, and those who see no bridge over it choose to exit, often in a romantic fashion, still acting according to the script of romanticism.

Edna must face reality, must face the abyss—one of many such images of infinity in *The Awakening*. Edna seeks to lose herself in the infinity of the sea, just as she tried to lose herself in the infinity of the bluegrass meadow when she was a child. She has not succeeded in defining herself or her relation to the world. Her passion is for life, but she chooses death—what Nikolai Berdiaev calls the "absolute solitude,"[5] an appropriate epithet here since Chopin's working title for *The Awakening* was "A Solitary Soul." Edna's attempt to find or forge her own identity, to find a room of her own fails, both because she does not have a "brave, courageous soul" and because she does not realize that solitude can be as seductive as a man—and infinitely more dangerous.

A FATE WORSE THAN DEATH

Luísa and Ana, the protagonists of *O primo Basílio* and *La Regenta*, do not have children and do not actively take their own lives in the end. Both novels have been studied as imitations of Flaubert's masterpiece,[6] yet the changes made to plot and character are significant enough to merit in-depth and comparative studies of these three novels in place of mere "influence studies." The protagonists are romantics who have affairs, then fear public humiliation, but Luísa does not have a bovine, obtuse husband, and Ana's is perhaps equally influenced by the books that he reads. His immersion in the "*capa y espada*" (cloak-and-dagger) dramas of the *Siglo de Oro* (Golden Age) induces him to carry out the duel that leads to his death. Art may have reflected life in realist literature of the nineteenth century, but at the time of Clarín's writing, duels were no longer the norm; thus, Ana's husband lives according to his dramas, and "life" reflects art.

The parallels between Luísa and Emma Bovary are greater than those between Ana Ozores and Emma, for Ana Ozores is of a higher class and more determined by psychology than is her counterpart in the French tradition. Luísa, on the other hand, shares a comparable social status (just slightly more elevated than Emma) and is similarly bored with life and inflamed by the novels that she reads and the theater that she attends. In fact, her boredom opens the door to temptation, which she herself admits: "*Se ele* [Jorge] *estivesse ao pé dela! Mas tão longe e demorar-se tanto!*" (If only he [Jorge] were at her side! But so far away and to delay so!) (119). Her cousin seems so appealing, in part, because Jorge is not present. Would she have committed adultery if Jorge never left on business? Her love for Jorge after his return and her overwhelming desire to conceal her affair, which she now wholeheartedly regrets, would seem to indicate that she would not have. She is more like Effi in welcoming the chance to put her indiscretion behind her and resume the role of the dutiful wife. Their adultery is a balm for boredom.

We learn from the analepsis to Luísa's youth that Luísa enjoys similar pursuits and shares common dreams with Emma, despite their very different upbringing, milieu, and motive for marriage. Luísa spent summers, as a child, on her uncle's estate in Sintra and winters in Lisbon. She was not educated in a convent (indeed, no description of her education is given beyond a casual allusion to "school days") and seems to have enjoyed more freedom than Emma since her mother was a rather lax chaperone who would fall asleep while reading a volume from the Ladies' Library, which left Basílio and Luísa virtually alone. Her social status is slightly higher than Emma's since she and Jorge live in Lisbon (the cultural center of Portugal); he is an engineer (one of the new intellectual elite), and they are able to maintain *two* servants as opposed to Emma's one, whom Emma tries to turn into a ladies' maid.

Luísa, furthermore, does not marry out of boredom. Once she recovers from the rupture with Basílio, and once her mother is convalescing from her illness, she entertains the passion of a lieutenant in the military and reflects, "*Foi um tempo muito alegre, cheio de consolações*" (It was a very happy time, full of consolations) (23). She is clearly not pining away on a farm in the provinces, alone with her father. She seems to have had plenty with which to keep herself occupied . . . so why marry Jorge?

Aside from the obvious need for all women to marry, enter a convent, or become a dependent upon the family for life, Luísa marries to appease her mother and society and because Jorge is comfortable and comforting, and he offers protection from bodily harm and gossip. Fanny Burney's *Evelina*, an eighteenth-century British novel, shows the dangers that a young, unprotected woman faces in society. Without the supervision and protection of a father figure, she is susceptible to the flattery of ne'er-do-wells—a veritable assault upon her virtue. Perhaps women never needed the supervision and protection of a male to the extent that Burney's novel suggests (this being the manifestation of paternalistic thinking through an immasculated viewpoint); nevertheless, the protection of a male is deemed necessary in Queirós mostly because it was expected. When Luísa wanders the streets at night with Juliana as her sole companion, she is taken for a prostitute and pursued by a man with a straw hat. Once safely at home again she berates herself: *"Que imprudência, por-se a passear pelas ruas de noite, com uma criada! Estava douda, desconhecia-se"* (What foolhardiness, to walk through the streets at night with a servant! She was sickened and did not know herself) (222). Well-bred women simply did not walk about unescorted, particularly at night, which Luísa well knows and which explains why she is beside herself when she returns home. She has acted rashly, uncharacteristically, and unwittingly identified herself as a woman of the streets.

Jorge (when he is around) provides Luísa with the necessary protection, and Luísa feels comfortable with him: *"E sem o amar, sentia ao pé dele como uma fraqueza, uma dependência e uma quebreira, uma vontade de adormecer encostada ao seu ombro, e de ficar assim muitos anos, confortável, sem receio de nada"* (And without loving him, she felt a certain weakness, dependence and fragility when she was around him, a willingness to sleep leaned up against his shoulder, and to remain thus for many years, comfortable, without fear of anything) (24). Luísa admits to never loving Jorge and even goes so far as to admit that his physical appearance did not please her at all when she first made his acquaintance. With time, she comes to appreciate his nice eyes, the *frescura* (freshness) about him, and the comfort that he brings her.

Aside from his tender disposition, Luísa is comforted by the mere fact of her engagement to Jorge since it will relieve her mother: *"Estava noiva, emfim!Que alegria, que descanso para a mamã!"* (She was engaged at last! What happiness, what a relief for her mother!) (24). Thus, like many marriages of the nineteenth century (including those discussed here), Jorge and Luísa's union is adulterated from the start by subconscious motives for marrying. As Vronsky presages in *Anna Karenin*, "[H]ow often the happiness of *mariage de convenance* falls to pieces just because the very passion that was disregarded asserts itself later!" (153). Naturally, not all marriages of convenience ended in adultery. What exacerbated the dispassionate socioeconomic union was a spouse's desire for perpetual passion and excitement.

Expectation plays a significant role in the women's disillusionment with first marriage, then adultery. Luísa, like Emma, constructs an imaginary world where everything is beautiful and refined, where lovers are like chivalric knights, and where love is both passionate and good. She has always enjoyed and continues to read romances, such as those written by Walter Scott and Alexander Dumas. When she was 18, she wanted to live in a Scottish castle and was enamored of Ivanhoe, Ervandalo, and Morton, whose images spawn the image of ideal lovers: *"apareciam-lhe de gravata branca, nas ombreiras das salas de baile, com um magnetismo no olhar, devorados de paixão, tendo palavras sublimes"* (they appeared to her with white ties, in the door-posts of ballrooms, with a magnetism in their eyes, devoured by passion, speaking sublime words) (20). Jorge, though capable of giving love, like Charles Bovary, is found wanting by Luísa, whose ideal is literally a knight in shining armor.

Although Jorge reminisces about "nights of passion" as he watches Luísa's hair being lopped off during her deathbed fever, he does not seem to be "devoured by passion" when we meet him in the opening scene of a leisurely July luncheon. The predominant element in the description of Jorge's feelings is "tenderness." His disposition is inherited from his mother—"*o génio manso*" (a gentle nature) (15). Any passion that he might have felt for Luísa lies dormant until the end of the novel when her illness revives it. The reality of Jorge does not match Luísa's mental picture of him: she at first believes him capable of stabbing her, which excites her; only later does Luísa perceive the placid temperament of Jorge and take comfort from the constancy of his love and protection. Although he does not match the ideal of romance, Jorge ironically dies a very romantic death—by pining away for love of Luísa. Either Jorge is a sentimentalist like Luísa, or he has become polluted by sentimentalism after his wife's death, as Charles does after Emma's.

Part of Luísa's detachment from reality is revealed in her inability to envision the development of life in the future; she sees life through the colored spectacles of romance, where the characters are ever-youthful and the passion always scintillating. She imagines Jorge "*sempre amante, novo, forte*" (always the lover, new and strong), and she sees her imagined child "*sempre dependente do seu peito, da maminha, ou gatinhando e palrando, louro e cor-de-rosa*" (always dependent on her breast, on her milk, or crawling and babbling, blond and pink) (56–57). The psychonarration continues: "*E a vida aparecia-lhe infindável, de uma doçura igual, atravessada do mesmo enternecimento amoroso, quente, calma e luminosa como a noite que os cubria*" (And life seemed endless to her, of a like sweetness, pierced with the same loving, hot, calm and luminous compassion as the night that covered them) (57). Jorge's absence and Basílio's presence shock her out of this "sweet sameness," and she realizes, first, that she has the chance to experience the happiness about which she has always read and dreamed, and subsequently, that such happiness exists only in the newness of a relationship and that Jorge's love is something more precious because it is more sincere and constant.

Luísa, unlike Emma, has a greater awareness, in her more lucid moments, that she and Basílio are playing a very dangerous game. She vacillates throughout the novel between her longing to be chic and her intuition that her marriage with Jorge is far preferable to her affair with her cousin. Even as she begins to engage in nostalgic memories of her maidenhood and dreams of visiting Scotland, Paris, and Venice, she queries, "*Não era melhor viver num bom conforto, com um marido terno, uma casinha abrigada, cochões macios, uma noite de teatro as vezes, e um bom almoço nas manhãs claras?*" (Wasn't it better to live comfortably, with a tender husband, in a warm house with soft mattresses, an occasional night at the theater, and a good breakfast on clear mornings?) (71). When Basílio does not appear for his daily visit one day (before they begin meeting at the "paradise"), Luísa decides not to receive him anymore, and the narrator comments, "*E o seu grande amor, de repente, como um fumo que uma rajada dissipa, desapareceu! Sentiu um alívio, um grande desejo de tranquilidade*" (And her great love, suddenly, like smoke that a gust of wind dispels, disappeared! She felt relieved and a great desire for tranquility) (51).

The passage then moves directly into internal monologue: "*Era absurdo realmente, com um marido como Jorge, pensar noutro homem, um leviano, em estróina!*" (It was absurd, really, with a husband like Jorge, to think about another man and a frivolous, extravagant one at that!) (151). When Leopoldina, Luísa's close friend from her "school days," echoes Emma's lamentation about wishing to be a man, for then she could do anything, Luísa responds, "—*São tolices, no fim, andar, viajar! A única coisa neste mundo é a gente estar na sua casa, com o seu homem, um filho ou dois*" (They are foolish notions in the end, going abroad and traveling! The only thing that matters in this world is that we are at home with our men and a child or two) (162). Luísa reiterates the values of her society here, but she herself is not thoroughly convinced at this point that the life of domesticity is preferable to the life of adulterous love. She vacillates as Anna Karenin does regarding her need for her son Seriozha. After a slight from Basílio, Luísa is content to stay home. When inflamed by passion, however, she is ready to abandon her home and exchange her bourgeois life for the life of a mistress in Paris.

Luísa's bovarism[7] and materialism prevail over these "moments of truths"; nevertheless, these flashes of insight, momentary though they are, show a greater awareness of Basílio's duplicity than Emma ever has of Rodolphe's. It is only after she wears herself out with Léon that Emma finally tires of adultery. Luísa vacillates early in her one and only affair; she is propelled by boredom, her highly impressionable character, and her naive acceptance that happiness would come with life's luxuries. We have seen how she questions the sincerity of Basílio's proclamations of love; she is also equally persuaded by them. She is a puppet who moves in whatever direction the puppeteer pulls her. When Basílio is attentive, and her secret is safe, then Luísa is a willing partner in crime, willing to cast off bourgeois life, but when Basílio slights her, then she scorns Basílio's love and takes consolation in Jorge's. When it looks as if exposure is imminent after Juliana steals two of Luísa's love letters, then Luísa consoles herself with the thought that this "disaster" was at least forcing her to make a move that she would not otherwise have had the courage to make: "*O que havia de infeliz em abandonar a sua vida estreita entre quatro paredes, passada a examinar róis de cozinha e a fazer* crochet, *e partir com um homem novo e amado, ir para Paris! para Paris! Viver nas consolações do luxo, em alcovas de seda, com um camarote na Opera. . . ! Sem ele [o desastre] nunca teria tido a coragem de se desembaraçar da sua vida burguesa* (What was so sad about abandoning her narrow life between four walls, spent examining kitchen items and crocheting, and going to Paris with a new man whom she loved! To Paris! To live in the consolation of luxurious living, in silk bedrooms, with a box at the opera. . . ! Without it [the disaster] she would never have had the courage to disencumber herself of her bourgeois life) (234). Luísa is anxious, as is Emma, to live the fashionable, cosmopolitan life of high society. Unlike Emma, however, Luísa is, at times, quite content with her bourgeois life, though nevertheless sensitive to her cousin's criticism of it.

Basílio best plays on Luísa's susceptibilities by telling her how aristocratic ladies live. He overcomes her bourgeois morality by making adultery seem almost like the duty of the aristocracy and her hesitancy to try it, a defect of the bourgeoisie: "*O adultério aparecia assim um dever aristocrático. De resto a virtude parecia ser, pelo que ele contava, o defeito de um espíritu pequeno, ou a ocupação reles de um temperamento burguês.*" (Adultery seemed thus like an aristocratic duty. Besides, virtue seemed to be, according to how he described it, the defect of a small spirit or the despicable occupation of a bourgeois temperament) (126). The force of Basílio's persuasive powers more or less convinces Luísa that adultery is something like "an aristocratic *duty*"—an obvious exaggeration on Basílio's part that adds humor and foregrounds Luísa's naïveté—but if not a duty, adultery certainly was an expectation of aristocratic, arranged marriages, particularly in Europe. D. Camila bears out the truth of this statement, for she is a woman "*ilustre pelo seus amantes*" (famous for her lovers), and yet she can take a stroll with her illegitimate children and host soirées and be the toast of the town—none the worse for her nefarious reputation. As Luísa notes when she sees her, "*Era muito festejada, ninguém dizia mal dela*" (She was very celebrated; no one spoke badly of her) (243). Though she does not fully realize or comprehend it, such would not be Luísa's reception in society after an affair because of her social class.

Adultery may have been tolerated by the aristocracy, but it was strongly censured by the moralizing middle class. Had she lived, Luísa would not have been celebrated like D. Camila but rather ostracized from her social circles. Luísa senses the disapproval that would follow her in her own social milieu, but Basílio is able to mold her to his way of thinking, to the point where she pretends to disdain the virtue so typical of her class. She is shaped to the point of "*afectar, sem o sentir, um desdém pela gente virtuosa, para imitar as suas opiniões libertinas*" (affecting, without really feeling it, a disdain for virtuous people, in order to imitate his [Basílio's] liberal opinions) (203). Basílio cannot undue her moral education; she does not truly feel such disdain, but she affects it, much as Emma becomes a ferocious consumer as a means of separating herself from the thriftiness and moral rectitude of the bourgeoisie.

Ana Ozores, a member of the upper class, might be expected to have an affair; instead, she is renowned for her virtue, with only the slightest "inclination" (her term) for Don Álvaro Mesía. She never does long for a lover in the way Emma Bovary does, in the end merely resigning herself to Don Álvaro (Melón Ruiz 83). The virtue that she maintains up to that point is at the expense of her health, for her attempts to suppress physical needs and desires produce nervous attacks wherein her pulse races and her vision clouds. More than any other adulteress, Ana is victimized by the religion to which she clings so strongly. Don Fermín, the synedochal embodiment of the church, plays upon Ana's sensibilities (as Basílio does upon Luísa's) and orchestrates the exposure of Ana and Mesía's affair and the duel that follows—all with such a pious veneer that Ana actually repents of her former suspicions and slander of *el magistral*. *La Regenta* ends as it began: with Don Fermín refusing to hear the confession of Ana. When we first meet *el magistral*, he refuses to enter his confessional out of pride (to show the former Regent's wife that he is not at her beck and call), and in the end, Don Fermín nearly strikes Ana out of his *ressentiment* for a deception that he feels more profoundly than Don Víctor. Despite Don

Fermín's shortcomings as a spiritual father, Ana never questions the sanctity of the church, begs for its absolution, and only dimly becomes aware of her illusions through the sensation of the kiss of a toad.

Our first glimpse of Ana is through the eyes of this prominent church officer, through the lens of Don Fermín's eyepiece. The power and importance of the church are described in greater detail in *La Regenta* than in *Madame Bovary*, which is indicative of the more conservative and reactionary nature of Spanish society well into the modern era. Aside from two very memorable scenes between Emma and Fr. Bournisien (before catechism class and when Fr. Bournisien performs the last rites), Fr. Bournisien appears more in opposition to the positivist ideas of the pharmacist Homais than in the role of an ineffectual spiritual guide for Emma. Don Fermín, unlike Fr. Bournisien, is one of the four principal figures in the narrative; consequently, we are privy to much more of his mental discourse, which is so often at odds with what he says and does.

Ana's religious fervor masks deep-seated longings for affection and carnal love. As with Emma Bovary, Ana's devotional readings and meditations become stepping-stones to flights of fancy. As she reads a question-and-answer book about the sacrament of confession, for instance, she stops reading: "*Su mirada estaba fija en unas palabras que decían:* Si comió carne" (Her glance was fixed on some words that said: *If you ate meat...*) (70). These words, more particularly, the mention of "flesh" (the same word, *carne*, in Spanish is used for both "meat" and "flesh"), send Ana into a hypnotic trance in which she is unaware of her surroundings. When she recovers her senses, it is as if her thoughts were returning from "*no sabía qué pozo negro*" (she knew not what black well) (70). A "black well" suggests yet another abyss—this one, of the inferno and the stain of mortal sin. Ana's loss of consciousness implies that the abyss holds an attraction for her that she is powerless to deflect, inducing her to have lewd thoughts during her preparation for a general confession.

On this same occasion, after she gets into bed with her devotionary, Ana turns the pages, all the while thinking (without knowing why) of Don Álvaro Mesía. She then stops with "*Los parajes por donde anduvo*" (The places where you walked), which recalls her childhood preparation for the sacrament of reconciliation: "*[P]ase la memoria por los lugares que ha recorrido*" ([R]eflect on where you have been) (74), and Ana reflects upon the night that she spent in the boat with Germán, which caused her to be branded immoral like her mother the seamstress and which she considers the great sin that she has committed without having any knowledge of it: "*aquel gran pecado que había cometido, sin saberlo ella*" (74). Ana only knows what her aunts have told her and what society at large has made her feel. She is too naïve to understand that there can be no personal sin without foreknowledge of the same. These citations manifest the psychological realism so often discussed as typical of Clarín's style, but more importantly for our discussion here, they demonstrate how frequently Ana's religious devotions spawn secular (and what the church might consider sinful) reflection.

Much later in the novel, when Ana is trying so desperately not to give in to her carnal attraction for Mesía, she tries to displace the draw of carnal love with spiritual fervor. After saying good-bye to Mesía one evening, for instance, Ana takes out a crucifix and puts her lips to the "hot" ivory—a scene quite reminiscent of the passionate kiss that Emma Bovary plants upon the crucifix that Fr. Bournisien extends over her deathbed. Ana enjoys kneeling or sitting on the tiger skin at the foot of her bed, where "*gozaba la voluptuosidad dúctil de imaginar el mundo anegado en la esencia divina*" (she enjoyed the tractable voluptuousness of imagining the world flooded with the divine essence) (593). On the verge of consummating victory with Ana, Mesía finds her on the balcony and exclaims, "¡Ana!"—to which Ana replies, "¡Jesús!" (789). Later, when Ana thinks about losing Don Álvaro, it is with the same fear that she once had about losing Jesus (795).

Ana is not alone in finding religion sensual, nor is she unaware of her tendency to romanticize it. The bishop himself, Fortunato Camoirán, delivers poetic sermons and is the author of five books on the Mother of God, "*y sabía alabarla en estilo oriental, con metáforas tomadas del desierto, del mar, de los valles floridos, de los montes de cedros en estilo romántico*" (and he knew how to praise her in an Oriental style, with metaphors taken from the desert, the sea, flowered valleys, and cedar mountains—in a romantic style) (310). Both in his writings and sermons Camoirán combines aestheticism with religious fervor.[8] Ana notices the similarity of the emotions raised by contemplating secular art and religious images and ideas and is horrified that they seem to be one and the same. She immediately wishes that she could escape consciousness (a very modernist conception), for she would rather not be capable of recognizing that religion does not hold a hierarchical position of superior value in the kind of sentiment that it can arouse.

During her convalescence from her illness after her father's death, Ana begins to create "*poemas, novelas, dramas, poesías sueltas*" (poems, novels, plays, and loose poetry) in her imagination, all of which she admires so much that she breaks into tears, just as she does "*cuando pensaba en el amor del Niño Jesús y de su Santa Madre*" (when she thought about the love of the Child Jesus and his Holy Mother) (119–120). What Ana does not realize is that the emotions stirred by the image of the Madonna with Child are physiological longings that she experiences for a child of her own, not the affect of contemplating the beautiful or the religious or the beautiful religious object/idea.

Confused by the similarity of feelings, Ana wonders whether aestheticism could be religious and whether vanity might explain her reaction: "*¿Sería que uno y otro sentimiento eran religiosos? ¿O era que en la vanidad, en el egoísmo, estaba la causa de aquel eternecimiento?*" (Could it be that both sentiments were religious? Or was it vanity and egoism that were the causes of that emotionalism?) (120). Since Ana would much rather intuit than analyze, she wishes that she did not complicate her life with such insights. She does not want her mind to control her feelings since thought consumes sentiment, and Ana lives to feel. Like a modernist of the twentieth century, like a D. H. Lawrence or a Joseph Conrad, Ana envies life forms without the power of reason since they are free of the burden of consciousness.

Not only is Ana more analytical than Emma Bovary, but she is also more self-reflexive. Clarín uses Ana's own flashbacks, in the form of quoted monologue and occasionally narrated monologue, to convey to the reader information about her youth, which increases this impression of self-reflexivity. The narrating voice does not intrude in these moments to give us the necessary information. For instance, the first analepsis that we encounter in Ana's background is couched within the framework of her examination of conscience for the general confession that Don Fermín has mandated for the following day. Thus, Clarín not only opens and closes *La Regenta* with the church but even places his presentation of Ana's background within a religious context.

Ana's imagination, as we saw with the others, causes her more agony than it relieves. After her first confession with Don Fermín, she looks about her in the streets and sees everyone paired off, which only increases her sense of loneliness: "*con la imaginación iba juntando por parejas a hombres y mujeres según pasaban. . . . Sólo ella no tenía amor; ella y los niños pobres . . . eran los desheredados*" (her imagination was pairing off the men and women as they were passing by her. . . . She, alone, did not have love; she and the children of the poor . . . were the disinherited ones) (237–238). This causes her to rebel slightly against her fate, which she immediately tries to suppress, having just gone to confession, but she cannot quiet her inclination for Don Álvaro, and in both this instance and the following, the latter fortuitously appears on the scene to capitalize upon the chinks in Ana's armor.

Ana, like Emma and Luísa, longs to experience the romantic love that everyone talks about; unlike the latter, however, she is resigned to her marriage, considers herself on the threshold of old age at 27, and thus despairs of ever tasting the nectar of romantic love: "*Tenía veintisiete años, la juventud huía; veintisiete años de mujer eran la puerta de la vejez a que ya estaba llamando . . . , y no había gozado una sola vez esas delicias del amor de que hablan todos, que son el asunto de comedias, novelas y hasta de la historia*" (She was twenty-seven years old; youth was passing her by; twenty-seven years for a woman is the doorway to old age, which was already calling . . . , and she had not even once enjoyed the delights of love, which everyone talks about and which are the subject matter for comedies, novels and even history) (253). When she is at the theater (a scene analogous to the one in *Madame Bovary*), she thinks, "*¡Ay!, sí, el amor era aquello, un filtro, una atmósfera de fuego, una locura mística; huir de él era imposible*" (Oh! Yes, love was like that: a magic potion, an atmosphere of fire, a mystical madness; to flee from it was impossible) (457). The reality of such a love is called into question by the nineteenth-century novel of adultery. Literature, history, and legend would have you believe that romantic love is endless, inexorable, mystical, and aflame with passion, but realist novels question everlasting, inevitable, passionate love and posit instead the determinism of physical appetites, heredity, and milieu. A different kind of love shines forth in realist novels: a constant, unconditional love given by mediocre characters, but none can recognize it due to the prior distortion of love in romantic literature.

In *La Regenta*, the abyss, or "*sima*," is endowed with yet another meaning. It represents for Ana not so much real life as opposed to self-deception but the absence of youth, love, and light. In this respect, the image functions as in *The Awakening* since both protagonists suffer in their solitude and give in to appetites when they feel no love. The abyss in *La Regenta*, however, is not associated with other symbols of infinity; it is used to describe Ana's feelings about aging without ever experiencing love. Ana, like Edna, exercises the pathetic fallacy of the romantics: she looks up at the sky and sees a metaphor of her life written amid the moon and clouds. She is the moon, and silver clouds are passing by her quickly—a metaphor for her fading youth. Now the moon is racing across the sky, toward the abyss (*sima*) of a huge, black cloud (old age) that swallows the moon up in its darkness (255). Note the verb *abismarse* in the following passage of quoted monologue: "*Lo mismo era ella; como la luna, corría solitaria por el mundo a abismarse en la vejez, en la oscuridad del alma, sin amor, sin esperanza de él*" (She was like the moon which coursed alone through the world to be absorbed in old age, in the darkness of the soul, without love, and without hope of it) (255). Thus, once again, we see the "abyss" in the nineteenth-century novel of adultery as an infinitude of despair. In contrast to the fate of the other five protagonists, Ana's tragedy is that she must live with the despair, without hope, without forgiveness, without love. Her fate to live with the despair and public ignominy is a fate worse than death.

The women we have seen in this chapter all believe that they are lacking something in their marriages. To some degree, more so in some cases than others, they are right, but they are mistaken, as they learn, in thinking that adultery will satisfy their longings and give them life. They are all influenced by romantic notions; some have more insight than others, but all fall susceptible to the promise of fulfillment that they envision in their imaginations. Education and milieu foster the unchecked growth of their imaginations and create insatiable desires. Many women have lost their mothers at an early age, which is an interesting link with their husbands, many of whom were also orphaned as youths, but whereas this makes the women starved for affection, it causes the men to become cold, and it is to these men that we will now turn our attention.

NOTES

1. This is particularly evident in José de Alencar's *A Senhora*, wherein we see the protagonist forced to stand in a doorway lintel so as to attract a husband and make unsuitable suitors suffer.

2. *Madame Bovary*, 159.

3. Heinrich von Kleist, letter to Wilhelmine von Zenge, 22 March 1801, reprinted in Phillip B. Miller, 95.

4. Anna tells Dolly at Vozdvizhenskoe, "Do you see, I love . . . equally, I think, but both more than myself, two beings—Seriozha and Alexei". (671). By "Alexei" here she is referring to Alexei Vronsky and not Alexei Karenin—an interesting twist that they should both have the same name, as Anna herself notes in her delirious state after childbirth.

5. Berdiaev, *Solitude and Society*, 104.

6. For a brief analysis of Flaubert and Queirós, see Peter Gay's *The Tender Passion*. A more in-depth comparison is made in Silviano Santiago's *Eça, autor de* Madame Bovary. For a discussion of *La Regenta* and *Madame Bovary*, see Melón Ruiz de Gordejuela's article in *Archivum* titled, " Clarín y el bovarysmo." For a comparison of the protagonists and motifs of *Anna Karenin* and *Madame Bovary*, see Priscilla Meyer's

article in *The Russian Review*: "*Anna Karenina*: Tolstoy's Polemic with *Madame Bovary*." Biruté Ciplijauskaité in *La mujer insatsifecha* looks at four nineteenth-century realist novels of adultery in depth: *Madame Bovary, Anna Karenina, Effie Briest*, and *La Regenta*.

       7. Mendonça defines bovarism as an attitude toward love, an attitude of obligation to die for love since death is both the "origin" and "horizon" of love (*Bovarysmo & Paixão* 9).

       8. Ana also combines religion and art in her verses addressed to the Virgin Mary (Clarín 109–110).

3

Tower of Babel

The Moor is of a free and open nature,
That thinks men honest that but seem to be so,
And will as tenderly be led by th' nose
As asses are . . .
—*Othello* I. iii. 399–402

Alison Sinclair in *The Deceived Husbands* (1993) analyzes the figure of the deceived husband from the cuckold of the Middle Ages, to the "man of honour" of Spanish Golden Age drama, to the more complex figures of the novel of adultery. Of the three, only the man of honor occupies a central position in the text. In fabliaux, the source of many tales of cuckoldry, the husband is a source of ridicule but never developed as fully as are the characters of the wife and lover. In the novel of adultery, as we can deduce from the extent of the foregoing chapter, the adulterous wife takes center stage, displacing both husband and lover. Her inner turmoil replaces the ridicule of the cuckold and the vengeance of the man of honor.

Though not as central to the novel of adultery, the husbands and lovers of these novels must be discussed before judgment can be assigned—if, in fact, it can be. If the deceived husband is in the mold of the cuckold, for instance, this might be a means of justifying and pardoning the wife's infidelity since the cuckold is often portrayed as weak and consequently deserving of his wife's deception (Sinclair 35). The wife's defense with a tale of cuckoldry, according to Sinclair, "is constructed on the base of a recognition of her as someone with expectations and desires that are not being met within marriage and showing her therefore as justified in seeking elsewhere" (97). While the husbands discussed here do offer some justification, it is not through their falling neatly into the category of the cuckold. Charles Bovary most closely approximates this type, as described by Sinclair, and even he deviates from it in his "clumsy essays at fatherly love and by his spontaneous entry into abject grief as the denouement of Emma's adulterous adventure is reached" (Sinclair 175). Don Víctor in *La Regenta* begins as a cuckold but ends as a man of honor—a type that he very consciously imitates and complicates by his insights and emotions after his personal epiphany. The others—Karenin, Pontellier, Jorge, Innstetten—do not fit any stereotype of the deceived husband. Jorge *claims* that he would respond as the man of honor and kill his wife were she unfaithful, yet in the end, he can do no such thing and mourns Luísa's passing as Charles mourns Emma's: to the point of self-abnegation. Innstetten, Karenin, and Pontellier reflect the changing face of society. New options, aside from the classic duel to the death, had become available to husbands in the nineteenth century to preserve their honor: separation and divorce. A woman, such as Edna Pontellier or Anna Karenin, could always separate herself from her husband physically, but in many countries only a husband had the power of divorce. Both Innstetten and Karenin contemplate this power; Innstetten alone exercises it in addition to killing Crampas in a duel.

HUSBANDS

Interestingly enough for a novel entitled *Madame Bovary*, the novel opens with the childhood of *Monsieur* Bovary. The reader might expect that a novel with an eponymous title would begin with this title figure, and yet Flaubert chooses to open *Madame Bovary* with Charles, a secondary figure, through whose eyes we first see Emma. Indeed, we do not actually see with Emma until Chapter 6 of Part One—the focalization being fixed with Charles until this point. As Lilian R. Furst notes, there are actually *three* Madame Bovarys in this novel, a seemingly trivial detail that serves to emphasize that Emma's identity is not her own, not unique, and utterly depends upon her husband.[1] Thus, the reader can understand Emma's concern for keeping up appearances: her status and identity are but reflections of Charles'. Similarly, Charles' honor becomes linked with Emma's in the marriage contract. Emma knows in the end that her exposure will not only ruin her reputation but Charles' and Berthe's, as well (though her own reputation seems to be all that concerns her).

Flaubert could be said to be perpetuating male patriarchy in demonstrating the privileged position of men in society by structuring this novel so that Charles precedes Emma. As with most names in *Madame Bovary*, Emma's title serves to mock her. She is a "Mrs.," a married woman, but she is married to such a bovine creature. The juxtaposition is highly ironic. Charles is the embodiment of mediocrity: he has no intelligence or talent to recommend him and is overly malleable; moreover, he is quite content to be mediocre, only making feeble essays at a better life due to the prodding of his mother and Emma. Even more pitiable still is that Charles must work *hard* to even be considered mediocre.

When Charles first began medical school in Rouen, he attended every lecture, though he understood "absolutely nothing of any of it," and never missed a visit to the hospital: "*Il accomplissait sa petite tâche quotidienne à manière du cheval de manège, qui tourne en place les yeux bandés, ignorant de la besogne qu'il broie*" (He accomplished his daily tasks in the manner of a work horse that turns in circles with blinders over his eyes, ignorant of the work he is grinding) (43). But though he was diligent at the start and filled with good intentions, very soon his "natural irresponsibility" takes over, and he stops attending the lectures and visiting the hospital. Instead, he spends evenings playing dominoes in a tavern, whose very door handle used to give him "*une joie presque sensuelle*" (an almost sensual joy) when he touched it (44). Inevitably, he fails his examinations the first time and passes the second only by memorizing the answers in advance. Any critical thinking would seem to be beyond his limited capacities, in keeping with the bestial images used to describe him and as his bovine name suggests.

Flaubert, the ironist, plays with the dichotomy between the inner and outer man in his characterization of Charles Bovary. Outwardly, in his pursuits and habits, Charles is very bestial. As a child, for instance, he *played* during recess, *worked* in study hall, *slept* soundly, and *ate* heartily. He does not engage in any intellectual pursuits or physical activity beyond those required for school, and even those intellectual endeavors are performed without any comprehension. He is not at all spiritual (in any sense of the word) but rather finds fulfillment in the satisfaction of his physical needs. Later, in Rouen, he does engage in social pursuits, such as the aforementioned domino-playing, learning bar songs, attending parties, and finally "coming to know love," but the fine arts, literature, and the theater are not among his interests and certainly not among his aptitudes. Perhaps his greatest folly is that he thinks that marriage will give him greater freedom, and so he marries the Dieppe widow whom his mother procures for him. In so doing, he merely exchanges the tyranny of his mother for the control of his wife. Freedom eludes him.

Despite all the numerous instances of his mediocrity, however, Charles is quite extraordinary on the inside. He is, ironically, capable of just such romantic love as that about which Emma dreams. He does not have the semblance, behaviors, or aptitudes of the romantic heroes of Walter Scott, but he is every bit as capable of intense, enduring, passionate love, a love that corrupts him after Emma's death. We should keep in mind, as well, that just as Emma cannot see the inner man that is her husband, her view of his outer appearance and comportment may also be tainted. Nearly all the descriptions of Charles' crude manners are focalized through Emma, and Emma cannot see the difference between the inner and outer man. Since Charles does not wear the trappings of love, he must not be a lover. Indeed, as Alison Sinclair notes in *The Deceived Husbands*, "He loves, but he is not a lover" (182). Emma, unfortunately, cannot perceive that he loves her deeply because she sees the mannerisms of a doting fool.

Ironically, Charles and Emma are more compatible than Emma can imagine: both desire love and freedom (Charles thinks he has found both in Emma), and both see life through the distorting image of colored glass. In the same way that Emma idealizes Léon and Rodolphe as genteel lovers, so Charles sees Emma as strangely sensual and refined for her surroundings. He thinks that she is so rich and beautiful that she will surely marry well—not pragmatically considering Emma's limited opportunities to do so, just as Emma refuses to acknowledge the practical concerns of borrowing from Lheureaux until she is ruined.

If Charles only had more ambition and a greater sense of what was expected of him as a husband and lover, he and Emma might have been very well suited; however, Charles is not knowledgeable enough about the conventions of romance to recognize and respond to Emma's initial attempts to instill a spirit of romance in him. Ironically, when Charles rather romantically kisses Emma's neck as she is preparing for the ball, Emma shakes him off because she thinks he will muss her up. He is more devoted than Emma could ever wish, but since she cannot perceive his devotion, and since he in no other way fulfills her image of the ideal husband, she very quickly becomes critical of him: "*ne savait ni nager, ni faire des armes, ni tirer le pistolet*" (did not know how to swim, fence, or shoot a pistol); he cannot explain to Emma a riding term she comes across in one of her novels; and his conversation is full of "commonplaces" (76). He doesn't even have the desire to attend the theater—not even in Paris! Thus, poor Charles has neither beauty, wit, renown, nor talent to recommend him, and his manners become only cruder with time. We see with Emma as he begins whittling the cork from the wine bottles after meals, running his tongue over his teeth, and gulping his soup. He does not mind his dress and is often quite shabbily attired, which mortifies Emma for her own sake, not his (96). Emma is disillusioned by the dissonance between the ideal and the real; she expected that her husband would instruct her in the ways of the world, but "*il n'enseignait rien, celui-là, ne savait rien, ne souhaitait rien*" (he taught nothing, knew nothing, hoped for nothing) (76). He has no ambitions and no pride. When another doctor speaks slightingly of him, he merely brushes it aside without taking offense. Most annoying of all—he is happy and believes that he makes Emma happy.

During certain periods, such as when Emma's health is suffering from depression, Charles becomes cognizant of his wife's dissatisfaction with married life and immediately takes measures to make her happy. Like Don Víctor, Innstetten, and Mr. Pontellier, Charles tries to combat his wife's failing health with distractions and greater liberty. While all these husbands have their wife's health and happiness in mind, all unwittingly place their wives at the disposal of their seducers by encouraging more activity outside the home or, as in the case of Mr. Pontellier, do nothing to curb their wife's capriciousness.

Thus, when Emma's health begins to fail, and Monsieur Rodolphe Boulanger suggests horseback riding to improve her spirits, Charles eagerly adopts this plan and urges Emma to accept Rodolphe's offer of a horse and go with him. She finally agrees when Charles offers to buy her a riding habit: "*Quand le costume fut prêt, Charles le écrivit à M. Boulanger que sa femme était à sa disposition, et qu'il comptait sur sa complaisance*" (When the habit was ready, Charles wrote to Monsieur Boulanger that his wife was at his disposal and that he counted on his kindness) (186). Ironically, Charles, by encouraging the contact between Rodolphe and his wife, does, quite literally, put her at his disposal, giving him the opportunity to seduce Emma, just as Innstetten affords Major Crampas the opportunity to do the same with Effi, again in accompanying her horseback riding.

Charles similarly throws Emma into Léon's arms, though it should be noted that Emma becomes the aggressor in this affair. Charles and Emma renew their acquaintance with Léon at the opera in Rouen where Charles has taken Emma, yet again, with the aim of reviving her spirits. Once more, Charles exhibits his ignorance as he spends an entire day trying to buy the tickets and declares that he cannot follow the story "*à cause de la musique, qui nuisait beaucoup aux paroles*" (because of the music, which interfered too much with the words) (194). Opera, even today, is often a test of one's cultural IQ, with only the true aesthetes affected by its highly refined art. Charles, far from contemplating the sublime in the theater that evening, is like a beginning reader who can understand only the plot of a story; all levels of meaning aside from the literal are lost on him, and since the music and singing interfere with his understanding the words, Charles cannot even ascertain this.

After that night at the opera, Charles enables Emma to meet regularly with Léon in Rouen. First, he encourages Emma to remain behind without him in Rouen, under Léon's protection, in order to see the renowned final scene of the opera that they have missed by leaving early. Subsequently, he demonstrates an amazing lack of perspicacity in allowing Emma to go to Rouen and have a document notarized that will give her power of attorney. Finally, Charles permits Emma to take her piano lessons in Rouen, never suspecting for one minute, even after he accidentally bumps into Madame Lempereur and is told that she does know Emma, that she could be carrying on an affair.

Charles' ineptitude, for the most part, hurts only himself (and Emma's pride), but his failed operation on Hippolyte's, the stable boy's, club foot irrevocably scars that man and ruins Charles' career. Charles is persuaded by Homais and Emma to undertake the surgery, despite its being beyond his sanctioned powers as an *officier de santé*, because he wants to please Emma, who ironically believes that the fame will provide a more "solid" basis for their love. Charles' acceptance of her and Homais' plan demonstrates his suggestibility. Since he is incapable of critical analysis, all his actions stem from an instinctual desire to gratify his senses or accede to the will of someone whom he loves and/or fears.

Charles believes that he has considered all the possibilities in operating on Hippolyte; thus, when Hippolyte's leg becomes gangrenous and must be amputated, Charles accepts no personal blame, claiming that it was Fate, just as Fate is to blame for Emma's infidelity to Rodolphe. Charles' attitude is typical of the provincial: with limited formal education and a dependence on good weather and fertile arable land for crop production and a good harvest that would take them through the winter months, country people typically interpreted their fortune or misfortune as the handiwork of Fate or Providence, and yet the narrator tells us directly that Rodolphe has directed the fate of Emma and thus Charles. There is no Fate, only strong-willed people who direct the fate of the weak. Thus, Charles' assertion that "It was Fate" only further denigrates him in Rodolphe's and the reader's eyes since he evinces his victimization at the hands of Rodolphe and his shortsightedness in not seeing how he has enabled his wife's infidelity and how they were both manipulated by a consummate womanizer.

Charles' passivity intensifies after Emma's death, to the point of his wasting away, all the while neglecting the future of his daughter, until his eventual death. His passivity, blindness, and boring lifestyle (indicative of his lack of sexual virility) are all typical of the cuckold figure, according to Sinclair. Charles' one saving grace is that he loves Emma with a more than mediocre sentiment. He loves her so much, in fact, that her romanticism corrupts him from beyond the grave. He begins to dress as he thinks she would have wanted and signs promissory notes, just as she did. His senses never demand the refinements that Emma's do, but he has always enjoyed sensual pleasures, such as eating and sleeping or touching the doorknob of the tavern when he was about to play dominoes (an irony at his expense). He even refrains from opening the secret compartment in Emma's rosewood desk "*[p]ar respect, ou par une sorte de sensualité qui lui faisait mettre de la lenteur dans ses investigations*" ([o]ut of respect, or because of some sort of feeling of sensuousness that made him slow his investigations) (364). It is ironic that such tactile sensations as touching wood or metal should arouse such pleasure in Charles, but he is so diametrically opposed to the ideal of a romantic husband that it should not surprise us that is takes so little to stimulate him, and, at the same time, his stimulation by these things demonstrates the power of his imagination to make the ordinary exquisite and the insignificant significant.

After Emma's death, however, nothing stimulates Charles enough to want to remain in this life. Sinclair suggests that Charles' "nakedness of emotions" "sets him apart from the majority of other deceived husbands of the cuckold mold" (184). He is almost Werther-like in his rejection of society and brooding lifestyle. Right before his death we are told that he "*suffoquait comme un adolescent sous les vagues effluves amoureux qui gonflaient son coeur chagrin*" (suffocated like an adolescent under the vague amorous exhalations that swelled his sorrowful heart) (366). He seemingly dies of love, an occurrence that can mean two things: either we and Emma have underestimated a common man's ability to love profoundly, or even such a mediocre character as Charles can adopt the conventions of romanticism to an extraordinary degree.

Jorge is Eça de Queirós' response to Charles Bovary: what if the husband were not so despicable, not quite such a cuckold? Jorge is bourgeois, but he is not a dunce and actually seems quite fashionable when we first meet him. Indeed, if it were not for the deprecatory perspective of Basílio, we might think him "*um janota*, a "Petersburg dandy," a gentleman. He is not mediocre, socially inept, and obtuse, in the way that Charles is. Jorge works as an engineer and is respected among the society that he entertains—with the exception of his cousin, Julião, a free-thinking student who despises him for his complacency: "*Aquele parente, um mediocre, vivia confortavelmente, bem casado, com a carne contente, estimado no Ministério, com alguns contos de réis em inscriçoes— parecia-lhe uma injustiça, e pesava-lhe como uma humilhação*" (That relative, a mediocre man, lived comfortably, was well-married, physically content, esteemed in the Ministry, and had some paper *contos de réis*, and this seemed an injustice to Julião and weighed upon him like a humiliation) (38). As a freethinker, Julião is humiliated by his relationship to a middleclass engineer. The middle class could be so slavish in its imitation of the aristocracy and so bereft of moral value in its pursuit of wealth and comfort. As with *Madame Bovary*, however, we must be cautious not to assign the viewpoint of one of the characters to the author himself.

Edmundo Moniz asserts in *As mulheres proibidas* that Queirós was, in fact, on the side "*dos povos oprimidos contra os povos fortes e opressores*" (of the poor and oppressed against the strong peoples and oppressors) (16). Queirós was known to attack clerical hypocrisy, aristocratic decadence, and middle-class materialism in his writings, but with the possible exception of materialism, Jorge has none of these faults, and even a case for his materialism would have to be conjectured on the basis of his class and his commitment to his work. Jorge is bourgeois but would not seem to be avaricious or materialistic. On the contrary, his two most salient features are his tenderness and contentment, and it is his contentment, his satisfaction in being a public functionary, that causes his wife to seek excitement elsewhere. That Jorge bores his wife is the one attribute that he shares with the cuckold.

Jorge, like Charles, is a devoted husband. His dedication actually gives Luísa pause to think when she imagines running off with Basílio. She reflects on the time when she had pneumonia, and Jorge mothered her, fed and clothed her, held her hand while she slept, and entertained her by reading and drawing. Then, when the danger had passed, he covered her hand with kisses. He is best described as *mergo*, "tender," and this is the Achilles' heel of his and Luísa's relationship, for, from the romance novels that she reads and the operas that she attends, Luísa has come to expect a like passion and excitement in her own life. But such Elysian Fields were not expected to lie within the marriage bond; on the contrary, a certain amount of chastity was expected *within* a marriage as well as *before* it, and at that time and in that milieu women were not expected to enjoy married sex. It is only natural that, given this context, Luísa would turn to adultery for such pleasures, as did so many men of the age with society's unspoken blessing.

Jorge's relationship with Luísa, like Don Víctor's with Ana, is that of a parent to a child. While Don Víctor acts as a father to Ana, Luísa is the replacement for Jorge's mother. In a passage of narrated monologue (free indirect discourse) the narrator tells us how "*vinham-lhe melancolias lânguidas; . . . quereria enlaçar uma cinta fina e doce, ouvir na casa o* frou-frou *de um vestido! Decidiu casar. Conheceu Luiza*" (a languid melancholy came over him, wherein he would want to entwine a fine, sweet sash and hear the *frou-frou* of a dress in the house! He decided to marry. He met Luísa) (16). The juxtaposition of his *saudades* for his mother, with his decision to marry, with his meeting Luísa all suggest that he marries Luísa to fill the void left by the death of his mother; consequently, his relationship with Luísa is overly chaste. When he notices her naked breast through her nightgown, he covers it: "[*V*]*ia-se o começo do peito de uma brancura muito tenra, a rendinha da camisa: muito castamente Jorge abotoou-lhos*" ([H]e saw the beginning of a very soft, white breast, at the little lacework of her blouse; very chastely Jorge buttoned it up) (17). When Jorge leaves for his trip, he gives Luísa two kisses "*chilreados*" (birdlike). He is overly tender and, like Charles, overly complacent—precisely what Julião criticizes in him. He comforts Luísa but does not excite her.

The imagination developed through the books that one reads catalyzes the act of adultery. The husbands and wives typically have very different tastes in reading. Luísa craves the excitement that she reads about in the novels of Walter Scott, Alexander Dumas, and Paul-Henri Féval; she desires the euphoria that she feels while listening to the music of Giacomo Meyerbeer, Charles Gounod, and Verdi. Jorge, on the other hand, reads French economists, such as Frederic Bastiat, and naturalist writers, such as Luis Figuier. Jorge reads far more in the "realist" vein, while Luísa enjoys exercising her fancy in the romantic. Once introduced to the ideal, even in fiction, Luísa can no longer be satisfied with the real.

The narrator, while praising Jorge only on one occasion, that being his "heroic" behavior after reading Basílio's letter to Luísa while she was ill with the fever and concealing his anguish so as not to upset her, does not criticize him either, which is remarkable since almost every character in this novel, as in Flaubert's, is subject to ridicule. Jorge, however, is never portrayed as vain, artificial, or inane. He is always tender and, in the end, surprisingly passionate. As Luísa comes to realize after her disillusionment with adultery, Jorge's love was different *because of* its constancy: "*o seu amor era sempre o mesmo, vivo, mergo, delicado*" (his love was always the same—alive, tender, and delicate). Basílio, on the other hand, wanted her "*por vaidade, por capricho, por destracção, para ter uma mulher em Lisboa*" (because of his vanity, on a whim, for a distraction, and in order to have a woman in Lisbon) (214). Jorge is not the inept, obtuse husband that Charles Bovary is to Emma, but he is absent and complacent, and he is a husband. Married life, with its daily routines, its constant, unquestioned love, cannot compare with the exciting novelty of an affair—not unless one realizes, as Emma and Luísa do, that adultery can be just as boring as marriage and comes to long for the constancy of love instead of its novelty. The love inspired by Jorge's homecoming would likely have faded like the first bloom of newly wed bliss, though we will never know with any certainty since Luísa dies shortly thereafter, but her realizations about Basílio's love remain to caution other young women against adultery—especially when one has a husband as constant and loving as Jorge.

The marriage of Ana Ozores and Don Víctor in *La Regenta* is no more scintillating than is Jorge and Luísa's. The chastity of a son's love for his mother is mirrored in this novel by Don Víctor's paternal relationship with his wife, Ana. They share an asexual relationship of filial love, fostered by Don Víctor's being considerably older than Ana (some 20 years) and by hints of a homosexual relationship between Don Víctor and his hunting partner Frígilis—a name that suggests sexual frigidity. Since Don Víctor is over 20 years older than Ana, he naturally falls into the role of a father figure (and cuckold), attending to her well-being and prescribing activity to raise her spirits. He in no way fulfills his wife's need for sensual love and children; moreover, Don Víctor's propensity for hunting with Frígilis suggests that it is not only Ana but all women who do not appeal to Don Víctor, as he is described as a man who would prefer "*un buen macho de perdiz a todas las caricias conyugales*" (a good male partridge to all conjugal caresses) (249). Don Víctor would rather be with his "*querido*"

Frígilis or his birds than his wife and thus sleeps in a bedchamber closer to the aviary. His relationship with Ana is even more chaste than Jorge's with Luísa.

The paternal behavior of Don Víctor contributes to, if not catalyzes, Ana's nervous attacks since their sterile marriage precludes her sexual fulfillment and motherhood through that acceptable medium. The "*beso paternal*" that he is wont to "deposit" on Ana's forehead is described at one point as "*una escoba mojada*" (a wet broom) and again as "*un cepillo de yerbas hechas cenizas por la raíz y tostadas por las puntas*" (a brush of grass turned into ashes at the root and toasted at the points), which emphasizes not only the repulsive nature of such affections but the advanced age of Don Víctor through his graying mustache.

These novels of adultery all bear out the stereotype that "the husband is always the last to know." Charles and Jorge would never have suspected their wives if it were not for the letters discovered by each in turn (Innstetten also learns of Effi's infidelity through her love letters to Crampas). Don Víctor must be tricked into rising earlier than usual to go hunting in order to catch Don Álvaro sneaking over the wall. He, too, like Charles, actually places his wife at the seducer's disposal. He first insists that she go to the theater at least twice a week and *tertulias* and other social gatherings—all with the aim of improving her health through distractions; then he foolishly exclaims to his friend Don Álvaro Mesía that he would rather see her in the arms of a lover than have her become a religious fanatic: "*¡Antes de esto, prefiero verla en brazos de un amante! . . . ¡Sí, amigo mío! ¡Primero seducida que fanatizada!*" (Before this, I prefer to see her in the arms of a lover! . . . Yes, my friend! Seduced before fanaticized!) (729). Don Víctor is the quintessential cuckold in failing to see that his friend is seducing his wife and actually giving this friend the license to do so. He is so concerned about the power of the priest that he cannot see the greater danger that Don Álvaro poses because the rewards that he offers Ana are the ones that she seeks, and they are more immediate and physical than the ones about which her confessor speaks. The dishonor, moreover, that Mesía brings upon the Regent's house is no mystical abstraction and brings about Don Víctor's death and Ana's ruin.

Not until he is forced to confront his wife's adultery does Don Víctor realize that he has not provided the fulfillment that Ana needs: "[*C*]*laramente sentía que no era aquel amor de amante, amor de esposo enamorado, sino como de amigo tierno, y de padre . . . sí, de padre dulce, indulgente y deseoso de cuidados y atenciones*" (He clearly felt that this was not the love of a lover or that of an enamored husband, but rather that of a tender friend and father . . . yes, of a sweet, indulgent father desirous of care and attention) (817). He wants her "care and attention," but he does not love her like a lover or a husband in love. He loves her like a "tender friend" or a father, and, as her friend and "father," he wants to forgive her the transgression, but his honor is more important than his love, and it is out of offended pride, not jealous love, that Don Víctor fights the duel.

The theme of honor in Spanish literature dates back to the *Cantar de Mío Cid* and prevails into the late nineteenth century and beyond. The notion that honor is more important than life itself is not exclusive to Spanish literature, of course. Classic Greco-Roman texts contain this same theme, as do medieval romances, but the importance of honor as it combined with the chivalric code of the Middle Ages in Spain was slow to decline. Honor was more important than life itself; thus, Don Víctor risks and loses his life for a woman who has "wronged" him, and Ana's punishment of a life dishonored is a fate graver than ignominous death.

Don Víctor's love for Golden Age drama would have inculcated such a sense of honor in him, even if society at large did not. Whereas Ana reads Germán, San Agustín, and Chateaubriand, Don Víctor reads plays, especially comedies, particularly those of Calderón de la Barca, whose major preoccupation was *el honor*. His tastes are different from his wife's, but the effect of his reading is the same: to provide delight in, and a longing for, a lost or fictitious way of life. Both Don Víctor and Ana realize in the end that such scenarios about which they have read (adulterous love, "cloak-and-dagger" dramas) are horrifying in reality. Don Víctor, after making the analogy between his own life and one of his favorite dramas, does not see how he could ever have been amused by such a horrifying experience: "*Aquél era su drama de capa y espada. Los había en el mundo también. ¡Pero qué feos eran, qué horrorosos! . . . ¿Por qué recrearse en aquellas tristezas cuando eran ajenas, si tanto dolían cuando eran proprias?*" (That was his drama of cloak-and-dagger. They had them in the world, also. But how ugly they were! How horrifying! . . . Why does one enjoy oneself in those sad dramas when they were not his own if they hurt so much when they were?) (816). The cuckolded husband does not seem as amusing when he himself is cast in the role. Nevertheless, the duel is carried out at the sinister, occult prodding of Don Fermín, according to the dictates of honor perpetuated by the Golden Age drama and in a manner copied from a French novel since none present knows the proper protocol.

Although Don Víctor is aware of the leitmotif of the duel to resolve a conflict involving honor, he feels compelled to go through with the duel not because of literary conventions but, rather, because of societal ones: "*Era necesario según las leyes sociales, según lo que las costumbres y las ideas corrientes exigían, que don Víctor buscase a Mesía, le desafiase, le matase si posible le era*" (It was necessary, according to social laws, according to what custom and current ideas demanded, that Don Víctor look for Mesía, that he challenge him, that he kill him if possible) (843–844). Even though he is aware of the paltry significance of societal laws next to natural ones, Don Víctor persists in carrying out the custom since he is assured by Don Fermín that forgiveness would reap disdain when all of society comes to know of the affair: "*Con vivos colores, pintó [Don Fermín] el desprecio que el mundo arroja sobre el marido que perdona y que la malicia cree que consiente*" (Don Fermín painted, in vivid color, the disdain that the world casts on the husband that forgives, with which malice seems to agree) (844). Thus, although Don Víctor can ignore the prescriptions of literature, he cannot escape the impact that it has had on his and his society's conception of honor. Knowing that he has been cuckolded and that all will know and despise him for not seeking vengeance, Don Víctor challenges Don Álvaro.

Don Víctor, unlike Jorge, is more notable for his similarities with

Charles Bovary than his differences since, like Charles, he is foolish and content and blind to his wife's infidelity—typical cuckolds. In his contentment with life, Don Víctor fails to see that he does not please his wife. His concern over his wife's illness induces him to prescribe a course of action that throws Ana into Mesía's society, just as Charles encourages Emma to go riding with Rodolphe and as Innstetten cajoles Effi to go with Crampas. None suspects his wife's infidelity until he is confronted with the physical evidence of it. Indeed, the priest acts the part of the jealous husband more than Don Víctor.

Don Fermín knows of Ana's feelings for Mesía and suspects that something might be afoot at the Vivero, so he induces Don Víctor to accompany him on a search for them, but even after discovering a piece of Ana's undergarments in the shelter of the woods, Don Víctor suspects nothing and concludes that Ana must have made a present of the garment to her maid Petra. Don Fermín, however, senses the deceit and is offended—fully recognizing that it is not his place to be so: "*Oh, ¿quién es aquí el marido? ¿Quién es aquí el ofendido? ¡Yo, yo!, que siento la ofensa, que la preveo, que la huelo en el aire*" (Oh! Who is the husband here? Who is the offended one? I am! I am, who feels the offense, who foresees it, who smells it in the air) (769). Don Víctor, on the other hand, is conscious of no wrongdoing and thus feels no offense, and even after the offense is brought to his attention, he is willing to forgive the pair if it were not for the pressures of society, made manifest through Don Fermín. Don Víctor is not the hyperparanoid man of honor of Golden Age drama, even though he acts out the scripted conclusion to one of the dramas. In the end, he actively seeks to restore his wife's and, consequently, his own honor by killing the interloper (typical of cloak-and-dagger dramas), but he fails (atypical). He executes the duel as a "matter of propriety, and not as an act of jealous passion" (Sinclair 124), but he does not have the success of his Golden Age counterparts in that he himself is killed, and his wife's infidelity is thereby revealed to all the world.

In the minds of Vetustan society, Don Víctor dies an honorable death in defending his honor, but the narrator considers the custom of dueling "*[una] costumbre bárbara que habíamos heredado de la Edad Media*" (a barbarous custom that we have inherited from the Middle Ages) (849). The narrator does not have praise for this act, only compassion for its victims. His condemnation is for society, for it is society's custom to guard one's honor over one's life; Don Víctor is persuaded to uphold it, but it is to his credit that he must be convinced. Thus, in the end, instead of a husband who mourns the passing of his wife, in *La Regenta* we are left with a surviving widow who must bear the judgment of society and that which she inflicts upon herself for the death of her husband and the loss of her virtue.

In *Effi Briest*, the husband successfully defends his honor, though he betrays his inner moral compass. Innstetten, though like Don Víctor in his fleeting desire to forgive Effi, does not need to be encouraged to challenge Crampas and defend his honor. On the contrary, his confidant, Wüllersdorf, tries to dissuade him from such a course of action, promising to keep Innstetten's secret safe, but Innstetten, above all, is a man of principles. As Wüllersdorf notes, "[O]ur own cult of honour . . . is idolatry. But we must submit to it as long as the idol stands" (216). In the end, this idolatry of honor, Innstetten's inability to deviate from his principles, compels him to make Effi's shame public, challenge Crampas, and kill him.

For one brief moment it seems as if Innstetten might be capable of forgiving Effi. He, like Don Víctor, does not feel any thirst for vengeance and kills Crampas as "a matter of propriety," not out of jealous passion. The additional twist in Fontane's novel of adultery is the lapse of time: nearly seven years have passed since Effi's infidelity with Crampas; she has sincerely repented in her heart and is grateful for a chance to terminate the affair and begin anew in Berlin. The lapse of time, Innstetten's lack of vengeance, and the fact that Innstetten loves his wife all nearly tempt him to forgive Effi and keep up appearances, but he cannot ignore his principles; he feels that the rules that bind society together cannot be gainsaid; they compel him to act as he does because as a civil servant in the eye of the public, he cannot transgress his principles without despising himself and risking the disdain of society.

Innstetten does suffer remorse for sticking to his principles in this instance. It is not so much that he misses Effi as that he is haunted by the dying look of Crampas, a look that Innstetten hears saying, "Innstetten, always standing on principle. . . . You might have spared me that and yourself as well" (222). Innstetten thinks, "And perhaps he was right. I can hear myself saying something similar" (222). He would not have been happy to keep the secret and to live a life of dishonesty with Effi, but at least he would not be burdened by "the memory of that gentle questioning look of silent reproach" that he reads in the eyes of his onetime friend (222).

Gisela Zimmermann notes in her article "The Civil Servant as Educator: *Effi Briest* and *Anna Karenina*," that these novels of adultery are strikingly similar for the character of the husband. In each, Innstetten and Karenin are "bureaucrats first and husbands second," and both assume the role of educator toward their wives—an attitude that "has its mirror image in the patriarchal relationship between the State and the people that was typical of nineteenth-century Prussia as well as Russia and in which the civil servant was a vital element" (Zimmermann 817). Both Karenin and Innstetten are more than 20 years older than their wives; thus, they don the role of educator, not only as the civil servants that they are, but as a father is to his children. Effi and Anna must be pushed into their marriages—in Effi's case, by her mother, and in Anna's, by her aunt. Effi claims that anyone can be "Mr. Right"—"Of course, he's got to have a title and a situation in society and look presentable" (26), but she reveals in her homesick letters and her eventually falling prey to the attention of Crampas that she does look for more companionship and love in a mate than a civil servant, caught up as he is with the rules of the state and the rules of society, knows how to give.

Karenin is the consummate statesman and rationalist. He distrusts passion and sentiment and adopts a tone of derision when mimicking the discourse of the romantics. His adherence to the dictates of society "provides him with categories that allow him to avoid the emotional involvement of which he is afraid" (Zimmermann 826). He so distrusts his feelings that he usually masks them with a show of anger or impassivity. That he is an emotional man we know from the narrator, who tells us at the beginning of Chapter 13 that Karenin has a "weakness" of character that would not permit him to see or hear a woman or child crying. Presumably, he could not hide his emotions in such cases, so he tries to avoid them. The term "weakness" may be a conflation of narratorial and figural attitudes,[2] which is to say that Karenin's emotionalism is not judged a weakness by the narrator; it is the narrator's adopting the language of his character. It is Karenin who perceives his emotions as a character flaw and who tries to stifle their every manifestation.

The narrator tells us that whenever Karenin feels that "rush of emotional turmoil always produced in him by tears . .[,] he endeavored to suppress every manifestation of life in himself" (300). Anna's incompatibility with her husband becomes clear: Karenin lives an artificial construct; Anna is the embodiment of Schopenhauer's will-to-live. Karenin is not jealous out of a "personal trust"[3] in his wife and because it would not be dignified. When he is confronted, after returning from Princess Betsy's dinner party, with the possibility that Anna might love another, the very thought is incomprehensible to him, "illogical and irrational." As the narrator tells us, Karenin cannot fathom his wife's loving another because he was "face to face with life . . . and this seemed to him irrational and incomprehensible because it was life itself" (158). The rules of society may be very logical, but life is not; passions are not; human actions are not. Karenin is finally forced to face his wife's infidelity because it is not a silly, unfounded presumption. He would like to keep up appearances, somehow reconstruct the bridge over which he has walked to avoid the abyss of real life, but Anna chooses to live openly with Vronsky, thus obviating such a stratagem.

The basis of the artificiality of Karenin's life stems from his occupation as a high civil servant, which, in turn, compels him to follow convention, making him guilty of the "ultimate weakness" of the man of honor, according to Alison Sinclair, in that "he does not create his own standards of behavior but follows those established by society" (237). He does not see anything wrong, for instance, with Anna's sitting at a separate table at Princess Betsy's, but since everyone else does, he feels that he should talk to her about her behavior. When he considers options after Anna has revealed her affair to him, his sole concerns are to safeguard his reputation and punish Anna. Karenin is not foolish or complacent, like some of the other husbands discussed here. He is ambitious, rational, and proud, and because of his position in government and society, he commands respect and wields a great deal of power, which he will turn on Anna to wreak his vengeance.

Karenin is introduced even later than Anna in the novel—not until Chapter 30 of Part One. His role, like that of most of these husbands, is minor compared to that of the wife and lover, but his importance should not be underestimated: he holds the keys to Anna's happiness and is hell-bent on punishing her for her "crime." His trump cards are his power to divorce her and to deny her access to Seriozha. Chapter 13 of Part Three, the chapter that resumes the thread left dangling when Anna acknowledges her love for Vronsky (after the accident at the race course), most clearly delineates Karenin's priorities for handling this most unexpected situation. First and foremost, Karenin is concerned with keeping up appearances and with punishing Anna so that she does not profit by her crime. His needs are most important; Anna's are least. The effect of the gap of 16 chapters between the telling and the reaction is to suggest that Karenin has been mulling things over in the interim chapters, as any good rationalist fearful of making a hasty decision would, which makes the vengeful nature of his decision seem all the more calculated.

There is a moment in which real life and real emotions do intrude upon Karenin's ordered existence and force him to abandon his pride and his principles—though only for a moment. Just as Crampas' dying glance at Innstetten forces the latter to question his principles, so Anna's near-death experience in giving birth to Ani (her love child) fills Karenin with love and the desire to forgive her infidelity. Unlike Innstetten, Karenin does not idolize honor; he is its unwilling captive. He would like to succumb to the uplifting joy of forgiving, but he is under the ever-watchful eyes of society—in this case, of Princess Tverskoy, "the personification of that brute force which must govern the life he led in the eyes of the world and hinder him from giving way to his feelings of love and forgiveness" (Tolstoy 448–449). He cannot free himself from the conventions that bind him. To Karenin, that would be like breaking the law, and he is a civil servant, bound to uphold it.

Conventions similarly bind the socialite Mr. Pontellier in *The Awakening*. The first fact that we glean about the appearance of Mr. Pontellier is that he wears eyeglasses—a symbol of his myopia with regard to the needs of his wife. Pontellier never entertains the possibility of Edna's having an affair or that she could have any needs other than monetary ones. He treats his wife as "a valuable piece of personal property," and he cautions her, as Karenin does Anna, about keeping up appearances and respecting the proprieties. Mr. Pontellier is shocked, for instance, to learn that Edna was not at home for callers on their designated day at home. He reprimands her, "[W]e've got to observe *les convenances* if we ever expect to get on and keep up with the procession" (51). When Edna moves from their great house to her cozy "pigeon house" around the corner, Mr. Pontellier saves face by announcing their plan to renovate the house, thus deflecting the questions that would naturally be raised by Edna's move.

Mr. Pontellier, like Karenin, refuses to engage in feelings of jealousy, not because he considers this "dangerous romancing," as does Karenin, but because it is a part of his Creole class not to suffer the indignity of entertaining such a sentiment. He does see the changes in his wife and like the other husbands, tries to "cure" her with the advice of the doctor, who tells him to let her do as she pleases—not the best advice in retrospect. Pontellier wants Edna to be the woman she was when he married her. He cannot see that she is daily *becoming* herself or that, like a young child, she needs guidance, particularly at her very impressionable stage of development. It would not have helped Pontellier to have had such insight because he has been nothing but a hindrance to his wife's development; he would not have wanted her to discover or forge her identity. She has her identity, as far as he is concerned, and it is a relational one: his wife and his children's mother.

Mr. Pontellier's name is mentioned only once in *The Awakening*. As in the other novels of adultery (e.g., where Ana Ozores calls her husband

"Quintanar"), the use of such a formal name here places distance between the husband and wife and distances the reader, as well, from the figure of the husband. Pontellier is a great favorite with the other "ladies" in the novel, who enjoy the sweets that he sends Edna from the city and judge him to be "the best husband in the world." Edna must admit that she knows of none better, but as she comes to realize, it is better to be alone than to be poorly accompanied in life, but solitude is only for the courageous of heart.

LOVERS

Whether they be donjuanesque types or more Tristan-like lovers, the lovers receive far more attention in the novel of adultery than do the husbands. Boccaccio's salacious narrator Dioneo in *The Decameron* claims that "we are more inclined to laugh at scandalous behavior than virtuous deeds, especially when we, ourselves, are not directly involved" (432). This is Don Víctor's query: how could he have found those cloak-and-dagger dramas so entertaining when now that he was in the midst of his own like drama, he found it horrifying and ugly? As Tolstoy opens *Anna Karenin*, "All happy families are alike but an unhappy family is unhappy after its own fashion" (13). Since all happy families are alike, no one would be interested in reading more than one story about a couple who is happily married. Conflict makes a story interesting, and the nineteenth-century novel of adultery adds some new conflicts to the traditional, adulterous love triangle. For example, Emma Bovary takes two lovers. Edna Pontellier would have taken a second (her first choice really) if he had agreed, and Ana Ozores is attracted to both Don Álvaro and Don Fermín, though for very different reasons. *Anna Karenin*, *O primo Basílio*, and *Effi Briest* follow the pattern of husband-wife-lover established in ancient times, but the husbands and lovers are very different characters in each of the texts, fostering varying degrees of sympathy and judgment.

Monsieur Rodolphe Boulanger de la Huchette is, like many of the characters and places in *Madame Bovary*, satirized by his very name. He gives his full name to impress the people at the inn in Yonville, and they are all very impressed, but his name means "baker," and his estate is "the little bread box."[4] He sizes Emma up as a sportsman would a horse in this quoted monologue: "*De belles dents, les yeux noirs, le pied coquet*" (Beautiful teeth, black eyes, charming feet) (161). He is 34 years old, of a "*tempérament brutal et d'intelligence perspicace*" (brutal temperament and penetrating intellect) (161). He has had a great many mistresses; therefore, he knows women well. He judges Emma correctly, though brutally: "*Ca bâille après l'amour, comme une carpe après l'eau sur une table de cuisine*" (She is gaping for love like a carp on the kitchen table gapes for water) (162). He knows that she is bored with Charles and would be eager for an affair, so eager that Rodolphe cannot help but wonder how he will dispose of her when he tires—this even before he has begun his conquest.

Rodolphe is like a tactician studying "*la partie politique de l'entreprise*" (the strategic aspects of the undertaking) (162). His strategy is to play upon Emma's sympathies, and so he speaks of contemplating suicide, of having no friends, and of being completely and helplessly enamored of her. The nature of his flattery is exposed in the clever juxtapositioning of the discourse of the chairman of the agricultural fair with the entreaties of Rodolphe. As Rodolphe tells Emma, for example, "*Cent fois même, j'ai voulu partir, et je vous ai suivie, je suis resté*" (A hundred times even I wanted to leave, and I followed you; I stayed), the chairman awards the prize for "*Fumier!*" (Manure!) (178).

The dissonance between the character of Rodolphe, as we see it developed in his thoughts and actions, and the image that Emma has of him creates a great deal of irony within the text and further reveals the gap between the ideal and the real in Emma's head. Emma imagines Rodolphe to be the typical romantic hero, but though he is typical, it is more in the line of a Lovelace than an Ivanhoe. She is slightly troubled, consequently, by his comments and jokes about Charles, for she believes that they demonstrate a certain "*indélicatesse et [de] grossièreté naïve*" (indelicateness and vulgarity) (198). Rodolphe is not the least bit concerned, for instance, that Charles might discover their affair, which Emma at first takes as a sign of his preparedness to duel with Charles to protect his honor and her own, but Rodolphe merely laughs and says, "[*P*]*auvre garçon*," (Poor man), with a dismissive gesture, as if to say, "*Je l'écraserais d'une chiquenaude*" (I could crush him with the flick of the hand) (198). His pity for Charles only increases when he encounters him at the market at Argueil in the end, after Emma's death. After hearing Charles say that he does not hold it against him and that fate was to blame, Rodolphe "*qui avait conduit cette fatalité, le trouva bien débonnaire pour un homme dans sa situation, comique même, et un peu vil*" (who had determined that fate, found him quite easy-going for a man in his situation, comic even, and a little despicable) (366). Charles is not playing the role of the wronged husband, nor is he lashing out against Fate; he continues in his passive acceptance of events, which is the logical conclusion to a belief in "*la fatalité.*"

Basílio shows no more compassion at the death of Luísa than Rodolphe does for Emma. He is described from the very beginning, before we ever meet him, as "*um janota*"—a dandy (62). He is, like our any other Don Juans, extremely wellversed in the art of lovemaking, cosmopolitan and supercilious. He is the epitome of the materialist, judging Julião, for example, by his lack of fashionable footwear rather than his talent and ideas. After having lived in Paris, he finds Lisbon provincial. He knows how to play upon Luísa's feelings by insinuating that he never married because he could not have her. He claims that he broke off their relationship only because he was poor and without prospects, and he wanted her to be rich and happy "*mas o que eu sofri, as lágrimas que chorei*" (but what I suffered and the tears I cried) (109). Julião pronounces the most apt judgment on this seducer type in informing Sebastião, who has sought his advice, that Cousin Basílio "*quer o pracer sem a responsabilidade*" (wants the pleasure without the responsibility) (132). He wants to enjoy the fruits of marriage without the financial responsibility of maintaining a wife and household.

Without Queirós' style of variable focalization, our appreciation of Basílio's duplicity would be lost—as would Flaubert's judgment of Emma's romanticism in *Madame Bovary*. It depends upon our witnessing the role Basílio plays of the reformed rake and hearing his internal monologue. For example, after claiming that he never ceased loving Luísa and never married because of her, Basílio takes his leave, and at the bottom of the stairs, he says to himself, "—*Que bonita que ela está! . . . Está de apetite!*" (How pretty she is! . . . And how appetizing!) (69). As with Rodolphe, he views his cousin as a conquest— one of many. Indeed, this new conquest causes Basílio to think about others: "*A amante que deixara em Paris era muito alta e magra, de uma elegancia tísica. . . . as formas de Luiza decidiram-no.—A ela! exclamou com apetite: —A ela, como S. Tiago aos mouros!*" (The lover that he had left in Paris was very tall and thin, with a sort of consumptive elegance. . . . Luísa's figure decided him. "She is the one!" he exclaimed with appetite. "To her like Santiago to the Moors!") (69). Later, after their affair has become as monotonous as marriage, Basílio does not leave because Luísa still satisfies his appetite: "*Mas tinha pena dela, coitada! E depois, sem a amar apatecia-a*" (But he felt sorry for her, poor thing! And then, without loving her, his appetite was peaked by her) (248). What Luísa imagines as an undying, unquenchable love is really nothing more than the fulfillment of a physical appetite for Basílio.

Anna Karenin also displays some of this same discourse in talking of women as fulfilling an appetite. Anna's philandering brother, Oblonsky, tries to explain to Levin, an enlightened landowner enamored of the simple life, how "women are the pivot the world turns on" (54). He tries to solicit Levin's advice in the predicament of his wife, but Levin finds the problem incomprehensible:

"It's like this," Oblonsky says. "Suppose you are married, you love your wife, but you are attracted by another woman."

"Forgive me," Levin responds, "but I really find that absolutely incomprehensible. . . It's as if . . . as incomprehensible as if, after a good dinner here, I were to go into a baker's shop and steal a roll."

Oblonsky's eyes sparkled more than usual. "Why not? Rolls sometimes smell so good that you can't resist them!" (54)

Oblonsky, though he has his physical, sexual needs met with his wife, cannot resist other women because he finds them so attractive. He is like uncontrollable eaters who eat, not because they are hungry but because they cannot control their desire.

The analogy in *La Regenta* is that of going into battle, rather than whetting or satisfying the appetite (also implied in Basílio's saying, "like Santiago to the Moors"). Don Álvaro attacks the fortress of Ana's virtue as though going into battle and refers to the pursuit as "*la campaña*"(the campaign) (681). Ana's virtue is like a city with multiple layers of walls, and Don Álvaro plans his attack upon her virtue as a soldier would a city that he is ordered to take.

The preceding imagery might suggest that Don Álvaro is a virile *conquistador*, but Don Álvaro Mesía is as frivolous a lover as Basílio, only much older, and, like Vronsky, he is more captivated by his conquest than she is by him and than other lovers are by the wives in the novel of adultery. Don Álvaro maintains more control than Vronsky in the course of the siege and does eventually tire of the pursuit; nevertheless, in the beginning he must contain his emotions so as not to appear foolish in the eyes of society. Mesía is proud of his reputation as a Don Juan and does not want to be thought a lovesick fool, like a character in some romantic novel. He approaches Ana as a conquest, disappears after killing Don Víctor, and makes no attempt to assuage the grief, humiliation, and life-in-death existence that Ana must endure as the result of his actions. The end of their affair does not have the same impact on his life that Anna's death has on Vronsky.

Don Álvaro shares Rodolphe's and Basílio's disdain for the provinces and prides himself on his cosmopolitan manners and dress. He dresses in the latest fashions from Paris and Madrid, speaks four languages, and does not speak with Vetusta's provincial accent—thanks to his frequent trips to Madrid, which he uses to brush off his contact with the provinces, leaving behind "*muchas víctimas de su buen talle y arte de enamorar*" (many victims of his fine figure and art of lovemaking) (132). The characterization of Don Álvaro as a Don Juan is no leap for the reader. The narrator himself calls him "*el Tenorio*" and evinces little respect for his type, contradicting Álvaro's assumptions, calling him a "materialist" and pointing out that he expresses opinions about literature that he has not, in fact, read.

Don Álvaro may not have read the plays of Molière (as he claims to have done), but he is certainly familiar enough with the romantic novels that Ana has read, for he knows to address her in just such a style, the style of a "perfumed novel." Ana, in her "*exaltación*," cannot see "*la falsedad del idealismo copiado de su interlocutor*" (the false, copied idealism of her interlocutor) (459). In thinking of a place where he and Ana can meet for "*horas y horas de voluptuosa intimidad*" (hours and hours of voluptuous intimacy), Don Álvaro knows that he must find someplace that would not be repugnant to Ana, for that would make her see adultery in a similar light: "*[C]omo en Ana la imaginación influía tanto, el desprecio del albergue podía llevarla a la repugnancia del adulterio*" ([S]ince in Ana the imagination was so influential, her disdain for the shelter could lead her to a repugnance for the adultery) (797). Don Álvaro knows just how to fuel her imagination. He must convince her that theirs is an eternal love, for, otherwise, Ana would consider it "*um bochorno, . . .un crimen infame, villano*" (a shameful thing, . . . a villainous, infamous crime) (795).

Don Álvaro does admire Ana, perhaps more than any other conquest, but he will not die for love of her. He does not love her with the undying passion that he feigns. He risks his life in dueling Don Víctor to protect *his* honor, but he is clearly not concerned with Ana's. She is, despite his fascination with her, another conquest, unusual only in the sense of precipitance that he feels in wooing her before he decays before her very eyes, for Don Álvaro is an *aging* Don Juan. He is not the typical lover in the triangle of adulteresses, cuckold, and lover since he is not significantly (if at all) younger than Don Víctor, though he is infinitely more virile.

Alexei Vronsky is not like his seducer counterparts in that he does not view Anna as a conquest but as his "single blissful goal" and is reported to love her with a "Werther-like passion" (120, 191). At the outset there may be a question of Vronsky's staying power, but there is certainly no question that his feelings are genuine and that he does not possess Rodolphe's or Basílio's cold and calculating ways.

Our introduction to Vronsky is dialogic in nature. First, Oblonsky describes him to Levin as "a fine sample of the gilded youth of Petersburg. . . . Awfully rich, handsome, influential connexions . . . a capital fellow. . . . cultured and very intelligent" (53). The narrator gives us a physical description just a few pages later, which is not unflattering: "Vronsky was a dark, squarely built man of medium height, with an exceptionally tranquil and firm expression on his good-natured, handsome face. Everything about his figure . . . was simple and at the same time elegant" (64). Kitty and her mother consider him a good catch as a "well-bred man-of-the-world" (60). But Kitty's father, the prince, sees through Vronsky's outward demeanor and judges him a "Petersburg dandy—they turn them out by the dozen, all alike and all trash" (69). His assessment would seem to be borne out by Vronsky's hypocritical attitude toward his mother: the narrator relates that the more outward respect that he paid his mother, "in accordance with the ideas of his set and with his upbringing . . [,] the less he respected and loved her in his heart" (74). Thus, in the beginning, like the other seducer types, Vronsky is duplicitous, though never in terms of the feelings that he has for Anna.

At first, Vronsky does seem to fall into the conventional donjuanesque stereotype. He thinks that husbands are ridiculous and therefore never considers that he himself will marry. He tells Stiva that he prefers courtesans to well-bred women because he knows that they judge only his monetary value, not his character: "If you don't succeed with them [women of the *demi-monde*] it only means you've not enough cash; but with the other [well-bred women] it's our merits that are weighed in the balance" (74). His "code of principles" is clear-cut but inconsistent. It includes such precepts as "one must not lie to a man but might to a woman" and "one must never cheat anyone but one may a husband" (327). As the narrator evaluates them, "These principles might be irrational and not good, but they were absolute and in complying with them Vronsky felt at ease and could hold his head high" (327). How ironic to consider Vronsky a "man of principles" when he is so far from the principles of a character such as Innstetten, for example, or even Karenin, though Vronsky's principles are really no more self-serving than those of either. Vronsky's ethics develops a posteriori from his behavior, merely sanctioning what he has already decided is the right thing to do, which is precisely the role that religion serves for Karenin in his decision after Anna has revealed the truth to him.

If we were to judge Vronsky by the company that he kept before Anna, then his character would be much maligned, but Vronsky changes, as he himself realizes when he is forced to entertain a visiting foreign prince in Petersburg. Vronsky's closest friend in the regiment is Yashvin, "a gambler and a rake, a man not merely without moral principles but of immoral principles"—a man not unlike Vronsky himself! (194). Vronsky begins to change after hosting the foreign prince since he sees himself mirrored in the prince and does not like what he sees: "The prince was a very stupid, very self-satisfied, very healthy and immaculate man, and nothing else" (379). Vronsky begins as a similarly shallow "Petersburg dandy" and makes the single pursuit of his life for an entire year the seduction of a married woman; nevertheless, his commitment to Anna endures, despite the changes in her character and their relationship after the consummation of their affair.

If the men's reaction to the women's deaths is any indicator of their feelings toward them, then Vronsky truly did love Anna, for her death induces him to shoot himself and for six weeks not speak a word and barely touch his food, nor does Vronsky's melancholy diminish with the passage of time. After two months her death is as vivid as when he first witnessed it. He goes abroad to fight in Serbia as a means of expiating his guilt and with the hope of dying in battle, for he says, "As a man I have the merit that my life is of no value to me. . . . I am glad there is something for which I can lay down the life which is not simply useless but loathsome to me" (814). Anna has her revenge, but she cannot be said to be the victor in this struggle of wills, for all that was beautiful and gracious and winsome in her is snuffed out long before her actual death.

Alcée Arobin in *The Awakening* shares Vronsky's affinity for horses and the racetrack, and it is on just such a day at the races that he and Edna strike up their friendship. He, too, is a socialite, "a familiar figure at the race course, the opera, the fashionable clubs" (73). He dresses as "the conventional man of fashion" and appeals to Edna's romanticism by showing her a scar that he acquired in a duel in Paris when he was eighteen (74). His case is distinct, however, in that, although he sets out to seduce Edna and does, Edna, for her part, is never as emotionally involved as her counterparts. She is really far more taken with Robert Lebrun, but she cannot disguise or assuage the reflexive reaction of desire that Arobin's attentions arouse in her, insincere though they are.

Edna knows that she does not love Arobin, but she cannot help feeling attracted to him and so does eventually succumb to his entreaties. His manner of talking to her, the narrator tells us, appealed "to the animalism that stirred impatiently within her" (78). Her awakening to her self was an awakening to her needs as a woman—physical, emotional, and spiritual. Arobin appeals to the physical, which will not be denied, even though emotionally and perhaps even spiritually, Edna knows that he is not the right person for her. After their first dinner alone and Arobin's warm kiss on the back of her hand, Emma thinks, "Alcée Arobin was absolutely nothing to her. Yet his presence, his manners, the warmth of his glances, and above all the touch of his lips upon her hand acted like a narcotic upon her" (77). She is wise enough not to mistake the narcotic for the real thing, for after their first kiss Edna regrets that her body should have responded as it did, despite her not loving Arobin: "There was a dull pang of regret because it was not the kiss of love which had inflamed her, because it was not love which had held this cup of life to her lips" (83). She has always imagined that such feelings could be aroused only by the passionate embrace and kisses of a lover (in the true sense of the word), but she has found that her body has needs independent of her emotions. Emotionally she longs for the love of Robert Lebrun; spiritually she needs solitude to develop toward self-definition; physically she craves sensual pleasures.

Just as the actual affair is given short shrift in Fontane's *Effi Briest*, naturally so, too, is the character of the lover—Major von Crampas. Crampas is not introduced until nearly halfway into the novel, in a letter that Effi writes her mother, wherein she notes that the new commandant of the district militia has a reputation for love affairs and even has a shattered shoulder due to a duel—quite like Arobin in this respect. Effi goes on to describe him in this missive as "extremely gallant and extraordinarily quick-witted," and later we learn that he is an "excellent conversationalist" (101, 123). Like Vronsky, likewise an officer, Crampas adopts a self-serving ethic: "Helping a friend and deceiving him five minutes later were things that fitted very well into his conception of honour" (127). So it is that Crampas can so profoundly affect Innstetten with his dying glance. Though in the military corps, he does not share Innstetten's antiquated code of honor. He has dispensed with that "Calderonian sense of honor," as Ciplijauskaité puts it, and his silent reproach forces Innstetten to question his adherence to such principles when the feelings of anger, hatred, and vengeance that once inspired them are absent.

FRIENDS?

Robert Lebrun, like Alexei Vronsky, is rehabilitated in the course of the novel. We are led to believe from our introduction to Robert that he will be our Alcée Arobin, that he will complete the love triangle in the role of seducer-lover. After all, he has spent the last 11 summers attached to 11 different ladies—most of them married. Madame Ratignolle notices his attentions to Edna and requests that he leave her alone since she might take him seriously, but Robert claims that she should have warned *him* against taking himself seriously, for "[y]our advice might then have carried some weight and given me subject for some reflection" (22). But Edna does take him seriously and realizes after he departs for Mexico that she loves him as she loved the tragedian and the cavalry officer as an adolescent. It is a sort of idealized love, not based on the reality of his person, for just as Emma preferred her daydreams about Léon to his actual presence, Edna feels closer to Robert in her imaginings than when she actually sees him once again: "She had been with him, had heard his voice and touched his hand. But some way he had seemed nearer to her off there in Mexico" (102). When he returns, there is "no return to personalities," to the roles that they had played that summer (99). It has become too dangerous for Robert to resume the playful banter and "*camaraderie*." Genuine love is at stake, such a love that induces Robert to spare Edna from harm rather than yield to physical desire.

When Edna kisses Arobin, she feels unfaithful, but to Robert, not her husband. She believes that Robert caused her awakening that summer and later comes to understand that his seeming aloofness since the summer is because of his feelings for her. His love for her induces him to go to Mexico, and it compels him to return and then leave again, for once back in her presence, his desire overtakes his nobler sentiment, and he begs Edna not to go to Madame Ratignolle. Reluctant to break her promise, Edna goes to her friend, allowing Robert time to compose himself and leave her the note: "I love you. Good-bye—because I love you" (111). Robert's love is more noble than that of any of the lovers. He loves Edna enough to want the best for her and is willing to sacrifice his own desire and happiness for the sake of doing what he considers right. It remains to be seen whether his rejection is the sole reason for Edna's suicide and, if so, to what degree he is to blame for having awakened these feelings in her and then abandoned her to them.

Don Fermín in *La Regenta* also transforms the classic love triangle into a rectangle. It is through Don Fermín's eyes (and eyepiece) that we first glimpse Ana Ozores. She is, in fact, an insignificant speck at the mercy of the powerful *magistral*, who occupies the highest point in Vetusta in this opening scene, a metaphor for his position of authority and his power in Vetustan society, as he surveys his surroundings as a lord would his estate. In the end, he is still above Ana, forcing her to cower at his feet, his power bruised but intact.

The narrator explains Don Fermín's penchant for heights and climbing with an aside: "*Era montañés*" (He was from the mountains) (23), but a less literal interpretation can be inferred from Don Fermín's dreams of power: "*[E]ra él mismo que ahora mandaba a su manera en Vetusta!*" ([I]t was he, himself, who ruled now, by his own inclination, in Vetusta) (26). The narrator's commentary immediately follows: "*En este salto de la imaginación estaba la escencia de aquel placer intenso, infantil y material que gozaba De Pas como un pecado lascivia*" (In this leap of the imagination was the essence of that intense, childish, and materialistic pleasure that De Pas enjoyed like a sin of lasciviousness) (26). The narrator makes the connection between De Pas' ambition for money and power and other sins of the flesh, such as the one that Ana commits with Don Álvaro, which makes Don Fermín De Pas hypocritical in his judgment of her. He himself is guilty of the very same sin; they are both guilty of "excessive love."[5]

If Don Fermín were honest with himself, he would have to admit that his sudden revulsion toward Ana stems not from any sense of moral indignation but from wounded pride that she should have chosen Álvaro over himself. Ironically, Don Fermín, more so than Don Víctor, occupies the role of the deceived husband. Don Fermín may be a slave to societal norms; he may be afraid of the murmuring of the townspeople, afraid that they will discover his servile relationship with his mother or his lascivious desire for the regent's wife, but he not the ineffectual priest that Fr. Bournisien is in *Madame Bovary*. Don Fermín effects his revenge on Ana and avenges his wounded pride through a proxy. Like the man of honor of the Golden Age, he uses the power that he has "to judge and reject, rather than forgive and accept" (Sinclair 216). He orchestrates the events in the novel from the affair's disclosure to Don Víctor to the "barbaric" duel and is further able to avenge his honor by refusing to confess Ana, threatening her with bodily harm, and turning away from her.

Ana does not know what to make of her relationship with Don Fermín, but she does believe that he contains "*promesas de luz y de poesía*" (promises of light and poetry) (352). After confessing to him, she feels as though he is "*la salvación, la promesa de una vida virtuosa sin aburrimiento, llena de ocupaciones nobles, poéticas, que exigían esfuerzos, sacrificios, pero que por lo mismo daban dignidad y grandeza a la existencia muerta, animal, insoportable que Vetusta la ofreciera hasta el día*" (the salvation, the promise of a virtuous life without boredom, full of noble, poetic occupations that required effort and sacrifices, but, at the same time, which gave dignity and grandeur to the dead, animal, and unbearable existence which Vetusta had offered up until then) (352). Ana is searching for spiritual meaning to fill the void left by a morally bankrupt, materialistic, provincial society; she is never attracted to Don Fermín as a lover, but, rather, to an idealized vision of him and his ability to guide her to a virtuous life and Elysian Fields. Like Emma and, to a lesser extent, Luísa, Ana tries to quench her appetite for love and affection with religious piety; however, the role of the devout penitent is soon replaced by more tangible pleasures.

NOTES

1. Furst, Lecture, Chapel Hill, 1992.
2. See Vaheed Ramazani's *The Free Indirect Mode* (47ff.) for more on the conflation of narratorial and figural attitudes.
3. Zimmermann 826.
4. This last translation is suggested by Elizabeth Sabiston in *The Prison of Womanhood*.
5. A reference to Dante's *Divina Commedia*, where sins of incontinence (lust, gluttony, and avarice) are seen as less offensive to God because they are not malicious, stemming rather from "excessive love" of a person, food, money, or power.

4

Judgment Day

> For as you judge, so will you be judged, and the measure with which you measure will be measured out to you.
> —Matthew 7:2

"As a rhetorician," Wayne Booth writes in *The Rhetoric of Fiction*, "an author finds that some of the beliefs on which a full appreciation of his work depends come ready-made, fully accepted by the postulated reader as he comes to the book, and some must be implanted or reinforced" (177). How is it possible to "implant" beliefs in the reader? An author may do this through explicit commentary, irony, symbolism, "mood manipulation"[1] (i.e., scene setting), or characterization (i.e., by creating sympathy or distance from the characters). Booth asserts that some beliefs are "ready-made," by which he means those beliefs that are shared by both reader and author before the experience of the text; however, Booth also acknowledges that "the precise relationship of love to sex can never be taken for granted," and so "each novelist is left to establish the world in which the loves of his characters take place" (180). Thus, we must analyze the worlds of Tolstoy, Clarín, Fontane, Chopin, Queirós, and Flaubert in turn, for none can a priori be said to share the same norms, nor can the authors suppose that their readers will share theirs.

Realist writers did tend to follow Flaubert's intention to be like God in his universe—"everywhere present and nowhere visible."[2] However, just as philosophers like Thomas Aquinas have offered proof of God's existence through his effects, through creation, we can use the modal terms in a text to determine an implied author's/narrator's attitude toward the story that he is telling. These modal terms often take the form of adjectives that the author uses to describe his characters that reveal his or her attitude toward the character in question. In these novels of adultery, these terms, as we see in the forthcoming pages, are nearly always sympathetic in nature with the adulteress.

In this chapter we concern ourselves with the value judgments, whether implicit or explicit, made in the discourse of each of our narrators/implied authors. We begin with the most authoritative, explicit judgments of *Anna Karenin* and end with the more indirect, implicit ones of *Madame Bovary*.

ANNA KARENIN

Anna Karenin does not offer a severe criticism of the adulterous wife—whatever were the intentions of Tolstoy when he began.[3] The novel calls for catharsis, not judgment. We pity Anna's fall from noble wife to selfish mistress and fear that we in her situation would suffer a similar fate. To borrow from Tolstoy's philosophy of art: we are not to judge but to *feel* for Anna,[4] and we are encouraged to refrain from judgment from the opening epigraph to the scene of Anna's death.

If one philosophy influences the creation of *Anna Karenin* more than any other, it is Christianity. The epigraph is a direct quote from St. Paul's epistle to the Hebrews, which, in turn, is a reference to the Song of Moses in Deuteronomy 32: 35-36: "Vengeance is mine; I will repay" (Hebrews 10: 30). The message is twofold: live in fear of the Lord's judgment and do not seek vengeance yourself, for God will punish your enemies on Judgment Day. The chapter from Hebrews begins by acknowledging the unique nature of the sacrifice of God, which takes away the sins of the world, thereby reconciling sinners to Himself. Similarly, in *Anna Karenin* there is this mingling of judgment and forgiveness. Those who are willing to forgive are cast in a sympathetic light, whereas those who judge are either the one-dimensional, secondary figures or anonymous characters of the upper strata of society, and those who seek vengeance (Karenin and Anna) bring their own misery upon themselves.

The theme of forgiveness, like the theme of adultery, is foregrounded in the opening of the novel with Dolly's forgiveness of her husband's indiscretions. The implied author is quite clear here, in the opening, that Stiva Oblonsky, Anna's brother, is the one at fault: "Oblonsky was entirely in the wrong as regards his wife, as he himself admitted" (26). Dolly is an exemplary wife and mother who further exalts herself by forgiving her husband's infidelity (with some encouragement from Anna, who mediates the pair's dispute). Dolly is held up for our admiration not only here but throughout the novel with her repeated acts of kindness toward Anna and particularly for her fulfillment of the ideal of the maternal figure.

The novel is rife with instances of forgiveness granted and withheld. Kitty can forgive Levin for his sinful past, about which she has read in his diary, but she cannot forgive Anna for stealing her beau (Vronsky). Karenin forgives Anna in his heart for her infidelity, but he cannot express this forgiveness publicly, for he could not live with himself for breaking the code of society and dishonoring his name; thus, he withholds his forgiveness and allows feelings of vengeance to direct his actions. Likewise, Anna seeks vengeance on Vronsky and on herself for her lonely situation as his mistress. In the end, Dolly is our best model for forgiveness. She says to Anna at Vozdvizhenskoe that if one loves someone, one loves the whole person, just as they are, not as you would have them be (645). Her unconditional acceptance of Anna (and of her very weak and flawed husband) earns her forgiveness in turn—measure for measure—for Anna replies, "All your sins, if you had any . . . would be forgiven you for this visit and what you have just said" (645). Inasmuch as Dolly has been forgiving of the shortcomings of others, she will presumably be forgiven her shortcomings in the afterlife (though she does not manifest any in the course of the novel). The final plea for forgiveness in the novel is one that Anna makes to God before killing herself; she asks that He forgive "everything" (802).

When Karenin experiences his moment of forgiveness for Anna, which causes him to experience "a blissful spiritual condition . . [,] a new happiness he had never known," the implied author is quick to point out that this is not the result of a sense of Christian duty. At that moment Karenin "was not thinking that the Christian law which he had been trying to follow all his life enjoined on him to forgive and love his enemies" (438). He is transformed by the "joy in forgiving" that turns his suffering into inner peace (444). Such is his joy that he even forgives Vronsky, who is so mortified by Karenin's magnanimity that he tries to commit suicide.

Karenin's joy is short-lived, however, for the brute force of society, personified in the figure of Princess Tverskoy, governs Karenin's life and "hinders him from giving way to his feelings of love and forgiveness" (449). Karenin sadly realizes after the Princess' visit that he "would not be allowed to do what seemed to him now so natural and right, but would be compelled to do what was wrong, but seemed the proper thing to them [the moralizing circle of high society]" (451). He is guided henceforth in the novel by an external sense of honor, not the inner voice of conscience that brought him such peace. Though willing to forgive Anna and Vronsky in his heart, Karenin allows himself to be manipulated in his decisions regarding Anna by Lydia Ivanovna and hides his magnanimous spirit from all. Given that Karenin does have magnanimous impulses that are stifled by his milieu, readers might summon some sympathy for this easily maligned character since he, too, is a victim to the external forces of his milieu.

In addition to a character's propensity for forgiving, the female characters can be judged by their proximity to the ideal of motherhood, embodied in Dolly. Even in the midst of her quarrel with Stiva, Dolly has only to hear the cry of a child, and her face softens. Her realization at Vozdvizhenskoe that she and Anna have little in common reflects negatively upon Anna since Dolly represents the ideal of motherhood from which Anna has strayed; moreover, Anna herself knows that her "better part" is being smothered by her surroundings and that Dolly's presence arouses feelings of remorse because she is a touchstone of goodness: "To have those feelings awakened was painful but yet she knew that they belonged to the better part of herself, which was fast becoming smothered by the life she was leading" (673). Anna judges herself here and finds herself dominated by an "evil spirit" that has possessed her since her return to Moscow and continues to do so until her vengeful death.

Anna diminishes in stature inasmuch as she plays the role of lover more than that of mother. When we first meet her, she is devoted to Seriozha, to the point of bringing out his picture at her brother's house because she misses him and longs for the opportunity to speak of him. Once her affair with Vronsky begins, however, she is only too willing to abandon her son as long as Vronsky's love satisfies her—an observation she herself makes; moreover, Anna takes an extreme measure for her era in having a hysterectomy to prevent her becoming a mother again. The surgeon would seem to have excised her maternal feelings along with all or part of her uterus since Anna cannot seem to summon any maternal feelings for her and Vronsky's love child, Ani. Thus, part of the "better part" of Anna that is smothered by her environment is her maternal part, for the more immersed she is in her lover, the less maternal she is or wants to be or can be.

Levin, the simple landowner whose thoughts are most often confirmed by the implied author, shares the implied author's positive evaluation of motherhood. Levin divides women into two categories: courtesans and mothers, and "his future wife was to be a repetition of that exquisite and holy ideal of womanhood which his mother had been" (109). He cannot imagine a wife who is not a mother or marriage without a family. According to the narrator, motherhood is a "gigantic" task, and it is a task that Anna leaves unfinished. The task is so immense because of its importance, because the "truths" by which children need to live must be instilled with their mother's milk. Levin finally realizes after much mental anguish and years and years of searching for the meaning of life that he can live only as he was raised to live—according to the habits of his youth. Without even realizing this, Levin was unwittingly doing so, despite his doubt: "He had been living (without being aware of it) on those spiritual truths that he had imbibed with his mother's milk" (832). There really is no other way: "Now it was clear to him that he could only live by virtue of the beliefs in which he had been brought up" (832). Not only does Levin's line of thinking here demonstrate the importance of motherhood, but it also supports the Naturalist tenet that we are the products of biology and environment. If this is the case with Anna, if Anna is a victim of physical needs conflicting with unenlightened society, then can we blame her for her actions? We cannot assign responsibility without moral agency, so we must first consider whether Anna is a victim of deterministic laws of nature.

Anna's environment does stifle what is good in her. At the start of the novel, she has a suppressed joie de vivre, a Schopenhauerian will-to-live. When we first see her through Vronsky's eyes, "It was as though her nature were brimming over with something that against her will expressed itself now in a radiant look, now in a smile" (75). Her joie de vivre is suppressed due to her marriage to a civil servant many years her senior: "But the time came when I [Anna] realized I couldn't deceive myself any longer, that I was alive, that I was not to blame, that God had made me so that I need to love and live" (314). Dolly excuses Anna for this same reason: "How is she to blame? She wants to live. We were born with that need in our hearts" (639). Whether God implanted such a need, or the world *is* such an impulse, as Schopenhauer suggests, this will-to-live is something inescapable.

Anna changes after leaving the proper environment of the Karenin household to live the bohemian life with Vronsky. Once noble in her attempt to repair a broken marriage, after the consummation of their affair Anna lives either to serve Vronsky or to satisfy herself. She becomes more and more self-absorbed, self-pitying, and jealous, and her acts of charity are nothing more than self-serving attempts to end her boredom. Even her death is a vindictive attempt to wound. She lives to serve Vronsky, then only herself. She must take morphine to sleep at night and believes that only by keeping her figure, that is, by having a hysterectomy so that she cannot be impregnated, can she keep her man. As Dolly thinks when she hears this, "It seemed . . . too simple a solution for too complicated a problem," and "If that is all he [Vronsky] looks for, he will find dresses and manners still more attractive and charming" (668, 669). Indeed, Anna's hysterectomy and fancy dress do not ease her mind, and she becomes a jealous harpy, suspicious of Vronsky's every absence. Her self-esteem needs constant reassurance, so she tries to enamor all the men with whom she comes in contact. Her dress no longer frames her beauty; it becomes the locus of beauty, becoming more and more dazzling. Whereas once she wore simple, black gowns, like the one she wears to the ball in Part One, which sets off her beauty as a frame does a picture, she changes to gowns of the sort that she wears to the opera: a "low-necked gown of light silk and velvet that she had had made in Paris," and she places "rich white lace" on her head (571). The dress overtakes her physical beauty, which was once so attractive due to its emanation of life itself, but Anna no longer cares about life, only the dark fires of passion.

Anna claims that she is not to blame, that things could not have been otherwise,[5] but Anna does make a significant choice in the novel: she chooses Vronsky over her son Seriozha; she chooses life with Vronsky and the possibility of happiness over maternal duties and her son. Ironically, Anna is more a prisoner in adultery than she ever was in marriage. Those who view adultery as a means of liberation for women in the nineteenth century should pay close attention to Anna's position as a lover, for though these women break societal and religious laws, they are not liberated. As a wife, Anna was unhappy, but she had certain rights, and she had dignity and respect. As Vronsky's lover, she forfeits all privileges, dignity, and respect; consequently, she is more a slave in adultery than she is in marriage.

The analogy between the sex drive and an appetite for food appears in more than one of these novels of adultery. Basílio and Don Álvaro, for instance, describe their readiness for sex in terms of the appetitive nature of Luísa and Ana Ozores. Oblonsky has an ever-present appetite for food and sex even when he is not physically hungry; he is, in other words, insatiable. Priscilla Meyer goes so far as to assert that Oblonsky is the embodiment of sensualism in the novel[6] and, as such, represents "the Enemy . . . the destructive force of Tolstoy's novel, for it is this life force and sensual appetite that lead Anna to go against her moral principles and precipitate suicide" (258). Anna does not have the appetite that her brother has, and yet she, too, expresses the belief that "[y]ou can't get away from yourselves" (795). Is Anna a slave to her appetites? She certainly thinks so. Anna claims in a paragraph of quoted monologue, "We all want what is sweet, what is nice. If we can't have bon-bons, then dirty ice-cream!" (793). Anna could not fulfill her need for passion in any acceptable, "pure" way, so she did so in a "dirty"—that is, immoral—way. Abstinence is possible only for so long before the damn breaks and the nervous tension created by repressed desires becomes unbearable and washes away all restraint. Anna claims that she was born to live and love, that God made her thus. Should she have to struggle against a God-given nature? She may have been made to live and love, as she believes, but was she made for the dark fires of passion? If Anna is will-to-live, then she is not made for disordered passion, for such passions are destructive in nature.

As if the tragic conclusion to Anna and Vronsky's affair were not enough, we are given numerous reminders throughout the text of the destructive nature of passion. Typically here, as elsewhere, passion is opposed to reason, as when Anna recalls Vronsky's confession of love to her on the train to Petersburg and thinks, "He had said what her heart longed to hear, though she *feared* it with her *reason*" (118; emphasis added). In Vronsky's set, "the important thing was to be elegant, handsome, broad-minded, daring, gay, and ready to surrender unblushingly to every passion and to laugh at everything else" (129). Thus, Vronsky throws himself into the pursuit of a married woman for a year, incurring neither the censure of his class nor any feeling of humiliation. Only his family seems to worry about his "Werther-like passion" for Anna. Others in his circle consider it quite romantic and even commonplace.

The allusion to *The Sufferings of Young Werther*, while conjuring up images of the typically misunderstood hero and the impossibly eternal love, should also remind us of the destructive nature of Werther's passion for Lotte. Werther commits suicide at the end of the novel because he despairs of ever being considered more than a brother by Lotte. Anna also commits suicide—out of despair, certainly, since death seems the only solution, but out of vengeance, as well, and Vronsky also attempts suicide *à la Werther* when Anna and Karenin seem to be reconciled and when the obstacles to his loving Anna seem to mount. We must not think, however, that the destructive nature of passion is limited here to successful suicides or suicide attempts. Its destructive work begins, as it does with Werther, long before the actual suicide/suicide attempt.

When Anna returns from Princess Betsy's dinner party, when her husband first begins to suspect something amiss, the narrator describes Anna's vivacious glow not as a "joyous glow" but as "the terrible glow of a fire on a dark night" (161). There is something "terrible" about Anna and Vronsky's love for one another when its consummation is described in criminal, sinful terms. Anna droops her "once proud, gay" head after the consummation and begs God for his forgiveness, a plea that she ends up directing at Vronsky since he is all that is left to her in this world and since she is sacrificing any life in the next. She will sacrifice her position in society and the few rights that she had as a wife and mother and be a social outcast. Similarly, Vronsky "felt what a murderer must feel when he looks at the body he has robbed of life" (165). As is typical of our authoritarian narrator, he explains the metaphor for the reader: "The body he had robbed of life was their love, the first stage of their love" (165).

At least at this point in the story, the opening of Chapter 11 of Part Two, the implied author is casting much of the blame for the crime of adultery upon Vronsky, for he is the so-called murderer of the first stage of their love— the most pure stage. He is the one who has pursued Anna for nearly a year. Though the implied author tells us that he has some sense of wrongdoing, that he feels the death knell of their love, he continues to cover Anna with caresses and kisses "as with fury and passion the murderer throws himself upon the body [he has just killed] and drags it and hacks at it" (165). From this point on in the novel, Vronsky struggles to hide his crime. He makes sacrifices in order to remain with Anna, like passing up a good post in the service, and tries to pretend that he is happy in their love, but the implied author informs us that Vronsky makes the same mistake that others have in thinking that the fulfillment of his desires will bring him happiness: "He soon began to feel that the realization of his desires brought him no more than a grain of sand out of the mountain of bliss he had expected. It showed him the eternal error men make in imagining that happiness consists in the realization of their desires" (490–491). *If* happiness were the end and *if* the fulfillment of desire were the means to happiness, then Vronsky's actions might be justified; however, as it is in the novel, goodness, not happiness, is proposed as the *telos*, so Vronsky is censurable for pursuing pleasure at the expense of the "public welfare."

The implied author's judgment of Vronsky is subsequently manifested in his refusal to mitigate the blame that Vronsky assigns himself and in the rather overt parallels suggested by Vronsky's breaking Frou-Frou's back at the races and his breaking of Anna's will-to-live because he is chafing at the reins.[7] Vronsky feels sorry for Anna when she is pregnant with his child and at the mercy of Karenin, for "he could not help her, and with that, he knew that he was to blame for her wretchedness, that he had done wrong" (340). The wrong that he does is metaphorically represented in his breaking Frou-Frou's back at the races. Vronsky was "in the clear" that day at the races when "for some inexplicable reason" he makes "a dreadful, unforgivable blunder," which results in breaking his mare's back. The description of the broken mare on the ground reminds us of Anna: "Frou-Frou lay breathing heavily before him, bending her head back and gazing at him with her beautiful eyes" (218). Not realizing what he has done, Vronsky tugs at the rein; Frou-Frou tries to regain her feet but sinks back to the ground in agony; then, in a fit of passion, Vronsky kicks his beloved mare in the belly. There is no hope for her; she must be shot, and "[f]or the first time in his life he [Vronsky] knew the bitterest kind of misfortune—misfortune beyond remedy, caused by his own fault" (218). He is responsible for his mare's death, and, by implication, he is responsible for Anna's. He has murdered their love with its physical consummation, and for Anna, life and love are inextricably intertwined.

Vronsky receives the most overt censure from the implied author; however, Anna alone receives the judgment and punishment of society and her husband. Vronsky's mother speaks for society at large when she pronounces, "[S]he [Anna] ended as such a woman deserved to end. . . . [H]er death was the death of a very bad woman, a woman without religion" (812). In weighing the authority of such a judgment and whether or not it is confirmed by the narrator, we should recall that the countess herself was accustomed to taking lovers and that Anna's last words are addressed to God, praying for forgiveness—surely she was not without religion, only without society's hypocrisy and a strong beacon to guide her along the right path.

What must have surely come easily for the countess with her numerous lovers is torture to Anna. Anna is never at ease with her position, though she is not the first or only adulteress in Russian society. What is easy for countless other women is torture to Anna since she has always been distinct from other women of society. She is an intelligent, independent thinker graced with beauty and nobility of character, which makes her fall all the more tragic because she, who was once so great, becomes so petty. We cannot fear and pity the fate of one who was never admirable or extraordinary, but we do experience catharsis with Anna's death because she fights valiantly against her fate until she is overcome by her milieu.

Since it was clearly not unusual for aristocratic women to take lovers, we well might question why Anna and, later, Ana Ozores in *La Regenta* are ostracized for their affairs. In the first place, Anna Karenin and Ana Ozores choose not to associate with society proper, which is to their credit since the principal preoccupations of the *grandes dames* are fashion and the latest gossip. In the beginning of the novels, both Anna and Ana choose to distance themselves from these women who expect and overlook marital infidelity, thus placing themselves above the herd of society proper and creating feelings of envy and *ressentiment* among other members of the aristocratic herd. It should come as no surprise, consequently, that Anna and Ana's connections in society proper are only too happy to facilitate their affairs, for they are resentful of the respect that Anna and Ana garner for their purity and noble bearing and happily see them weaken and fall.

Thus, as each proves that she is really no "better" than the society around her, those envious members of society are quite pleased—even more so when they are able to hypocritically snub the protagonists once their affairs are revealed. Adultery is tolerated in high society provided it is not flaunted, and although Anna Karenin and Ana Ozores are certainly not eager to flaunt their indiscretions, Anna's living with Vronsky and Don Víctor's duel with Don Álvaro thrust their affairs into the open and elicit the aforementioned ostracization. As Boccaccio writes in the fourth tale of the first day of *The Decameron*, "A sin that's hidden is half forgiven." Provided that one keeps up appearances, infidelity can be enjoyed with impunity, but once revealed, especially a wife's indiscretions, then punishment is incurred.

To confirm an assessment of the detrimental effects of passion, sensualism, and vengeance, we have only to look to Levin and the children. Levin is most unlike any other character whom we encounter in *Anna Karenin* because he is from the country and has simple tastes, intellectual curiosity, and genuine concern for the laboring class. He, too, feels as though his better nature were smothered by the environment of high society in the city, as when he stays out late with Stiva and pays a visit to Anna (a destructive force at this point). On his briefer visits to the city, Levin maintains his simple lifestyle. He does not enjoy dinner with Oblonsky in Part One of the novel since Oblonsky, like any socialite, lingers over eating (it is a social occasion), and Levin is accustomed to dispatching with meals in the country in order to return to work—a very utilitarian view of food and mealtimes. Levin's appetites, thus, have been conditioned by the environment in which he was raised, an environment that is closer to the land, the peasants, and simplicity. It is only natural that with this kind of milieu,

Levin is said to have a "childlike light-heartedness," which endears him to Dolly, Kitty, and Dolly's children—all positive touchstones.

Children, because of their simplicity and lack of affectation, are good indicators in *Anna Karenin* of the moral probity of the characters. Seriozha is the touchstone of innocence who reminds the pair how far they have erred: "This child, with his innocent outlook upon life, was the compass which showed them the degree to which they had departed from what they knew but did not want to know" (204). The implication here is that maternal love is more pure than erotic passion; thus, Seriozha's disgruntled reaction to Anna and Vronksy connotes how far the pair has strayed from the path of righteousness. Anna and Vronsky pretend that their love and passion are all that matter—that they can disregard society, wasted career opportunities, and family, but they learn that the fulfillment of desire does not yield happiness or peace of mind and that individuals cannot live without society.

We might similarly look at how Dolly's children accept Levin, confirming this character as a positive foil for the course of Anna and Vronsky's affair. Although Dolly's children do not really know Levin, they "did not show towards him any of that strange shyness and hostility children so often feel for grown-up people who 'pretend'" (288). The narrator's presence is evident in the phrase "so often feel" in the foregoing passage and in the following commentary: "Pretense about anything whatever may deceive the cleverest and shrewdest of men, but the dullest child will see through it, no matter how artfully it may be disguised" (288). To ensure that we draw the proper conclusion, he adds, "Whatever failings Levin had, there was not an atom of pretense in him" (288). Thus, with the children's affection, his lack of pretense, and his simple country manners, Levin is a positive foil to Anna's gradual impoverishment.

The character of Levin may not, at first, seem pertinent to a discussion of the implied author's judgment of adultery in *Anna Karenin*, but Tolstoy has chosen to weave the stories of two couples together structurally: one of them is a cautionary tale (Anna and Vronsky), and the other, an exemplary one (Kitty and Levin). It is important, thus, to look at Levin and Kitty's relationship to see where Anna and Vronsky go wrong. For example, Levin and Kitty love each other almost like brother and sister. Anna and Vronsky, conversely, hide their emotions and battle one another for freedom and power; theirs is a love of dangerous passions. Kitty forgives Levin when she reads his diary, and Levin forgives Kitty for tolerating the courtship of Veslovsky. Anna and Vronsky withhold forgiveness from one another in order to gain the upper hand.

The couples, in addition, experience parallel lives. Their differences cannot be attributed to very different circumstances. Levin and Anna experience similar feelings and conflicts, as do Kitty and Vronsky. Anna is ashamed after she reveals her affair to her husband, as is Levin after he makes Kitty an offer of marriage that is refused. Anna's difficulty with Karenin is matched by Levin's difficulty with his peasants in the following section. Finally, Vronsky's feelings of confinement in his relationship with Anna are echoed in the subsequent chapter by Kitty's literal confinement due to her pregnancy. Though they experience similar emotions, these couples nevertheless react very differently because of their natures and the nature of their loves.

If we were to recapitulate the positive values established in *Anna Karenin*, we would see that Anna fails to exhibit more than one as a result of her time spent as Vronsky's mistress. Her vengeful suicide evinces her unwillingness to forgive; she loses her maternal affection, and she gives in to her destructive passion. She acts contrary to all that is positive; nevertheless, the implied author's suggestion that Anna's character is determined and his very poetic description of her death provide a rationale for withholding judgment and empathizing with the tragedy of a lost soul. Our judgment is mitigated by our final glimpse of Anna's psyche: "And the candle by which she had been reading the book [of life] filled with trouble and deceit, sorrow and evil, flared up with a brighter light, illuminating for her everything that before had been enshrouded in darkness, flickered, grew dim and went out for ever" (802). Anna's book of life is filled with "deceit," but it is also filled with "trouble." She becomes possessed of an "evil spirit," but she also has her share of "sorrow." Anna's greatest mistake, her tragic flaw, if you will, is neither her passionate affair nor her suicide; it is that she never heeds the divine revelation purportedly revealed to all men; she never learns, as Levin does, to endow her life with "a positive meaning of goodness." She rejects divine as well as worldly wisdom.[8]

Levin discovers in the end that his life is no longer meaningless, that even though he may outwardly act the same and make the same mistakes, his "whole life . . . every minute of it is no longer meaningless as it was before, but has a positive meaning of goodness with which I have the power to invest it" (853). Levin finds the meaning of life in irrational altruism. Anna, conversely, demands personal satisfaction from life and places happiness instead of goodness as the end of all striving. Like Vronsky, she, too, comes to realize that the fulfillment of desire does not lead to happiness, but her death proves that she has not learned that there is a higher good than personal happiness. Happiness, for Levin, comes as a by-product of his pursuit of the general welfare. He knows that serving the public welfare is countercultural and irrational, but he decides that revelation cannot be explained by reason, and so he will unquestioningly endow his life with the purpose that it had when he was a child, with the truths that he ingested from his mother's milk. Even though Levin cannot be sure in all cases what is best for the "general welfare" (the Serbian question is his most immediate problem), "he knew beyond doubt that this welfare could only be achieved by strict observance of that law of right and wrong which has been revealed to every man" (845). "Man" here can be understood as humankind since Levin is not referring to any truths learned in school but those revealed by God and passed on through a mother's milk.

Tolstoy's novel advocates absolutes. Although certainly a number of factors create sympathy for Anna's plight—the character of her husband, her determined characterization, and her tragic death—what she does is nevertheless clearly presented as a crime; however, judgment, too, is "wrong." Happiness lies in forgiving, working for the common good, and living the simple life away from society and closer to our roots in nature. We have the exhortations not to judge or seek vengeance in the epigraph and in the words of Levin, the positive representation of the Christian concept of forgiveness, and Levin's final inner peace in submitting himself to irrational revelation. Vronsky is never censured by society, but he is explicitly judged by the implied author. He is the murderer of his and Anna's love. Whatever was good and pure in their love for one another takes a terrible turn, and the destructive nature of their passion prevents them from heeding reason; moreover, in their selfish pursuit of happiness, they are deaf to the revelation of divine wisdom, perhaps best heard in the natural realm of God's creation.

LA REGENTA

Tolstoy is an anomaly among late nineteenth-century writers for advocating an absolute, divinely revealed law of right and wrong. There may be hints of determinism in *Anna Karenin* but nothing like the clear representation of a wife at the mercy of her physical appetites that we have in Clarín's *La Regenta*. Naturalists, such as Clarín, may have considered themselves more objective than Realists, producing photographs of reality rather than portraits, but their tenets of the determinism of heredity, moment, and milieu override their intention of objectivity and dictate the pessimistic outcomes of their works. Ana Ozores, like Anna Karenin, is a tragic figure because, though she drives herself to physical illness in a futile attempt to repress desire, she is unable to surmount her environment and fulfill her longing for love and life. The figure of Ana, moreover, demonstrates how our very imagination can make us prisoner and create such intense desires that their repression causes nervous disorders.

Ana, in contrast to the unnatural sexual practices of Celedonio, possibly Frígilis and Don Víctor, and the *"anafrodita"*[9] English governess Camila, does not go against Nature in her sexual fantasies and practices. She wants heterosexual love—the accepted, conventional, even clichéd love of romances. There is nothing perverse in her appetite for carnal love and offspring, though her social milieu would not have understood the sexual needs of a woman. When there is a perceived hint of such a perversion in her desires, as when Ana thinks about a priest's loving her, she immediately turns away. Although Ana's appetites are in accordance with Nature, they do not meet the socially acceptable norms of proper conduct, and so Ana fights her impulses and desires and tries to lose herself in a mystic union with God—exercises that lead to her psychosomatic illness.

Since she is ignorant of the concept of natural law, Ana continues to fight very natural inclinations. Her fight is noble but tragically motivated by conformity to the mores of an unnatural society driven by the traditions of a "timeless" church whose precepts are not altered to accommodate scientific advances and so-called biological needs. The narrator of *La Regenta*, thus, in mocking the unthinking clergy who are the supposed exemplars of good conduct and in condemning the machinations of the manipulative magistrate, conveys his respect for a more universal and inescapable law—that of Nature. These men of God are as susceptible as laypeople to carnal love, petty jealousy, boredom, ambition, an avenging spirit, and a gossiping tongue. What's more, they do not fight their baser passions with all the rigor that Ana does hers. If the "paragons of virtue" in Vetusta cannot refrain from sinning, how can we expect Ana to withstand the temptation? Is it possible for her to win the fight against desire when the fight itself turns a perfectly "normal," healthy woman into a physically and mentally sick member of society in need of a cure?

Ana Ozores, like Anna Karenin, cannot escape herself, cannot suppress her appetite for love. Raised by three aunts who are "*frías, secas y caprichosas*" (cold, dry, and whimsical) and an androgynous English governess, Ana learns to repress desire in the interest of appearing respectable. Levin says in *Anna Karenin* that we must live by the truths that we imbibe with our mother's milk, but what if we never had such nourishment? Ana never has the guidance or love of a mother, a fact that she uses to explain her vices to Don Fermín: "*Yo no he tenido madre . . . no sé ser buena . . . no quiero la virtud si no es pura poesía, y la poesía de la virtud parece prosa al que no es virtuoso. . . . Por eso quiero que usted me guíe*" (I have not had a mother . . . I don't know how to be good . . . I don't want virtue if it is not pure poetry, and the poetry of virtue seems like prose to the one who is not virtuous; therefore, I want you to guide me) (509). Ana wants virtue to be pure poetry, but she confesses to Don Fermín here that she is not virtuous, that she would be unable to recognize the poetry of virtue; therefore, he must guide her.

Ana is the product of a motherless upbringing. When she first begins her examination of conscience, for instance, in Chapter 3 of the novel, her first thought is that she has never known a mother's love and that "*[t]al vez de esta desgracia nacían sus mayores pecados*" ([p]erhaps from this misfortune were born her greatest sins) (73). As a child she does not dream of marriage but motherhood. She uses her imagination not to envision her spouse but to substitute for the caresses of a mother.

Clarín establishes a logic of cause and effect to explain Ana's development; hence, we have in *La Regenta* the most in-depth flashback to the adulteress' youth of any of the novels of adultery studied here. And when Ana muses that perhaps her most serious offenses against God can be accounted for by her lack of maternal affection and proceeds to rub her face against the softness of her sheets (one of her substitutes for the caresses of a mother), the narrator notes that "*Aquella blandura de los colchones era todo* lo maternal *con que ella podía contar; no había más suavidad para la pobre niña*" (That softness of the mattress was all the *maternalness* on which she could count; there was no other gentleness for the poor child) (72). The narrator emphasizes that the inanimate sheets make a poor substitute for a mother in his stressing the word "*maternal*" and adds the adjective "poor" before "child" to convey his sympathy for Ana directly. Later he will return to this characterization of Ana as "*la pobre niña sin madre*" (the poor child without a mother) when he tells us that "the poor child" averts a nervous attack by releasing her emotion in tears (104).

Ana's fate is her character, which is determined by a loveless background, with little formal education. Though she has a governess as a child, she would be more aptly described as self-educated since she undertakes the vociferous reading in her father's library, and it is from these books that she gleans her limited knowledge of the world, knowledge that is, like Emma Bovary's, erroneously attuned to sentiment rather than conceptual understanding. Ana cannot, for instance, understand the more theoretical and philosophical final books of Augustine's *Confessions*. Since her knowledge of the world comes to her

Judgment Day

from books, when she leaves the convent of her father's house, she inverts the accepted relationship between life and art and expects life to imitate poetry. Her only consolation in her solitary youth and virginal adulthood is her imagination, which she is unable to suppress or control and which both facilitates and impedes her encounters with God, for it enables Ana to experience a mystical union with the divine being (albeit a "false" one, as the narrator characterizes it in the end) and simultaneously distracts her from her meditations and induces flights of fancy of a more physical nature, catalyzed by the feel of tiger skin on her naked flesh or the softness of her sheets or the flattery of Don Álvaro. Ana knows that her flesh is weak, that she needs guidance, which is why she seeks out Don Fermín, her confessor and spiritual guide, who fails her because he, too, is all too human, with his jealousy and vengeful spirit.

Since Ana is more clearly a victim here, the critique of society is all the more biting. The society in question is the fictional Vetusta; however, Paciencia Ontañón argues that *La Regenta* is primarily a criticism not of Vetustan society but of the erroneous principles of society in general that perpetuate from generation to generation and that "*se permite convertir a un ser humano pleno de posibilidades en un enfermo*" (allow a human being, full of possibilities, to be converted into a sick person) (11). Noel Valis does not interpret the criticism of Vetusta quite so broadly; she asserts that Vetusta is emblematic of the problems inherent in Restoration society, the setting of the novel. Whether the criticism is directed at society in general, provincial society, or Restoration society, no one denies that Vetusta is under attack.

The town is ironically presented as a "noble and loyal" and "heroic" city—which is taking a nap! It is a moribund place where "*[l]a tierra fungosa se descarnaba como los huesos de Job*" (The spongy earth was becoming fleshless like the bones of Job) and "*toda la campiña entumecida, desnuda, se extendía a lo lejos, inmóvil como el cadáver de un náufrago*" (all the stiff, naked countryside extended in the distance, immobile like the cadaver of a shipwrecked person) (489). Nature, itself, resigned to the sadness of its death, seems to hope that the rains will "dissolve" its "useless, inert" body (489). The cathedral spire during the rainy season is like "*un mástil sumergido*" (a submerged mast) in the "*negruzca*" (blackish) city (489). All these images of the city serve as metaphors for the stultifying, tomblike atmosphere in which Ana drowns.[10] Ana suffers in Vetusta, as Effi does in Kessin, from a "desperate tedium" and repression because she cannot express her erotic desires in an acceptable, satisfying manner (for Effi the repression is augmented by her fears, which are fostered by her husband). The sole acceptable means of expressing such desires was in religion, which only augments Ana's nervous disorder to the point of physical illness and in which Effi professes not to believe.

The narrator's criticism of Vetustans in general is most vituperative at the end of the novel. No one visits Ana after her husband's death; the Vetustans feign compunction but are secretly glad of thc scandal caused by the duel since it relieves the boredom of their provincial existence: "*No entraban. Vetusta la noble estaba escandalizada, horrorizada. Unos a otros, con cara de hipócrita compunción, se ocultaban los buenos vetustenses el íntimo placer que les causaba* aquel gran escándalo que era como una novela, *algo que interrumpía la monotonía eterna de la ciudad triste*" (They did not enter. Noble Vetusta was scandalized, horrified. The good Vetustans, with faces of hypocritical compunction, hid from one another the intimate pleasure the *great scandal that was like a novel* gave them, something that interrupted the eternal monotony of the sad city) (862). The italicized phrase in the original text is a subtle reminder that we readers are guilty of the same pleasure as the gossiping Vetustans when we turn the pages of the novel, ourselves eager for more scandal. We readers, like the "noble" Vetustans, enjoy the conflict, transgression, and punishment of Ana from a safe distance. Could we be as hypocritical, bored, and sad as Vetusta?

In the midst of the town's murmuring about the scandal, the comment made by the Marqués de Vegallana sticks out and characterizes the hypocritical self-righteousness of the Vetustans. The Marqués exclaims that the whole affair is "nauseating"—to which the narrator adds: "*Esto lo dijo el marqués de Vegallana, que tenía en la aldea todos sus hijos ilegítimos*" (This was said by the Marqués de Vegallana, who had all his illegitimate children in the village) (863). The ironic juxtaposition of the Marqués' exclamation with the narrator's seemingly innocent identification of the speaker, whose corruption in political matters has already been suggested earlier in the novel,[11] calls attention to the hypocrisy of those who would cast the first stone. The narrator's judgments of Don Álvaro, Don Fermín, and Petra are not nearly so subtle.

Don Álvaro is clearly identified as a donjuanesque figure. The mere mention of his name is often accompanied by epithets (modal terms) such as "*Tenorio*," "*seductor*," and "*materialista*." His declaration of love for Ana is "*toda idealismo, llena de salvedades y eufismos*" (all idealism, full of exclamations and euphemisms) (774). As Don Álvaro well knows, this is precisely what Ana needs to hear, for it feeds her girlhood dreams of love. Like Emma Bovary, she cannot conceive of a love that is not manifested in a conventional manner (even taking a lover is conventional). The narrator, however, does not allow the reader to be taken in by the trappings of love, by the posturing of Don Álvaro, as our protagonist is. Don Álvaro envelops Ana in a "*delirio amoroso*" (amorous delirium), "*como en una nube envenenada con opio*" (as in a cloud poisoned with opium) (803). Don Álvaro's love poisons Ana and also serves to justify her infidelity since she is unaware that she is being "poisoned" by Álvaro, that his passion is not transcendental and will destroy her, or that Don Álvaro sees her as an appetizing drop of candy ready to eat.

Before succumbing to Don Álvaro, he who most influences Ana's behavior is her confessor, Don Fermín. His is the power that Innstetten wields over Effi—fear. The significant role that Don Fermín is meant to have in the novel is demonstrated by the fact that he and Ana are the only characters dealt with from infancy and those whose victimization at the hands of society is dealt with in any depth.[12] Whatever sympathy we might have for Don Fermín due to the description of his youth and the narrator's labeling him a "*víctima*" of "*las dionisíacas de la injuria*" (the Dionysian excesses of insult), for his frustrated plans and desire for Ana, for his inability to express himself as a man given his office as a priest, this sympathy is dissipated by Fermín's subsequent vengeful actions. The deal that he makes with Petra to expose Ana and Álvaro's affair is characterized as "*una intriga asquerosa y vil*" (a vile and loathsome intrigue) (810). By the end of their conference together, Don Fermín and Petra are speaking together "*como dos cómplices de un crimen difícil*" (like two accomplices of a difficult crime) (810), and Clarín ends the scene of their collaboration with the following explicit denunciation: "*Había allí dos criminales apasionados, y ningún testigo de la ignominia; cada cual veía su venganza, no el crimen del otro ni la vergüenza del pacto*" (There were there two passionate criminals and no witness to the ignominy; each one saw his own vengeance and not the crime of the other nor the shame of the pact) (811). This personal vengeance, passionately undertaken out of feelings of rejection and resentment, is judged "criminal" and "shameful" by the narrator. No such modal terms are used in the discussion of Ana's adultery. The former would seem to be the greater crime.

Though not criticized by name, Don Fermín is subject to the irreverent observations that characterize the clergy in general. For example, the narrator describes the clergy's manner of praising God as a daily drudgery that they complete between yawns: "*El coro había terminado: los venerables canónigos dejaban cumplido por aquel día su deber de alabar al Señor entre bostezo y bostezo*" (The choir had ended: the venerable religious had fulfilled, for that day, their duty of praising the Lord between yawns) (49). These members of the religious order worship their divinity with about as much enthusiasm (a word that literally means "with God's spirit") as a student undertakes a subject that he finds uninteresting, and yet how can these "men of God" have so little zeal for their "work"? Even if they had no enthusiasm, they might at least demonstrate an intellectual curiosity, a faith in God based on their theology, but their intellects are no more engaged than their emotions, for bringing up theology only proves to be the best way to end an argument; it was like "*echarle agua al fuego*" (throwing water on a fire) (469). The "venerable dignitaries" have a "*respeto singular*" for theology "*que consistía en no querer hablar nunca de cosas altas*" (which consisted of their not wanting to ever speak of "elevated things") (469). Even the clergy of Vetusta would rather gossip about the Regent's wife than discuss matters of God.

Don Víctor, since he assumes responsibility for Ana's adultery and refuses to judge her, is spared the narrator's biting criticism. He is "*el mísero*" when Ana and Álvaro are carrying on their affair. He does not escape satirization—he is a classic cuckold—nevertheless, like Karenin, he is willing to forgive his wife and her lover, though he, too, finds himself unable to go against the expectations of society and his own imagination, cultivated by the "cloak-and-dagger" dramas of the Golden Age. His attention to propriety and to his role as a type of *bonhomme* blinds him to the very real drama that transpires under his roof through the contrivance and treachery of his old friend. His foolishness notwithstanding, Don Víctor is granted keener insight into the workings of Nature than any other character in the novel, for Don Víctor sees that while societal laws and laws of honor are accompanied by their own harsh punishment when trangressed, they are not as important or essential to people's well-being as is an imitation of natural law:

¡[Q]ué hermosa era la naturaleza!, ¡qué tranquilmente reposaba . . . ! ¡Los hombres, los hombres eran los que habían engendrado los odios, las traiciones, las leyes convencion-

ales que atan a la desgracia del corazón! . . .Y todas las ciudades, y todos los agujeros donde el hombre, esa hormiga, fabricaba su albergue, ¿qué eran comparados con los bosques vírgenes, los desiertos, las cordilleras, los vastos mares . . . ? Nada. Y las leyes de honor, las preocupaciones de la vida social todas, ¿qué eran al lado de las grandes y fijas y naturales leyes a que obedecían los astros en el cielo, las olas en el mar, el fuego bajo la tierra, la savia circulando por las plantas? (825)

[H]ow beautiful was nature! How peacefully it rested! Men, men were the ones who had engendered the hatreds, treasons, and conventional laws that tie the heart to disgrace. . . . And all the cities and all the holes where man, that ant, would build his shelter—what were they compared to the virginal forests, the deserts, the mountain ranges, the vast seas . . . ? Nothing. And the laws of honor, all the concerns of the social life—what were they next to the great and fixed and natural laws that all the stars in the sky, the waves in the sea, the fire under the earth, and the sap in the plants obeyed?

Such a profound observation would be out of character for the vacuous, obtuse husband that Don Víctor has been thus far if the crisis of learning of his wife's infidelity were not apt to engender other awakenings.

Don Víctor is spared the narrator's explicit judgment, for he judges himself: he acknowledges that he has loved Ana like a daughter and that he has not given her the passion that she needed. Although he realizes that life is not like one of his "cloak-and-dagger" dramas and that societal expectations should not weigh greatly against natural law, he is convinced by Don Fermín that it is his duty to fight Don Álvaro or else be the butt of much mockery. Don Víctor is so inured to the fear and loathing of dishonor through socialization and Golden Age drama that despite his recognition of the superiority of natural law, he proves the cogency of the imagination, tradition, and conformity.

Ana has relied on her imagination to provide what life has not: physical, sensual pleasures. Because of her deprived youth (her motherless upbringing and orphaned state as an adolescent), she longs to give and receive affection. While it is true that the word "flesh" can send her off on a tangential memory, it is not an erotic one. The physical sensation of the softness of her sheets does not send her into ecstasies because it is a surrogate for the touch of a lover; the softness of her sheets is all the maternal softness about which she can only fantasize. Ana's "false mysticism," as the narrator characterizes it, is her sanctioned means of experiencing and expressing love—an inadequate substitute, as Ana comes to realize once she experiences the more immediate and tangible lovemaking of Don Álvaro. Though never the focus of her fantasies, this lover receives what was once mystical passion for God and has now become *"puramente material"*—an epithet that is italicized twice within the same paragraph. She becomes immersed in her body, in its carnality, and ceases to seek the transcendental love of God, though the narrator never criticizes her for this change. Her mysticism had not been genuine; her affair with Don Álvaro is completely natural and inevitable given her cold upbringing and her distant marriage to a father figure.

Ana thinks to herself while watching Zorrilla's *Don Juan Tenorio* that since her body belongs to Don Víctor through matrimony, she would be immune to the temptation to which Doña Inés succumbs in Zorrilla's nineteenth-century romantic drama about the familiar figure of the womanizer. This play is one of a palimpsest of texts alluded to in *La Regenta*; however, Ana's identification with Doña Inés, Álvaro's role of el Tenorio, and the similar plot development of the two texts merit further analysis, for these parallels suggest further reasons for justifying Ana's infidelity to Don Víctor. Additionally, Ana's appreciation of Zorrilla's drama earns her the approval of the narrator,[13] who says that Ana sees the drama with "*todo el vigor y frescura*" (all the vigor and freshness) that it possesses but that few experience because they come to the theater either with certain predispositions or "*porque tiene[n] el gusto de madera de tinteros*" (because they have the wooden taste of inkstands) (455).

In Zorrilla's play Doña Inés is a novitiate who lives an isolated life brightened only by her "*sueños infantiles*" (childish dreams) at a convent in Sevilla. Her father, the Comendador, has placed her in the convent since birth; hence, she has never known the world or its pleasures, nor is she destined to. The Abadesa rejoices in this fact, exclaiming:

> *Dichosa, mil veces vos*
> *dichosa, sí doña Inés,*
> *que no conociendo el mundo,*
> *no le debéis de temer!* (3.1.1445–1448)

> Happy are you, a thousand times
> happy, yes, Doña Inés,
> that in not knowing the world,
> you ought not to fear it!

On the contrary, Doña Inés, precisely because of her sheltered life, should fear the world. She is too ingenuous to see through Don Juan's conventional posture of the lovesick fool, which evokes her compassion, as he knows it will. She has no firsthand knowledge of the world—certainly not of the seducer type—and so naively accepts what she is told, little suspecting that a man could use her preconceived notions about love to ensnare her.

Ana herself perceives the similarities between herself and the actress playing the role of Inés and between her upbringing in her father's house and Inés' in the convent: "*Al ver a doña Inés en su celda, sintió la Regenta escalofríos; la novicia se parecía a ella. . . . Ana se comparaba con la hija del comendador; el caserón de los Ozores era su convento*" (Upon seeing Doña Inés in her cell, the regent's wife felt chills; the novitiate looked like her. . . . Ana compared herself with the *comendador*'s daughter—the great house of the Ozores was her convent) (456–457). Just as Doña Inés goes from the sheltered life of the convent to the arms of Don Juan, without incurring any blame within the drama, so Ana goes from the sheltered life of her family home, her personal convent, to marriage with a fatherly figure (a continuation of the convent life really), to the arms of Don Álvaro—none of which she has consciously chosen. For both Doña Inés and Ana, their lovers are their first taste of a world from which they have been purposely protected and therefore against which they have no natural or learned defenses. Furthermore, both protagonists are aided in their fall from virtue by their maidservants or friends. Brígida encourages the suit of

Don Juan by playing upon the compassion of her mistress, telling her that Don Juan is desperate and dying for love of her, and Obdulia in *La Regenta* encourages the pursuit of Don Álvaro in a similar manner.

Ana, like Inés and a whole host of literary characters from the nineteenth century, exhibits the truth of Don Robustiano's challenge to Don Fermín that young women have no choice in how they will live the rest of their lives since they are sheltered from the possibilities: "*¿Cabe libertad donde no hay elección? ¿Cabe elección donde no se conoce más que uno de los términos en que ha de consistir?* (Can there be freedom where there is no choice? Can there be a choice where one does not know more than one of the options of which it consists?) (301). Don Robustiano argues that the young women of Vetusta, for instance, choose the convent (at Don Fermín's behest) only because they know no other life. Women cannot be said to freely choose the convent when they have not been exposed to the other choice, that is, life outside the cloister of their homes. Ana has not chosen the convent; neither has she chosen to marry Don Víctor. Naturally, her marriage was arranged; nevertheless, despite being married, Ana still has no idea what love is, or what its physical expression can mean, and she, too, like Inés and all the girls whom Don Fermín herds off to the convent, cannot ward off Don Álvaro's poison because she has been sheltered from the ways of the world and has no antibodies for it.

The parallels between the novel and the play are rounded out with the figures of the lover and father. To describe Don Álvaro as "el Tenorio" may seem more descriptive than evaluative for those unfamiliar with Zorrilla's drama, but for those who know these verses, the term becomes more of a judgment, for in *Don Juan Tenorio* even Don Juan's cohorts believe him to be a familiar of Satan, if not the devil himself. He is frequently labeled "*un Satanás.*" Don Víctor, since he loves Ana like a father, falls very nicely into the role of Doña Inés' father, who is killed by Don Juan in the fourth act, a sight that causes Ana to have a premonition of Don Víctor's death at the hands of her lover. Neither father figure blames his "daughter." They both know that the women are too innocent, and it is because of this innocence that they can become a means of salvation.

Doña Inés is a ruined woman by society's standards once she has run off with Don Juan, yet she becomes the means of his salvation, willing to place her soul in jeopardy in order to save her loved one's. Ana is also ruined in society's eyes, yet if we continue the parallel, she, too, becomes a means of salvation—to the readers of the novel, who learn from her example about the ways of the world and the dangers of false mysticism and unexamined tradition.

Ana is naive, but her naïveté is not censured since she is not responsible for her ignorance; her society is, for it does not educate women to have choices or to know the world in which they live. After all that transpires in the novel, the narrator is still affectionate toward Ana in the end. After she has recovered from her illness after the death of her husband and is ready to resume her religious duties, the narrator refers to her as "Anita Ozores," as he did in the description of her cold, motherless upbringing. The use of the diminutive here expresses affection and sympathy. Ana has learned from her experience, more than she could ever have learned from reading, particularly since the romantic novels popular at the time with young girls would have given her a rosy and inaccurate portrayal of reality.

When Ana does attempt to practice her religion again, unquestioningly in order to keep her peace of mind, she swears to herself that she will not let "*aquel* misticismo falso" (that *false mysticism*) conquer her again (869). Nevertheless, when she enters the cathedral after her illness, the smells and sounds of the place trigger the false mysticism, and as before, Ana is unaware of its falseness. Like Anna Karenin, she cannot escape herself. She is not will-to-live, but she is the product of her environment and her upbringing, and she has conditioned responses, like Pavlov's dog. She is a sensually deprived character whose only acceptable means of expressing and feeling passion is in the arms of the church.

The act of adultery itself is never censured in *La Regenta* and serves more as a manifestation of Ana's naïveté and the ability of others to manipulate this innocent than a violation of revealed laws of right and wrong. In the end, after surfacing from the abyss of madness, Ana cannot suppress a feeling of pleasure and complacency to come back to this solid earth. Her complacency is "*egoísta*" (selfish), however, as she sees it, which incites further remorse on Ana's part, once again for a feeling over which she has no control, "*que no podía evitar*" (that she could not avoid) (861). It is only natural that the familiar, tangible, solid world of reality should be comforting to Ana after her nervous breakdown, yet she feels compunction for her relief since she has been taught self-abnegation from the day of her birth, to sacrifice herself for the reputation of her family, the honor of her husband, and the sanctity of the Church. Coming back to the solid earth reminds her that she is alive to the physical world, that her husband is dead, and that the doors of spiritual salvation have been closed to her.

The fact that Ana is denied her final consolation should be viewed as a condemnation not of her but rather of the church, whose authority is out of natural proportion, as when the homosexual altar boy Celedonio steals a kiss from the ex-regent's widow while she is in a faint. The kiss is a "perversion of the perversion" of the boy's sexual identity and seems to Ana's awakening consciousness to be the viscous underbelly of a toad. Since this kiss is so degrading to Ana, we might be tempted to see it as a form of punishment, certainly as an expression of the status that she has abrogated through adultery; however, the toad appears earlier in the novel, when Ana returns to reality after a flight of fancy. On that occasion Ana believes that the toad is mocking her illusions. Her sensation of the viscous underbelly of a toad in the end recalls this earlier scene and suggests that Ana's hope for a return to normalcy is indeed an illusion. There is no doubt that Ana no longer stands on the pedestal of her virtue before Vetustan society; however, what Celedonio's kiss demonstrates is Ana's impotence before the unnatural power of the church, a church whose most powerful clergyman follows the laws of society more than those of God or Nature. The altar server, ironically, achieves what Don Fermín has been denied, and he does so out of curiosity and with impunity. Not only is the church's power greatly exaggerated, but the balance of power within the church is similarly upset and perverted.

La Regenta leaves the reader with the least closure of the six novels here discussed precisely because the adulteress lives. Whether the others commit suicide actively or passively or are punished or released in death, their deaths do provide a certain closure to the novel, closure that is absent in *La Regenta* because Ana must live with her dishonor, with the death of her husband, the flight of her lover, the disillusionment of her affair, and the excommunication of the church. Her life-in-death existence, dead as she is to Spanish Restoration society, is non-narratable, to return to D. A. Miller's term. Clarín cannot describe Ana's life further because it is tantamount to dying, an experience that is as impossible to narrate as extreme happiness. Nevertheless, Ana is alive at the end of the novel, and as indescribable as her life becomes, without Clarín's closure, we cannot help but imagine the possibilities and be horrified by them.

EFFI BRIEST

The question of honor figures prominently in the nineteenth-century novel of adultery, not only in Spain with its glorious tradition of Golden Age drama but in Germany, as well, where the end of the nineteenth century saw the meaning of the word *"ehre"* (honor) in flux. The Old German *ère* referred to an external conception of honor, an objective status, while the more modern concept of the High German *ehre* was evolving into a sense of personal integrity.[14] The duels that are fought in *La Regenta* and *Effi Briest* and longed for by Vronsky in *Anna Karenin* stem from a desire to protect an objective, external understanding of honor that would have one defend one's name before all society. Clarín's narrator labels this a "barbarous custom," and Innstetten lives with the regret of having sacrificed his own peace of mind to the external dictates of society. In the end he must be able to live with himself, must be confident that he has followed his own sense of right and wrong and not society's now primitive standard of what made a man honorable. George Fenwick Jones notes that by the end of the nineteenth century, "affairs of honor" duels "appeared as stupid survivals from a barbaric age, as brutish combats that favored the better shot rather than the better man" (191–192). He claims that an inner ideal of "disinterested virtue" had become the accepted ideal of the German people, at least in theory if not in practice, and that though duels continued to be fought, especially in Realist literature, the difference was that they were often morally censured (191).

Before we jump too hastily to judge Innstetten for his "primitive" conception of honor, his slavish idolatry of an external notion of honor, we should keep in mind that Fontane intended Innstetten to be seen in a positive light. Leslie L. Miller offers a defense of this "gentleman" in a 1981 essay in the *German Studies Review*, wherein she cites Fontane's letters and gives detailed textual support for a sympathetic reading of the character of Innstetten. Much of the criticism of Innstetten focuses on his decision to challenge Crampas to the duel, nearly seven years after the crime, and in the way he has raised Annie to be guarded around her mother, and yet, as Miller notes, there is plenty of evidence in the text that Innstetten is not the villain. As Henry Garland writes, "Faulty characters occur in his [Fontane's] novels but evil ones are absent" (282). The characters have their flaws and make their mistakes, but they are inherently good and none is wholly unsympathetic. No individual is judged because each is limited by his or her milieu and is at the whim of chance.

Around the bare skeleton of a true story about the adultery of the young wife of Baron von Ardenne, Fontane builds his novel. An important addition to his source that reveals the way in which Fontane meant for Innstetten to be seen is the prior relationship between Innstetten and Frau von Briest and the latter's rejection of the former to make a better marriage with von Briest. Innstetten, never expressive of his feelings since emotionalism can keep one from advancing, does not take the rejection lightly. He resigns his commission in the military, begins to study law "like mad," and even 20 years later cannot refrain from returning to the neighborhood of his first love despite his not having any relatives in the area (his ostensible motivation for returning)—seemingly drawn to see Effi's mother again and to try to recapture his lost love with her offspring, who is the approximate age that her mother had been when Innstetten was courting her.

The marriage between the man of principles and the child of nature is a mistake. Frau von Briest, as the marriage broker, bears the brunt of the blame for arranging such a match to placate her vanity and live vicariously through her daughter. She chose status over love and is asking Effi to do the same. Effi has a parallel affection for her Cousin Dagobert, but she sees him as only a boy and believes that she will go much farther with a man like Innstetten. When her mother questions whether she loves her cousin and would like to marry him, Effi's reply is: "Marry? Goodness me no! He's still half a boy! Geert is a man, a handsome man, someone I can cut a dash with, someone who is going to be somebody in life" (38). Nevertheless, after her death, Frau von Briest questions whether Effi were not too young really for the marriage. Rollo shakes his head to and fro as though to say, "No, don't blame yourself. No one is to blame." But Heide Dorsett unquestioningly places the blame for Effi's destruction on her mother. She writes, "Frau von Briest's actions become the basis for Effi's destruction because they are based upon the false assumption that Effi, like her mother, can be made to fit the model of the traditional German woman who will accept material well being as a substitute for inner happiness" (25).

Effi is too young to know what she wants. Her youth is stressed in modal terms throughout the novel, as when Innstetten puts the Christmas tree up for his "young" wife (94). She is not a "new woman," not yet, not at the time of the arrangement of her marriage. She is not sure whether love exists; she has never experienced it, and if it does not, then she wants honor, glory, and amusement— in that order (Fontane 36). Frau von Briest tries to temper some of Effi's romantic notions by suggesting, for instance, when Effi claims to have her heart set on a Japanese bedroom screen and a red light, that "lovely" and "poetic" are "just imaginings" and that "[r]eality is different" (35). Frau von Briest's mistake is that she does not give herself enough time to instruct Effi in reality. She hears her daughter say that she wants to "cut a dash" with Innstetten, but she doesn't caution Effi that life with such a man will not be as amusing as Effi hopes, and she has no words of wisdom for Effi after the latter's confession that she fears Innstetten because she has no principles at all. Despite Effi's youth—in mind and body—Frau von Briest does not call off the marriage, and so she is to blame for setting Effi and Innstetten on the road to destruction. She does not, however, cause either's.

Despite the difference in years and temperaments, the marriage between Effi and Innstetten is not doomed from the start. Although a man of principles with a preference for his head over his heart, Innstetten is not immune to love and passion, and he does love his child of nature; only he does not understand a woman's need to hear and see such love expressed. The narrator tells us that Innstetten "felt he loved Effi, and his good conscience in this respect led him to neglect making any special effort to show it" (99). Frau von Briest troubles her daughter with her teasing about Effi's "love for the alchemist" Gieshübler, for it forces Effi to confront the lack of attention that she receives from her husband. Innstetten loves Effi, but, like all the other husbands discussed here, he is no lover. He manifests few of the accoutrements of love, the small attentions that young girls expect to be present when love is present. That Innstetten is capable of deep emotions, of love, is evident in his reaction to his unrequited love of Frau von Briest, his "well-meant" caresses of Effi, and in his willingness in his heart of hearts to forgive her. That he does not express it well or at all is evinced in the many critical articles that vilify him.

In Chapter 1, we noted Innstetten's preference for Wagner—what Leslie Miller calls his "unexpected weakness" (389)—and the narrator's unwillingness to definitively tell us why, offering us two possible explanations, both of which "were probably right": the first is that "although he [Innstetten] seemed such a sobersides, in reality he was a nervous person" (hence his predilection for this passionate, romantic composer), and the second is that Wagner appealed to a certain strain of anti-Semitism in Innstetten (99). Ignoring this evidence of the inner man has led to the large body of criticism of Innstetten as a calculating rationalist, not unlike Karenin. They are both civil servants; they are both educators; they both fear the revelation of the depth of their feeling; and they both fear the loss of external honor more than they fear the loss of their personal integrity, but in *Effi Briest* we have a much more explicit description of just how much Innstetten loves.

The final evidence of the power and depth of Innstetten's feelings that I would like to offer is the words of the character himself. In themselves, they could not be offered as proof that Innstetten truly loves Effi, but given all that has gone before, his previous attachment to Frau von Briest, the narrator's comment that he loves Effi, his "well-meant" caresses, we might put credence in their sincerity. Innstetten responds to his fellow civil servant Wüllersdorf, whose counsel he seeks after reading Effi's love letters, in the following manner:

I'm infinitely unhappy, I'm humiliated, I've been shamefully deceived and yet in spite of that I have no feeling of hatred at all, or even a thirst for vengeance. And if I ask myself why not, then the first reason that comes to me is merely—the lapse of time.... And then the second thing is that I love my wife, yes, strange to say, I still love her, and however frightful all these things appear to me, yet I'm so much under her spell, she's so lovable and so gay, she has such a special charm all of her own, that, in spite of myself, I feel tempted in my heart of hearts, to forgive her. (214)

Just as Karenin refrained from expressing his forgiveness for fear of appearing foolish before the eyes of society, Innstetten regrets his inability to stifle his distress upon reading his wife's old love letters and unburdening himself to Wüllersdorf, for now his shame is public, and he resorts to the primitive, barbaric means of the duel to restore his external honor. Internally, he feels no insult, which is why he is willing to forgive; in answer to Wüllersdorf's question, no, he does not feel so enraged and insulted that he cannot live on the same earth as Crampas. Innstetten's mistake is that he makes his shame public in relating his secret to Wüllersdorf; he cannot rely upon Wüllersdorf to keep his secret, and so he goes ahead with the duel and kills Crampas because he could not live without his principles, and he could not live with the dishonor to his name. What he never counts on is how difficult it will be living without a personal sense of integrity.

Fontane pits individuals against society in *Effi Briest*, and while the social code of "polite" society destroys individuals like Effi and Briest, society in general is not without its redemptive qualities. Stanley Radcliffe argues that "Fontane suggests a mutual obligation of individual and society, which grants the individual the opportunity to show the quality of his spirit; it is on this that the collective quality of society itself depends" (38). In order for society to be great, in order for society to not become a destructive force, it is necessary that individuals live according to their own sense of what is right and wrong. The greatness of the sum total of all the individuals' great spirits will make society great. Innstetten's flaw is that he is "unduly subservient"[15] to society and not faithful to his inner sense of honor and integrity and the disinterested pursuit of virtue.

The tendency to judge Innstetten comes not only from overlooking the inner man but as a reaction to the very likable character that Fontane has created in Effi. The narrator in Fontane is most like Clarín's in his open sympathy for his protagonist, which is again evinced through these modal terms. In the opening of the novel, when Frau von Briest glances admiringly, surreptitiously at her child, the narrator tells us that this "was a gesture of maternal pride which was fully justified" (16). He uses the modal term "poor" on more than one occasion—on the instance of Innstetten's and Effi's first separation: "Poor Effi! How was she going to spend the evening?" (69); after Effi is ostracized and takes up painting: "Her poor life was now less poor" (242); and when Effi contracts her fatal illness: "Poor Effi, you spent too long looking up at the marvels of the heavens and thinking about them and in the end the night air and the mists rising from the pond stretched her once more on a bed of sickness" (264). In this last apostrophe the narrator actually directly addresses Effi in empathy and attributes her death to cosmic irony.

It is so easy to sympathize with the child of nature and to censure the man of principles. Fontane's implied author never explicitly censures Effi—only society does. As with our other novels of adultery, there are plenty of reasons to mitigate the nature of Effi's crime. She has led the typically sheltered existence before marriage, agrees to an arranged marriage, and is subject to the boredom of provincial life, where her husband is absent a great deal and where there are few acceptable neighbors with whom she can socialize; moreover, she is suitably repentant and wants only to begin again. She never loves Crampas; she always regrets the deception, and she happily adjusts to married life in Berlin.

What is distinct about Effi, but ever so refreshing, is that she does not labor under any romantic misconceptions of love or excuse herself. She fears from the very beginning that there is too great a disparity between herself, who has no principles whatsoever, and the man she is about to marry, who is the oft-quoted "man of principles," and she is cognizant of the wrong that she is doing in deceiving her husband. The deception bothers her most since her character is as open and free as the light and wind with which she is associated. In the midst of her deception, the narrator tells us, "In one respect only she remained true to herself: she saw everything clearly and made no excuses" (157). Effi is ashamed of her lying but not of her adultery, which she says is destroying her: "But I don't feel ashamed of being guilty, not really, or at any rate, not ashamed enough, and that is what's destroying me, because I'm not ashamed" (200). She feels something must be wrong with her that she cannot even "feel properly." This is the point that the novel brings home: if we can train ourselves to feel properly, then we can trust our consciences, and when we remain true to what we personally believe to be right and good, then we will also have honor. When we abide by archaic, "primitive" notions of what bestows honor, then we will never be at peace with ourselves.

Effi accepts the social code at this point in the novel and judges herself by her inability to feel its truth. Innstetten intuits the right course of action in the end, but he chooses to rationally abide by the social code. Effi rebels against the code briefly after her meeting with Annie, when she is treated so coldly, and rails against her husband for the first and only time in the novel, but her deathbed conversation with her mother, where she asks Frau von Briest to convey her reconciliation to all that her husband has done in an attempt to console the man who has destroyed her happiness, demonstrates that the code has been restored in her mind. Ana Ozores makes herself physically ill with her unceasing battle to abide by a social code that prohibits the satisfaction of her physical needs, and Effi suffocates in her world of artificial custom and so dies of tuberculosis.

Susan Sontag in her *Illness as Metaphor* asserts, "The disease that individualizes, that sets a person in relief against the environment, is tuberculosis" (37). Disease metaphors, in general, she maintains, are used in literature to judge society "not as out of balance but as repressive" (73). Characters prone to tuberculosis in the nineteenth century, according to Sontag, were those who were both passionate and repressed (39). Such a death could be "redemptive . . . for the fallen or a sacrificial death for the virtuous" (41). Regardless of how likable Effi is or how justifiable her crime, she cannot be considered a virtuous woman; thus, her death of tuberculosis, representative of the repression that she suffers from artificial society, would be considered redemptive according to Sontag's delineation of the metaphor. Effi's aforementioned final request of her mother to ease the mind of Innstetten is typical of the nature of a disease such as tuberculosis, which "can clear the way for insight into lifelong self-deceptions and failures of character" (Sontag 42). Thus, Effi is not subversive in the end.[16] Her last days during her illness at Hohen-Cremmen are admittedly her happiest because she has such nostalgia for her childhood home, because she is a child of nature, and because with her newfound insight into her failings and character flaws, she can be at peace with Innstetten, Annie, her mother, and herself. She understands that Innstetten did not have any other choice but to kill Crampas because such is the nature of his flawed character, and knowing the importance that he attaches to objectified honor, she chooses to have "Effi Briest" on her tombstone rather than "Effi von Innstetten"—not as an expression of her liberation, for she has accepted the social code and her violation of it, but out of respect for Innstetten since, as Effi acknowledges, she did not bring any *honor* to Innstetten's name. When Effi says to her mother that Innstetten "'was as fine a man as any one can be who doesn't really love'" (266), she is not ironically undercutting her husband, just stating what is true for her. She does not know that Innstetten has loved her because she has never seen evidence of it; the careful reader, on the other hand, will have noted Innstetten's ability to love and will not fault him for this failure, perhaps only for his inability to express that love.

What of the figure of the typical villain, the lover, in this case, Crampas? Major Crampas is not introduced until fully one-third into the novel in a letter that Effi writes to her mother. She is aware of his renown for love affairs, and, like Arobin, he has a romantic wound from a previous duel. If she were not aware of his reputation, she has her husband there to caution her. Innstetten knows too well the code of men like Crampas; it is a code not unlike Vronsky's in *Anna Karenin*: "Helping a friend and deceiving him five minutes later were things that fitted very well into his [Crampas'] conception of honour" (127). Vronsky's, you will recall, is that he could not lie to any man but he could to a husband. Despite his infamy, Effi is drawn to Crampas' gallantry and quick wit—he amuses her. He is bold and adventuresome, as Effi once was and still longs to be, an "excellent conversationalist," and an insidious sympathizer for the cursory treatment that her fears receive from Innstetten. Compared with the role of the lover in the other novels, Crampas' role is greatly reduced, and, in contrast with the others, he is unhappily married himself. He does not receive any authorial criticism; he, too, is portrayed in a very sympathetic light.

The novel is silent about the actual act of adultery and the brief interlude of the affair. The scant details that we glean come from the love letters that Innstetten unwittingly discovers, only snatches of which are recorded to summarize the course of their affair. Crampas' first letter urges Effi to seize the day, make life worth living, and not let things go on "just as they happen to be"; however, in answer to a missive that we never see, wherein Effi is to have pleaded with Crampas to run away with her, Crampas responds, "Fate is responsible. Everything had to be as it is" (212). He does not, like Rodolphe, claim to have directed that Fate. In his final letter Crampas agrees with Effi that their separation will be their salvation. There are no further pursuit, no further contact, no remnants of affection evident on either's part. In comparison with other donjuanesque figures, Crampas is quite benign and likable. He, even less so than Frau Briest, causes Effi's destruction.

No one character can be blamed for Effi's adultery. Many characters make mistakes, and circumstances have coincided to make these mistakes possible. Effi, Innstetten, Crampas, Frau von Briest all play a part, yet no one factor can be cited as the single most important cause for Effi's fall. Crampas tries to convince Effi to maintain the status quo because "Fate is responsible," and though his words may be insincere, there is some truth to them. The role that chance and circumstances play should not be overlooked.

The role of chance in a novel is but the contrivances of the author. In this case, Fontane's recourse to chance to advance the plot exonerates his characters from judgment for their failings. By chance Effi meets Roswitha in the cemetery; by chance Mirambo is kicked, and Innstetten leaves Effi and Crampas alone; by chance Innstetten receives the ministry in Berlin; by chance the love letters are discovered. Certainly, the characters do not always make the best choices with the hand that Fate has dealt them, and yet they are in essence good people. Radcliffe notes that whereas Flaubert rejects the burgeoning bourgeois society, Fontane "does not reject summarily the society which he presents, seeing that social forms are essential for the preservation of civilised conduct and personal security" (76).

Society is undoubtedly criticized, but as Radcliffe asserts, "The old values [of society] *can* be reasserted positively; new understanding of them is required, not new standards or structures" (76). Effi's impression of her neighbors in Kessin is that they are strict and self-righteous; none is more so than Sidonie von Grasenabb, and yet there are also the Gieshüblers and the Roswithas, who brighten Effi's existence and never reject her after her fall. Society is at its worst when it rejects a repentant Effi, who wants only to make amends. She is barred from even works of charity. Her parents must cut her off or be excluded themselves from their society in distant Hohen-Cremmen. Polite society, in particular, has for too long neglected the inner person. So absorbed in externals are they that they have lost a sense of true virtue, personal integrity, and the value of the individual. Marriage, government, society—these institutions do not need to be abolished, only reformed. Marriages must be more than socioeconomic contracts; honor must be more democratic; society must be more accepting of individual greatness.

THE AWAKENING

As evinced by Clarín's *La Regenta*, the positivist law of cause and effect finds its way into characterization in literature. Ana Ozores' psyche is conditioned by the trauma of her youth; the effect is the consolatory role of her imagination. Chopin develops the character of Edna Pontellier along similar lines in *The Awakening*. Though Chopin gives only a cursory glance at Edna's upbringing, in contrast to Clarín's thorough examination of conscience and consciousness, we know that Edna faced similar repression of emotion and desire due to a strict observation of religious and social precepts. The atmosphere of a religious institution continues to stifle Edna as an adult, for she must leave the services at the church on the *Chênière Caminada* because of its stifling atmosphere. There is not, however, in *The Awakening* a complete rationalization of all that Edna does based upon the deprivations and repression of her youth, nor is there a biting criticism of individuals within her society. As a collective, society stifles individualism in demanding conformity, but when taken individually,

Edna's acquaintances are not without redeeming qualities, like Fontane's characters. Rather than focus on any one villain in the novel, the narrator's enormous sympathy with the process of Edna's awakening to self implies a criticism of all who would impede her progress, but as Edna progresses from individualism, to egoism, to despair, the narrator's judgment falls upon Edna. Thus, Edna's suicide represents the absence of a courageous soul, which is necessary in this life not only to live the life of our dreams but to continue to live after one has experienced existential solitude.

The force of Nature in Chopin's *The Awakening* is even greater than it is in Clarín's *La Regenta*. Nature is personified in Chopin's novella to such a degree that it is second in importance only to Edna. The sea, in particular, is endowed with seductive, soothing qualities and a "sonorous murmur" that entices Edna into its embrace and calls to her "like a loving but imperative entreaty" (14). The sea, thus, plays the role of the lover; it seduces Edna into suicide in the same way that our donjuanesque lovers seduce the wives into adultery, and where there are seduction and betrayal, there is room for sympathy with the victim laboring under the delusion. Edna does not see that the undifferentiated space and solitude of the sea are inimical to her growth as an individual. Like most lovers, the voice of the sea is deceptive; rather than help her define herself, it quiets her will forever.

Edna is deceived in her suicide. In her life, though she becomes childish and egotistical, she is never wicked—not, at least, by Nature's code. Dr. Mandelet, a man of science more attuned to the natural requirements of the body and mind through his direct observation of his patients, sees Nature at work in the illusions that young girls cherish, for it is through such illusions that Nature is able to "secure mothers for the race" (110). If women knew the reality of marriage, childbirth, and child-raising, offspring would never be conceived. Nature provides the "decoy," according to Dr. Mandelet, but the agony for women comes not from Nature but in being held to their role as wives and mothers by societal and religious mores. If the religious and social codes coincided with the natural, much anguish would be prevented.

In addition to the voice of the sea, other voices of Nature speak to Edna: some "deceive" her with their promises of hope; others speak to her "from the darkness and the sky above and the stars" in "mournful notes without promise, devoid even of hope" (73, 53). Like Ana Ozores, Edna Pontellier has no internal compass to guide her response to the voices. She has friends and acquaintances who advise her on how to act and express concern for her, but there is no one who can serve as a role model for the self that Edna would like to be. Thus, willfully cut off from society, Edna is at the mercy of the seductive voices of the sea and the conflicting voices of Nature that promise alternately hope and despair. She engages in a battle against the entreaties of her biological nature and the seductive voices of Nature, which may engage the reader's sympathy, though some of her subsequent choices may not.

As in *Effi Briest*, society in *The Awakening* is not without its redemptive figures and is generally not as malicious or hypocritical as it is in *La Regenta*, *Anna Karenin*, or *O primo Basílio*. In the abstract, society is a negative entity since it demands conformity and stifles individualism; however, none of the characters here is guilty of the hypocrisy of Vetusta, Petersburg, or Lisbon. Madame Ratignolle, though overly concerned about public opinion, is intuitive, beautiful, dignified, and affectionate toward Edna. Mademoiselle Reisz is an eccentric, artistic type who lives on the fringe of society and who counsels Edna on the importance of having a courageous soul. Dr. Mandelet is not sympathetic toward "pseudo-intellectual" female groups, but he understands Edna and is eaeger to help her: "I don't want you to blame yourself, whatever comes," he says to Edna as he walks her home after Madame Ratignolle has given birth (110). He understands that she is caught between natural impulses and the "moral consequences[,] of arbitrary conditions which we create, and which we feel obliged to maintain at any cost" (110)—the "arbitrary conditions" being marriage and familial obligations. Mr. Pontellier is a myopic husband, guided by the dictates of society, but he is neither ridiculous nor cold and is liked by all. As for the "lovers" in *The Awakening*, neither proves as destructive as Edna's nascent self or the seductive sea. Arobin is innocuous since Edna never responds to him in more than a physical way, and Robert Lebrun genuinely loves Edna and so does what he thinks best by leaving her in order not to commit adultery and sully their pure passion.

Edna's acquaintances never ostracize her as other societies do the adulteresses and transgressors of the social code—they cannot because Edna ostracizes herself. There is a greater freedom, in any event, in American society as opposed to European at the end of the nineteenth century, even though the society that Chopin describes here tried very hard to slavishly imitate European high society. Edna does not create a scandal by keeping company with Robert Lebrun, and though her husband must deflect criticism for her moving into the pigeon house, she is nevertheless able to live there alone, something we could not imagine any of our European heroines doing without causing a scandal as great as their adultery.

Edna is expected to respect *les convenances*, and between her flouting of them and the reputation that she is gaining for herself in the pigeon house, Madame Ratignolle warns her that she cannot continue to visit her. Nevertheless, Madame Ratignolle does not cut off ties entirely; rather, she extracts a promise from Edna that she will come to her when she goes into labor. She does not disassociate herself from Edna completely, only under certain circumstances. Furthermore, Madame Ratignolle tries to recall Edna to her duty as a mother and wife, rather than encourage her affairs, as do the acquaintances of Anna Karenin and Ana Ozores. Madame Ratignolle's reference to the reputation that Edna is gaining for herself in the pigeon house is the only vestige of social scandal-mongering in the novel. Since Edna has chosen to isolate herself, she robs society of its power to exclude; thus, they are not to blame for increasing the adulteress' pain or hypocritically judging her. Edna is responsible for her own solitude and death. She chooses her own punishment, or release, as the case may be.

Chopin's original title for *The Awakening* was "A Solitary Soul." The word "alone" is mentioned "some two dozen times"[17] in the course of the novella, and it is from her physical solitude that Edna's strength develops; however, it is also the solitude of her soul that engenders the despair that eventually induces Edna to swim out alone in what may or may not have been a conscious suicide.[18] The narrator foreshadows Edna's failure by exclaiming in the beginning that so many souls perish in the attempt to forge an identity out of chaos: "But the beginning of things, of a world especially, is necessarily vague, chaotic, and exceedingly disturbing. How few of us ever emerge from such beginning! How many souls perish in its tumult!" (15). Edna's adversary to her development is her own very chaotic nature, and it is with a sense of foreboding that we continue to read, for we have been warned that many fail to control the chaos out of which an identity is forged. Edna's inner world, her appetites, her intellect, her moral and spiritual being must develop out of the chaos of ignorance into the light of knowledge, out of slavery to uncontrolled desire to mastery of appetite.

Edna's individualism is supported by the narrator, for her awakening, while linked with sensual needs, is an awakening to truth. Edna's speechless sense of impotence in her husband's presence early in the novel is explained and rationalized by the narrator, who tells us that Mr. Pontellier could not see that Edna was finally becoming her true self. This implies, as the narrator makes explicit in the following, that the woman who Edna has been thus far in her life with her husband has been fictitious: "That is he [Mr. Pontellier] could not see that she [Edna] was becoming herself daily and casting aside that fictitious self which *we* assume like a garment with which to appear before the world" (57; emphasis added). This passage might be read as narrated monologue—Edna's internal outburst against her husband's insistence that she is not herself—if it were not for the presence of the first-person-plural pronoun ("we"), which fixes the entire passage in the voice of the narrator and signals a world outside the fictional one. Thus, the narrator supports the changes in Edna since they are making her more genuine. The changes all begin on the Grand Isle, sparked by the penetrating glance of Robert Lebrun and fostered by Mademoiselle Reisz's piano playing, whose music imparts a sense of "the abiding truth" (27).

Edna's physical solitude, her separation from her husband and society, effects the emergence of her authentic self since she is able to focus her attention on her natural reactions to the world. She becomes more attuned to the needs of her body and spirit—changes that are noted by both Dr. Mandelet and Victor Lebrun. Both are pleased by these changes: Victor finds her "ravishing" and "improved," and Dr. Mandelet describes a metamorphosis from "the listless woman he had known into a being who, for the moment, seemed palpitant with the forces of life. . . . There was no repression in her glance or gesture" (70).

The pernicious influence of solitude comes to bear upon Edna's emerging self when she realizes how alone she is in the world. None of her acquaintances lives the romantic life free from stifling tradition and societal obligations that Edna would like to lead. Mademoiselle Reisz courageously defies tradition, but she is not gracious or beautiful, and while her playing arouses passion in Edna, the artist herself is unmoved by it. Moreover, Mademoiselle Reisz lives a life of solitude, whereas Edna imagines personal fulfillment through the love of a soul mate such as Robert Lebrun. Thus, when Robert, her great passion, decides to respect the conventions and not wait for her to return from Madame Ratignolle's, Edna becomes disillusioned with passion and with life and in her solitude returns to the sea—the only "being" who seems to take in the breadth of her soul.

Edna's awakening sensuousness is particularly manifested in her relations with Arobin, for Arobin appeals to "the animalism that stirred impatiently within her" (78). Edna does not love Arobin; moreover, she knows that she does not love him, and yet she cannot help but respond to his physical presence: "He [Arobin] stood close to her, and the effrontery in his eyes repelled the old, vanishing self in her, yet drew all her awakening sensuousness" (76). Arobin senses her "latent sensuality" and knows how to cultivate it because he senses "her nature's requirements" (103). Edna's requirements are typical of her gender, and since Arobin is something of a rake, his vast experiences with other women serve him well in anticipating how Edna's body will respond to his touch.

In contrast to the European texts herein analyzed, sensuality is not a negative in this American text and is not linked with materialism. Edna does become more spiritual insofar as she casts off her husband's "bounty" and downsizes to the pigeon house; however, she at the same time engages in her exploratory physical relationship with Arobin to no apparent detriment to her spirit. The narrator reports, "There was a feeling of having descended in the social scale, with a corresponding sense of having risen in the spiritual. Every step which she took toward relieving herself from her obligations added to her strength and expansion as an individual" (93). Thus, Edna is more spiritual as she becomes more of an individual and as she frees herself from her husband, his wealth, and his social connections. Her awareness of her own sensuality and the needs of her physical body is an important stage in her development and awakening and does not cause her to slip down the spiritual scale or crave material goods. Such is not the case with Edna's willful and very childish outbursts.

The narrator has been supportive of Edna's nascent self, her growing sensualism and individualism, but the tone changes as Edna is described as mired in a childlike stage of development. When Edna is first compared to a child, it is to convey the exhilaration that she feels in accomplishing what has seemed an insurmountable feat without anyone's assistance: "[S]he [Edna] was like the little, tottering, stumbling, clutching child, who of a sudden realizes its powers, and walks for the first time alone, boldly and with over-confidence" (28). She, who had been trying to learn to swim all summer but lacked the confidence and needed the reassuring hand of Robert or her husband, experiences the joy of unaided achievement. Her overconfidence nearly causes her death as she prematurely reaches out for the infinite. She has only just begun to walk.

Childlike behaviors that express joy, wonder, simplicity, innocence, and trust can be very endearing; however, the nature of children is not so uniformly idyllic, and Edna soon manifests some of the uglier traits. Toddlers are often given to tantrums in their selfish desire to please only themselves, and Edna has two such tantrums in *The Awakening*. The first is after an altercation with her husband, shortly after their return to the city, when Edna takes off her wedding band, hurls it to the floor, and stamps upon it. In the second instance, Edna impetuously refuses to accept responsibility for her children's lives and tells Dr. Mandelet, "But I don't want anything but my own way"(110)—an attitude characteristic of the very young.

Some might see Edna's death as a step in her maturation since her suicide is her first act since her awakening that may be motivated by a consideration for others: she kills herself in order not to "trample" upon the lives of her children, in order not to disgrace them with her actions or slight them with her inattention. Her suicide follows so closely Madame Ratignolle's exhortation: "Think of the children, Edna. Oh think of the children! Remember them!" (109), which seems to cause Edna to reflect upon her responsibility as a mother, on her place not only in the universe but specifically in society. Unwilling to accept her role as mother, Edna would rather extinguish her authentic, emergent self, so that her children may live with the remembrance of a mother's love rather than the knowledge of her abandonment.

That Madame Ratignolle's words have an impact is evident by Edna's passionate avowal to Dr. Mandelet that she wants her own way. She does not want to be responsible to or for anyone else. In this case, her suicide is not a sacrifice of her *self* but a selfish refusal to sacrifice herself for others. Edna is trapped between what she perceives is enslavement to her children and an aversion to crushing her children with her freedom. She cannot "trample the little lives"; neither will she enslave herself to her children. On the beach before her final swim, her avowal to Madame Ratignolle that she would "give up the unessential, but . . . never sacrifice herself for her children" recurs in her mind, suggesting that what she is about to do is her way of avoiding such a sacrifice. She is willing to die for her children, as she confesses to Madame Ratignolle, but she is not willing to sacrifice her *self*—a distinction that her friend finds incomprehensible since she, like Dolly Oblonsky, is the supreme mother figure and unquestioningly accepts her identity as exclusively wife and mother. Edna spends the wakeful night of her suicide trying to find a connection to this world. Her "children appeared before her like antagonists who had overcome her; who had overpowered and sought to drag her into the soul's slavery for the rest of her days. But she knew a way to elude them" (113). We are told that she was not thinking of this as she walked down the beach, and yet this is when the narrator chooses to report the foregoing to us, inevitably linking her suicide with a means of eluding the prison of domesticity. In the end, one wonders, like Carol Christ, whether Edna was thinking at all or whether she was enticed by the seductive voice of the sea and its "soft, close embrace" (113).

Helen V. Emmitt in her study of what the sea means to women[19] notes that Jungian archetypes and male authors alike identify the sea as mother. It is also connected with the Narcissus myth, though Narcissus was masculine, for Milton's placement of Eve in Narcissus' role has encouraged us to place women in the mirror of men and in the imaginary realm. For some women, then, the sea becomes a means of liberation, a home-coming of sorts, an escape from the demands of a masculine world (Emmitt 315–316). It could represent Edna's baptism into a new, independent, and inviolate life at home in the watery depths, or it could signify Edna's defeat, her inability to make a place for herself in the world. Triumph, as Emmitt notes, is suggested in her nakedness on the beach, which makes Edna feel like some "new-born creature" opening its eyes on a familiar, but unknown, world; however, defeat is also implied in the imagery of Edna's final swim as a bird with a broken wing circles "disabled down to the water," recalling the occasion when Mademoiselle Reisz felt for Edna's wings and warned her that she must have "strong wings" to "soar above the level plain of tradition and prejudice" if she is to soar above the conventions and remake herself. Edna does not have the courage to defy tradition and prejudice and so, like the bird, comes crashing out of the sky, where she has been flying with her flaunting of *les convenances.* Edna recalls these very words of Mademoiselle Reisz as she swims out alone and thinks how her artistic friend would have sneered at her domestic life, a life that she can escape only in death.

Edna's tragedy, according to Carol Christ, is that "by choosing death she admits that she cannot find a way to translate her spiritual awareness and infinite possibilities into life and relationships with others" (39). Christ resolves the seeming conflict of the images at the novella's conclusion thus: Edna's death is both triumph and defeat, "spiritual triumph but social defeat" (27). The real tragedy, according to Christ, is that the "spiritual and social quests could not be united in her life" (27). Chopin's novella demonstrates that without the support of society, a mystical experience of spiritual awakening risks the annihilation of self. The two role models for a woman that Edna has are Madame Ratignolle and Mademoiselle Reisz—both of which she rejects. She does not want to be a "mother-woman," nor does she want the life of "solitude and bitter isolation from society" that the eccentric artist represents (Christ 28). Thus, without any role model or support for the way in which she wants to live, Edna loses herself in the sea. Her spirit is intact, but her suicide illustrates her inability to live in society, which she wishes to do.

We know that Edna's heightened awareness of herself as an individual, distinct from her husband and children, puts her on the road to truth, but her suicide is a wrong turn. Edna loses touch with reality and abandons herself to Fate after Robert returns to Mexico, and her thoughts and memories reveal a consciousness in turmoil and under the sway of romantic imaginings once typical of her youth. Like Anna Karenin, Edna's last thoughts are of her childhood: "Edna heard her father's voice and her sister Margaret's. She heard the barking of an old dog that was chained to the sycamore tree. The spurs of the cavalry officer clanged as he walked across the porch. There was the hum of bees and the musky odor of pinks filled the air" (114). The mention of the cavalry office, in particular, evokes that phase in Edna's life when she was prey to a series of infatuations—one of which was this cavalry officer. She thinks that she has put such romantic tendencies behind her when she marries Leonce Pontellier, but they are with her, even in death.

The tragedy of Edna's and Anna's suicides is conveyed in just such nostalgic returns to their youth, for it was in their youth that these protagonists cherished hopes and dreams. Their adult lives, particularly after the failure of extramarital affairs, become devoid of hope; the great extremes of hope and despair are brought home to the reader in these memories of childhood as they end their lives. Willa Cather suggests, in her review of *The Awakening* in 1899, that Edna perhaps throws herself into the sea out of the same motivation that induces Anna Karenin to throw herself under the wheels of a train: both are the loci where the women first meet their loves: Robert Lebrun and Vronsky.[20]

Chopin creates in Edna Pontellier a character from whom her female readers can learn in their search for self-definition. No model existed for Edna, nor any support; Edna herself can become a model for others, and as more and more awaken, they can mutually support one another. At the time of Chopin's writing, at the very end of the nineteenth century, she herself would not have had any model for Edna. What does she do with a character who cannot fit into society unless she retreats to a fictitious and loathsome role? Edna must die in order to preserve the advances that she has made in creating an authentic self. Her death is not a punishment, nor is it a victory; it is an inevitably tragic conclusion to a novella about the awakening of a socialite to her inner self. The imagery of the conclusion is mixed because *The Awakening* is, after all, only the beginning. It will take an awakening of all the members of society to the needs of each individual, particularly the obedient wife and mother, before true triumph, both spiritual and social, can occur. Edna has not lived to soar above tradition and prejudice, but she will not don the clothes of convention ever again.

O PRIMO BASÍLIO

The judgments of the implied author or narrator are increasingly difficult to discern inasmuch as the author adheres to the style of free, indirect discourse. Of the novels discussed here, *O primo Basílio* and *Madame Bovary* are written in this style. That said, it must also be added that the mere fact that these authors tried to minimize their presence in the novel does not preclude our unearthing an operative ideology behind the work's creation or ascertaining the judgments of the implied author or narrator based upon the more subtle techniques of modal terms, characterization, and irony. In obfuscating their presence, these authors have made the ideology invisible, but it is still there.

Queirós in *O primo Basílio* emphasizes the other side of the Naturalist's coin. While Clarín emphasizes Ana's physical needs, her biological need to be a mother, Queirós describes the milieu that accounts for Luísa's fall, for Luísa is a product of her environment, her lazy disposition a result of her decadent environment of sensuousness and leisure. Just as there is evidence in *La Regenta* of the importance of heredity and environment, so in *O primo Basílio* is there evidence that Luísa is dominated by natural impulse. Unlike Ana Ozores, however, Luísa is able to see beyond the veil and recognize the fictitious nature of her aspirations, and such insights redeem her in the end.

The narrator's judgments, while rarely explicit, lie with Luísa's bourgeois society and Basílio, the lover, not with Luísa or Jorge. As in *Madame Bovary*, *O primo Basílio* has only one character (Sebastião) who might be considered above reproach, and even he is overly concerned with appearances. Queirós, like Flaubert, was content to tear down what his readers would have considered positive institutions and values, such as the church, society, government, and positivist science, without establishing any alternative values in their stead.

Luísa's submission to Basílio is represented by the narrator as though she were giving in to an uncontrollable force. She at first rejects her cousin's advances, saying, "*Deixa-me, deixa-me!*" (Leave me alone! Leave me alone!) and tears herself away with a contrary force, "*uma força nervosa*" (a nervous force) (110). Her subsequent daydream of kissing Basílio is related in the passive voice, an indication that Luísa is not in control: an almost palpable vision of herself and Basílio comes to her as *"uma certa ideia, uma certa visão"* (a certain idea, a certain vision) that *"foi-se formando no seu cérebro, completando-se, tão mítida"* (was forming itself in her head, completing itself so clearly") (121). Lastly, the narrator interprets Luísa's impulse to go to the Hotel Central in search of her cousin after she has missed him at the *paraíso* as an "indomitable impulse": she goes because *"estava num daqueles momentos em que os temperamentos sensíveis tem impulsos indomáveis; há uma delícia colérica em espedaçar os deveres e as conveniências; e a alma procura o mal com estremecimentos de sensualidade!"* (she was in one of those moments in which sensitive temperaments have indomitable impulses; there is an irascible delight in tearing duty and convention to pieces, and the soul greedily seeks evil with shivers of sensuality!) (229). Is this narrated monologue, free indirect discourse? Is Luísa aware of how natural her impulses are or the delight that she takes in tearing convention to pieces? Not likely. Though not presented in an authorial tone or explicitly in the words of a narrator, this description of Luísa's actions implies a knowledge of the world that Luísa does not have. Luísa only feels overcome by an impulse, an impulse that permits her to enjoy natural, sensual pleasures in her (un)conscious flaunting of unnatural convention.

The life that Luísa leads is not directly censured, but the decadence of her environment and its pernicious effects are conveyed in the preponderance of images suggestive of a life of leisure. Just as Clarín sets the tone of *La Regenta* with the opening ironic presentation of the "noble" city of Vetusta, so Queirós establishes the mood of decadence from the opening paragraphs. The novel opens on a Sunday in July, the remains of lunch are still on the table, the canaries are asleep in their cage, and the monotonous drone of flies fills the room *"de um rumor dormente"* (with a sleepy murmur) (14). Moving from the set to the characters, we see Luísa in her dressing gown and read this single-line paragraph: *"Tinham acabado de almoçar"* (They had just finished eating lunch) (13). The day is the only thing that advances as Luísa plans to now linger in a leisurely bath and Jorge pages through his book at a leisurely pace (*devagar*); the characters speak *"devagar"*; Luísa puts her socks on *"devagar"* and later undresses *"devagar."* When Basílio arrives, he will approach the piano *"devagar,"* and when *"devagar"* is not employed, then the more pejorative term *"preguiçosamente"* (lazily) is. Whether one sees "leisure" as a desirable respite from responsibilities and work or, out of bourgeois *ressentiment*, as a negative entity since one should be working, the terms "indolence" and "laziness" have always implied a judgment such that one does not have the disposition to work or does not work well. Whether a positive or negative, too much of even a good thing can be destructive, and the excess of leisure causes Luísa to develop the *"natureza de preguiçosa"* (the nature of an idler). As she no longer seeks to occupy her time in worthwhile pursuits, she becomes bored and ripe material for any sort of amusing activity—enter her cousin Basílio. The one pastime that provides some small level of distraction has been reading; however, this activity only increases Luísa's longing for adventure and passionate embraces.

Since Luísa is characterized by her sensuousness from the outset, we cannot very well say that her sensual characterization is the product of her adultery, as might be the case with Emma Bovary. Her sensuousness is the product of her materialism, of the exchange economy in which she lives, where power resides in one's ability to buy and sell. Note in the following passage how Luísa's sensualism is linked to the presence of exotic items, all of which were likely suggested from her reading: Luísa dreams of being "*numa banheira de mármore cor-de-rosa, em água tépida, perfumada, e adormecer! Ou numa rede de seda, com as janelas cerradas, emabalar-se, ouvindo música!*" (in a marble, rose-colored bathtub, in tepid, perfumed water, and falling asleep! Or in a silk hammock with the openings sealed, rocking herself, listening to music!) (19). The perfumed bath, the silk netting, and the music are all self-indulgences symptomatic of Luísa's materialism, which she has acquired through her bourgeois milieu and the reading of romances.

Like Emma Bovary, Luísa enjoys romances; they fill her days with the excitement that her leisured existence with the exceedingly content Jorge does not provide. She, too, might be content with their marriage if her reading did not spawn a desire for a kind of romance and passion that Queirós shows to be impossible. One of Luísa's neighbors echoes the judgment of Charles Bovary's mother in *Madame Bovary* that the protagonist's illness is the result of the books that she reads. Although neither the neighbor nor Charles' mother is admirable or central to the novels, Luísa's and Emma's reading does foster dreams and desires that facilitate the adultery and augment their materialism.

The narrator's commentary on such sentimental compositions is delivered in his criticism of the poem that Leopoldina's lover writes; it is "*uma composição delambida, de um sentimentalismo reles, com um ar artístico, muito lisboeta, cheia de versos errados*" (a pointless composition, of a despicable sentimentalism, with a very Lisbonese, artistic air about it, full of bad verses) (31). Luísa and Leopoldina cannot see through the affected sentiment; hence, they are suitably touched by such "despicable" sentiment and impressed by the "bad" verses. Neither would have received any sort of education in literature that would afford them the ability to develop discriminating taste.

Even though Luísa has a much freer upbringing than the other adulteresses due to lax supervision, there is a sense in which she, too, is raised in a figurative convent. Because of her sheltered upbringing, Luísa cannot know that the nights about which she has read, the days of melancholy, the carriage rides, castles, and knights in shining armor are fictional idealizations. She assumes that they are possible with wealth, charm, and a dashing lover, and, like many of our adulteresses, she imbibes her first "knowledge" of the world through reading; hence, she expects life to imitate art and happiness to be in the arms of a lover. She believes that books really do imitate reality and so is able to exclaim, like Emma, "*Tinha um amante, ela!*" (She had a lover!) (173). Both women feel more beautiful after consummating their affairs because they feel as though they have joined the ranks of all those heroines about whom they have read. Paradoxically, the world becomes more real as it becomes more fictional, for the fictional world has always seemed more real to them.

Luísa eventually realizes that transcendental love and passion can be present without the physical, conventional proof of them. Where once she equates her champagne brunch with Basílio at the *paraíso* with the decadence that she imagines is typical of the love affairs of the upper classes, she later sees in Jorge all the undying passion for which she has always longed and always had. Her awakening to the reality of love and lovers, marriage and infidelity is foreshadowed in the following passage, an authorial analogy of a boat fitted for a romantic voyage, which runs aground: "*Assim um* yacht *que aparelhou nobremente para uma viagem romanesca vai encalhar, ao partir, nos lodaçais do rio baixo; e o mestre aventureiro que sonhava com os incensos e os almíscares das florestas aromáticas, imóvel sobre o seu tombadilho, tapa o nariz aos cheiros dos esgotos*" (Thus, a yacht that was nobly outfitted for a romantic voyage will run aground, upon leaving, in the mud of the low river; and the master adventurer that dreamed of the incenses and musk of the aromatic flowers, immobile on his quarter-deck, covers his nose from the smells of the sewers) (190). The word "*lodaçais*" is very apt here, for it has the figurative meaning of "dissolute life," which is precisely what Luísa embarks upon in her romantic voyage. Thus, her very short-lived journey to paradise, a realm of anticipated physical delight, bodes a disillusioning running amok in this authorial metaphor. Luísa is headed for some unpleasant waters; rather than please her senses, she will end by offending them (and those around her).

Luísa expects the *paraíso* to be something out of a Paul-Henri Feval novel (slightly shabby on the outside but elegant on the inside) but is disappointed to find that the "paradise" is as ugly on the inside as on the out. The narrator, focalized through Luísa's eyes as she sees the love nest for the first time, describes the room in all its sordid detail: from the worn-out steps of the staircase, to the iron bed with its dirty linen, to the humidity stains on the walls. The reality of the paradise does not live up to expectation; Luísa has been a "master adventurer" in her proclivity to dream the impossible dream, but in the course of her voyage she discovers the tawdry reality of what had always seemed so rich.

The narrator has been preparing us through Luísa's insights for the redemptive judgment in the end. Luísa is reprehensible for her idle life and her materialism; however, she realizes her error with respect to the frivolous Basílio and achieves a greater understanding of the nature of passion. Like Effi, her disease gives her deathbed insights. Her ability to recognize the "truth" and not persevere in the rosy-colored world of romance redeems her. Whereas in the beginning Luísa refuses to accept any blame for the affair, in the end she has some sense of what motivated her to commit adultery and can even speculate about the attractiveness of lovers in general.

In the beginning, Luísa attributes her crime to external forces: "*Tinha sido uma* fatalidade: *fora o calor da hora, o crepúsculo, uma pontinha de vinho talvez. . . . Estava douda, decerto*" (It had been Fate: whether it were the heat of the hour, the twilight, the small bit of wine perhaps. . . . She was crazy, surely) (175). She then proceeds to justify her actions with an *ad populum* argument: "*Quantas mulheres viviam num amor ilegítimo e eram ilustres, admiradas!*" (How many women lived an illegitimate love and were illustrious and admired!) (175). Everyone else is doing it; why shouldn't she? Moreover, those who were doing it were actually "illustrious and admired!" Luísa has no awareness of class difference. She cannot see that what may be permissible for the aristocracy (provided the sin was hidden) is not at all acceptable for a bourgeois woman. In any event, she is not to blame. She is merely a handmaiden of Fate.

After some of the newness of the affair wears off, Luísa is able to wonder why she ever engaged in it: it might have been "*não ter nada que fazer, a curiosidade romanesca e mórbida de ter um amante, mil vaidadezinhas inflamadas, um certo desejo físico*" (not having anything to do, the morbid, romantic curiosity of having a lover, a thousand inflamed vanities, a certain physical desire) (215). She realizes that her boredom, a product of her life of leisure, and reading romances have combined to whet her appetite for excitement, a conclusion that is supported by the narrator's descriptions throughout. Anna Karenin recognizes the desire that novels create for personal adventure, but even she never voices her understanding, as Luísa does here, of the mechanics of desire and motivation. Luísa, however, is not so wise as to be able to cure herself, only diagnose the ailment.

Luísa begins to question Basílio's love for her almost immediately and comes to realize that Basílio's professions of love are really "ridiculous pretensions"; she remembers how Jorge loves and questions why she puts up with Basílio, deciding that what had seemed to her to be love had come from "*novidade, do saborzinho delicioso de comer a maça proibida, das condições de mistério do* Paraíso" (novelty, from the delicious taste of eating the forbidden fruit, from the mysterious conditions of the *Paraíso*) (215). She concludes at the end of the affair that she never experienced anything like the happiness in illicit love like that about which she has read in romances and seen in opera houses. According to romance, she and her cousin should have been exceptionally happy: they were young, they were a mystery to one another, and they were faced with difficulties since Luísa was married (the romantic ideal of impossible love), but outside fictional accounts, what makes an affair exciting is its newness, and as soon as the newness wears off, so does the pleasure. Thus, it gradually dawns on Luísa that the only way to maintain the excitement of adultery would be to do as Leopoldina does and continually change lovers: "*É que o amor é essencialmente perecível, e na hora em que nasce começa a morrer. Só os começos são bons. . . . Seria pois necessário estar sempre a* começar, *para poder sempre sentir? . . . Era o que fazia Leopoldina*" (It is that love is essentially short-lived and in the hour in which it is born, it begins to die. Only the beginnings are good. . . . It would be necessary, thus, to always be *beginning* in order to feel? . . . It was what Leopoldina did) (215). Emma realizes that adultery can be just as boring as marriage, but she never ponders why, as Luísa does here, and these insights redeem her otherwise frivolous character.

To her credit Luísa does not despair as do other adulteresses over the end of the affair. She is too concerned with concealing her "crime" from her husband, because, like Effi, she fears losing his love, respect, and admiration. She is repentant and wants to make amends and so does not waste any time bewailing the loss of Basílio; her despair comes rather from her inability to pay off Juliana, whom she considers her punishment. Juliana becomes the mistress of the house and wields her power over Luísa with malicious delight. She uses her knowledge of the affair to extort money and humble Luísa with her insolence. The balance of power within the household is disrupted, and Juliana does not prove worthy of Luísa's role. Since Luísa is so repentant and suffers her punishment at the hands of a servant filled with *ressentiment*, Queirós concedes her the very romantic death of a brain fever—a romantic convention in an otherwise realistic novel.

Because Luísa is repentant and has been punished, the reaction of society to her death serves to condemn them for their insensitivity, hypocrisy, and general moral bankruptcy. The way in which each character responds to her death separates the sincerely good from the callous and hypocritical: the Conselheiro delivers a eulogy for Luísa, which is interrupted by the bellowing of *"um sujeito grosso"* (a gross man) and hurries the speech to its clichéd conclusion so that he may go to his mistress; Basílio drinks cognac and sleeps soundly; Jorge thinks about his dearly departed wife and sobs; Sebastião cries softly in his room; Julião reads a science magazine; Leopoldina dances at a soirée, and "the others" of Lisbon sleep. The reactions are given, much as they are here, one after the other, in synoptic fashion, chronicling what each is doing the night of Luísa's death. The paragraph ends with a description of the weather, which proves that, like Jorge and Sebastião, Nature weeps for Luísa: *"E o vento frio . . . ia fazer* tristemente *uma árvore a sepultura de Luiza"* (And the cold wind . . . was making a tree at the grave of Luísa wave *sadly*) (426; emphasis added). Just as Rollo, a symbol of the natural world in *Effi Briest*, mourns at Effi's grave, so the sad waving of the tree at Luísa's conveys an appropriate reaction to the protagonist's passing. The more admirable characters sympathize with Nature, which encourages the reader to do the same.

When society is criticized in the nineteenth-century novel of adultery, the blame placed upon the adulteress is lessened. Unlike Anna Karenin, Ana Ozores, and Effi Briest, Luísa is never ostracized by Lisbon society since her crime is never disclosed (though it is suspected). The townspeople in *O primo Basílio*, like those in *La Regenta*, are constantly monitoring Luísa's movements and murmuring about the visits that she receives from her cousin. Even if Luísa does not, others recognize the importance of keeping up appearances and the impropriety of receiving the calls of her cousin so frequently and without a chaperone. As Sebastião says to Julião, *"A questão não é por ela. A questão é pela vizinhança"* (It is not a question because of her. It is because of the neighborhood) (133). More important than guilt or innocence is the *appearance* of innocence. Sebastião is more concerned that Luísa *seem* virtuous than that she really *is* virtuous. He and those in his milieu are like Innstetten and society proper in *Effi Briest*, who are more concerned with external, objectified honor than the presence of real virtue or a real sense of personal integrity.

The figure of the Conselheiro bears further mention because he has a parallel in the figure of the pharmacist in *Madame Bovary*. The Conselheiro is similarly ridiculed by the speeches that he makes. He makes foolish mistakes such as *"al rivedere"* instead of *"arrivederci"* and *"S. Tiago"* instead of "Sant' Iago" (54, 324). He delivers lines laden with irony, as when he calls Basílio *"um verdadeiro fidalgo"* (a true gentleman) and Luísa *"uma esposa-modelo"* (a model wife) (281, 419). His being named a Gentleman of the order of Sant'Iago (like Homais' receiving the Legion of Honor in *Madame Bovary*) only further increases the irony that someone as inane and vapid as he should receive such distinction.

Edmundo Moniz sees Luísa's death as a form of punishment, though he does not believe that Queirós meant it as such—he simply could not free himself from the tradition of punishing the wrongdoer, even though he justifies her wrongdoing within the course of the novel.[21] In keeping with this line of argument, Alexander Coleman points to Basílio as "the center of gravity" in the novel, not Luísa. The reason, according to Coleman, that the novel is entitled *Cousin Basílio* and not "Cousin Luísa" is that Queirós' intention was to expose the seducer type: "Basílio is just as banal as Rodolphe and Léon, but his name gives the book its title because Eça was determined to expose all Don Juans, all seducers" (116). Queirós was not about exposing adulteresses; they were lambs before the wolves. Basílio is the true criminal here, who, unlike Luísa, demonstrates no character development in the course of the novel, stagnant in his materialism and lack of spirituality to the very last page of the novel.

Consider the following exchange between Basílio and Luísa midway through the novel:

Luísa: —*Diz que [Julião] tem muito talento....*
Basílio: —*Era melhor que tivesse botas.*
Luísa: "They say Julião has a lot of talent...."
Basílio: "It would be better if he had boots." (120)

It is more important to Basílio that the people with whom he associates *look* good, rather than that they have any talent or virtue. In the end, he is no different from the beginning, calling Luísa a "*trombolho*" (a stumbling block) and wishing that he had brought another mistress with him from France. This lack of spirituality, attributed to the materialistic aims of the bourgeoisie, is criticized in all these novels of adultery. Any criticism that the narrator has of Luísa is reserved for her sensual materialism and not for the actual act of adultery. As Antônio Sérgio Mendonça notes, Basílio "*é uma condenação a estética do frívolo*" (is a condemnation of the aesthetic of the frivolous one) (60). Luísa can be criticized for her frivolity, for loving such a character as Basílio, but she must be praised for her learning to appreciate Jorge's sincerity after having denigrated herself by loving her cousin, and her death must come as a release for one who has expiated her sin in the purgatory of an inverted relationship between servant and mistress.

MADAME BOVARY

Some of the first critics of *Madame Bovary* in 1857 could not distinguish between the thoughts of Emma and those of the narrator due to the novelty of Flaubert's free, indirect style, which permits a conflation of narrator and character discourse. Where was the authoritative narrator, telling us what he thinks, telling us what *we* should think? The difficulty with the novel is that Flaubert tears down provincial society of the mid-nineteenth century without reifying anything in its place. The positive values in the novel are but a whisper amid the roar of materialism, mediocrity, and vanity. Queirós may have set out to expose the seducer-type in *O primo Basílio*; Flaubert exposes the adulteress and, even more importantly, the reality of adultery itself. *Madame Bovary*, as one of the very first realist novels, certainly the first to take a realistic view on a greatly romanticized subject, is necessarily the point of comparison for later novels of adultery of the nineteenth century. In the laboratory of the novel the lovers become more likable and less calculating than Rodolphe; the husbands become less of a cuckold than is Charles; the adulteresses come to have noble aspirations—all to determine whether there ever is any justification for adultery, whether an adulteress can seem more sympathetic than Emma, whether marriage, not adultery, is not at the heart of the problem.

Despite Flaubert's attempts at invisibility within the text—that is, to not create an authorial presence in an authoritative narrator—there are parts of *Madame Bovary* where a rudimentarily dramatized narrator makes his opinions explicit and where the characters are mocked in the very language used to describe them and in the ironic contrast between romantic ideals and prosaic reality. The sentimental songs that Emma sings in music class in the convent, for example, which give her glimpses of "*l'attirante fantasmagorie des réalités sentimentales*" (the phantasmagoric attraction of sentimental reality) are, according to the narrator, composed of "*la niaiserie du style et les imprudences de la note*" (silly words and inept music). When Emma describes her passion in terms of a fierce storm, the narrator undermines her analogy by suggesting that Emma's drainpipes are in no condition to weather the storm.

With the exception of Dr. Larivière, no other character in the novel is above reproach and beyond mockery. Charles is pitiable at best. He fails to demonstrate more than rudimentary reasoning capabilities, is quite uncouth in his manners, and is ridiculous in his affection for Emma. We might sympathize with Emma's shattered dreams and fated mediocrity if the substance of those dreams were not so shallow and she herself so selfish. Rodolphe Boulanger's pretensions are mocked in his very name, and he is so calculating in seducing Emma, so jaded in the course of the affair, and so callous in its conclusion that he is an impoverished imitation of the great lover. Crampas and Vronsky, Arobin and Don Álvaro are much closer akin to the archetype of the noble seducer (even though Don Álvaro is an aging one). Léon is even more impoverished than Rodolphe since he lets Emma take control of the affair and slavishly attends to Emma's every whim. The secondary figures are even easier to despise since they do not have the depth of the central characters and thus little opportunity to win our sympathy. The one exception is Dr. Larivière, who is very likely a reflection of Flaubert's own father.

Dr. Larivière's greatness is made all the more manifest by contrasting him with Dr. Canivet, the arrogant and condescending doctor whose advice is sought concerning Hippolyte's leg and subsequently Emma's poisoning. In the case of Hippolyte, Canivet demonstrates his complete lack of consideration for his patient, whom he sees only after he sees that his horses are being fed; in Emma's case he is berated by Larivière for prescribing an emetic. Since the narrator's comments are not often rendered explicitly and are so rarely sincerely laudatory, it is truly startling to see how verbose he becomes in singing Dr.

Larivière's praises: "*Dédaigneux des croix, des titres, et des académies, hospitalier, libéral, paternel avec les pauvres et pratiquant la vertu sans y croire, il eût presque passé pour un saint si la finesses de son esprit ne l'eût fait craindre comme un démon*" (Disdainful of decorations, titles and academies, hospitable, generous, a father to the poor, practicing virtue without believing in it, he might almost have passed for a saint if the keenness of his mind had not made everyone fear him like a demon) (339). Indeed, he does seem superhuman, for not only is he a man of science, an excellent physician, but he is sensitive and compassionate, as well. He actually cannot help but let a tear escape when he sees Emma in her death throes.

We can extrapolate from this uncharacteristic description of Dr. Larivière the traits that the narrator finds praiseworthy: an internalized pursuit of virtue (not the performance of a duty prescribed by a religious institution), modesty (he does not strive for public recognition as does Homais), generosity, wisdom, compassion, and skill—all traits that the people of Yonville lack. The narrator likewise exhibits compassion for Hippolyte and the blind man along the route of the coach, both of whom are labeled "*pauvre diable*[s]," and for Charles, who for 43 days attends to Emma in her sickness and weeps when she eats some bread and jam—"*le pauvre garçon.*" Since Emma manifests none of the good doctor's traits, and since Flaubert's ironic presentation of the way that she sees discourages identification with her, we might feel free to criticize her and all those members of her society who try to feed her with material things (Sabiston 46).

The narrator never explicitly condemns the values of this bourgeois society, yet his ironic presentation of what it holds dear sends a very clear message to the reader that its priorities are out of order. Yonville is both a marketplace and a cemetery.[22] Capitalistic instincts and materialistic gain prevail, but the road leads to a spiritual death. The scene at the agricultural fair not only offers the most comic dissonance between the language of love and the language of the marketplace but also emphasizes the disproportionate values assigned to goods and people. The highest monetary prize of 70 francs goes to the best crop, while the reward for 54 years of service at the same farm is a paltry 25 francs and goes to a woman with a shriveled body, wrinkled face, "knotty" hands, and the "mute placidity" of an animal. The vestiges of servitude, however, the tolls that it takes upon the body and mind, go unnoticed by the complacent townspeople, who look upon her with beaming faces.

Elizabeth Sabiston and Priscilla Meyer both identify Homais as the villain of *Madame Bovary*. Sabiston claims that Homais is actually *responsible* for Emma's death since it is his poison that Emma eats, and he is the one who invites the blind man to Yonville, "who so terrifies her" that he literally scares her to death (60). Meyer is not quite so literal in identifying Homais as the villain. She proposes that his clichéd use of language and "misapplied materialism" due to his faith in science presents "the degradation of Rousseau's progressive views and of Enlightenment ideas" (258). To try to assign the blame to any one member of society (that being anyone other than Emma) would be to ignore the ways that Fr. Bournisien, Rodolphe, and Dr. Canivet all fail her and the role that Charles plays in facilitating both affairs. We might just as easily lay the blame at

Fr. Bournisien's doorstep, for instance, for failing to minister to Emma's spiritual needs. As much as she tries to tell him that her suffering is not of a physical nature, Fr. Bournisien can only respond that he knows what it is to suffer because he has seen women without bread or firewood—he cannot grasp the longing that Emma has to transcend the material world, that she suffers a spiritual death in her adultery. In the end, Emma chooses death, which is further evidence of her ability to romanticize even this gruesome reality.

Thus, both science and religion fail Emma; nevertheless, there is not in *Madame Bovary* the same level of sympathetic justification for Emma's adultery as there is in *La Regenta*, *Effi Briest*, or *The Awakening*. Emma is bored, but she should not be. If she has the time to read romances and be bored, it is because she is neglecting her duties as a manager of the household.[23] Emma has always enjoyed reading romances. In the convent, for instance, she reads novels that are full of gentlemen who are "*brave comme des lions, doux comme des agneaux,* vertueux comme on ne l'est pas" (brave as lions, gentle as lambs, *virtuous as no one really is*) (72; emphasis added). This passage begins in the iterative mood; thus, the use of the present tense signals the position of the narrator in the present tense of narrating time and his judgment that romances depict an idealized image of virtue. Emma would be incapable of reaching such a conclusion; she always see through the colored glass. These romances "soil" Emma—literally, as the books she borrows from the lending libraries leave their dust upon her hands, and figuratively, as her satin slippers retain the wax of the dance floor at La Vaubyessard. Her reading of romances, like her contact with wealth at La Vaubyessard, leaves an indelible impression upon her whose effect stains the purity of her aspirations to transcend the mundane existence of provincial life.

Emma is further corrupted through her affair with Rodolphe. Effi and Edna Pontellier maintain their dignity in spite of their adultery since neither is particularly attached to her lover, and neither lover is portrayed as callous and calculating as Rodolphe. Flaubert chooses to dwell upon Emma's affair with Rodolphe in great detail, which dramatizes the effect that the various stages have upon Emma and shows all that Emma learns so that she can conduct her next affair with Léon. Emma is genuinely smitten with Rodolphe, who is so jaded that he cannot distinguish Emma's genuine sentiment from the licentiousness of his previous mistresses:

Il s'était tant de fois entendu dire ces choses, qu'elles n'avaient pour lui rien d'original. Emma resemblait à toutes les maîtresses; et le charme de la nouveauté, peu à peu tombant comme un vêtement, laissait voir à nu l'eternelle monotonie de la passion, qui a toujours les mêmes formes et le même langage. *Il ne distinguait pas, cet homme si plein de pratique, là dissemblance des sentiments sous la parité des expressions.* (219; emphasis added)

He had heard such things said to him so many times before that they no longer held any originality for him. Emma was like any other mistress; and the charm of the novelty gradually fell away like a garment, revealing in all its nakedness the eternal *monotony of passion, which always has the same form and speaks the same language.* He, this man of great experience, could not distinguish differences of feeling beneath similarities of expression.

The narrator (once again evident in the change to the present tense) mocks Rodolphe's experience here, that he should know women so well and yet not be able to differentiate true feelings from the merely affected. Emma will come to know such jadedness in her affair with Léon. The expression of passion is constant; the degree to which it is experienced varies. The narrator continues in the vein of the shortcomings of language in the following: "[*P*]*uisque personne, jamais, ne peut donner l'exacte mesure de ses besoins, ni de ses conceptions, ni de ses doleurs, et que la parole humaine est comme un chaudron fêlé où nous battons des mélodies à faire danser les ours, quand on voudrait attendrir les étoiles*" ([N]o one can ever express the exact measure of his needs, his conceptions or his sorrows, and human speech is like a cracked pot whereon we beat out melodies that make bears dance when we are striving to move the stars) (219). This is particularly true of Emma, who speaks in a conventional manner, and gives and receives love according to a clichéd formula, and yet the narrator implies here that she feels genuine love for Rodolphe, a love that he cannot recognize because she expresses it in the conventional trappings of passion. On the one hand, Emma is capable of poeticizing the mundane and crude (recall her impression of the Duc de Laverdière); on the other, she is limited by language and unable to express herself fully because she resorts to stock expressions, those about which she has read in her romance novels.

Regardless of the nature of Emma's passion for Rodolphe at the beginning of their affair, Rodolphe's treatment of her when he tires of the passion corrupts Emma's soul as she remains under his influence out of an "*attachement idiot*" (idiotic infatuation). Emma clings to Rodolphe because he satisfies her sensual needs, thus causing her soul to sink and drown in the intoxication of her passion, "*comme le duc de Clarence dans son tonneau de malvoisie*" (like the Duke of Clarence in his butt of malmsey) (219). From this point on in the novel, Emma becomes more and more depraved. She exchanges her ideal love stories for occasions of sensual surfeit and learns how to abuse language to feign feelings that she no longer has (i.e., for Léon). As the narrator declares on this occasion, "[*L*]*a parole est un laminoir que allonge toujours les sentiment*" ([S]peech is a rolling mill that always stretches out the feelings that go into it) (260). Whereas before, Emma did not know how to use language, could not convey the extent of her feelings with it, a more experienced Emma can stretch language to convey sentiment that she does not feel. She feigns melancholy over the time that she and Léon have spent apart (as does he) when both have been engaged in separate amorous encounters without so much as a backward glance at the time that they had spent together before.

In addition to corrupting language, Emma begins to corrupt her body and soul as well with material goods, lying, and finally poison. After the newness of each affair wears off, Emma tries to keep the flame of passion alive with recourse to material gifts, luxuries, and exaggerated professions of love. With Rodolphe she uses cold cream on her face, scents her handkerchiefs, wears all sorts of jewelry and fine lingerie, and continually buys new shoes to replace those scuffed in her morning trips across the meadow to visit her lover. With Léon she is more bold and "wanton." She and Léon have their own little paradise in Rouen (though much more refined than Luísa's—more in keeping with what Luísa imagined she would find) where they drink champagne out of thin glasses, and Emma wears slippers made of pink satin and trimmed with swansdown. She smokes cigarettes, walks about openly with Léon, and one evening dresses like a man for a party, where she becomes intoxicated and carouses all night with an unsavory bunch of rabble-rousers. She has no qualms about lying to Charles. In fact, she lies even when the circumstances do not warrant it—for the mere pleasure that she derives from it: lying "*était un besoin, une manie, un plaisir, au point que, si elle disait avoir passé, hier, par le côté droit d'une rue, il fallait croire qu'elle avait pris par le côté gauche*" (became a need, a mania, a pleasure—to the point that if she said she had walked down the right side of the street yesterday, it was almost certain that she had walked down the left) (294). Emma reaches the extremity of corruption in that she actually enjoys her depravity even as she is dominated by it.

First Emma poisons her soul. Then, she poisons her body. Charles' mother attempts to restore order in the household, but her admonitions to Emma only cause her to exercise her will more forcefully in her life with Léon since she is limited at home by the presence of her mother-in-law. The narrator explains what Léon cannot: "*Il ne savait pas quelle réaction de tout son être la poussait davantage à se précipiter sur les jouissances de la vie. Elle devenait irritable, gourmande et voluptueuse*" (He [Léon] did not know that her wholehearted reaction [to her mother-in-law] was pushing her even more to hurl herself into sensual pleasure. She was becoming irritable, greedy, and voluptuous) (299). The end of Emma's reactionary behavior is her "eating" arsenic—the height of recklessness. Her sensualism and materialism have poisoned her soul—indeed, have completely drowned it—and her corrupted sense of what is good for her body and her lack of restraint induce her to paradoxically nourish her body with poison.

Due to her corruption through her reading, her slavish imitation of high society, her adultery, her descent into sensualism and its corresponding materialism, Emma cannot be said to embody any of the positive values established with the character of Dr. Larivière. She does not serve the poor except for an occasional whim and even then is suspect, for the narrator wonders if her apparent magnanimity were not masked selfishness, for Emma does things for public recognition, like Homais, and can be just as calculating as Rodolphe in the pursuit of her desire. She gives to the blind man who hangs onto the carriage from Rouen only because she feels that the almsgiving is a grandiose gesture—something like Lady Bountiful. She does not exhibit compassion for Hippolyte or the blind man or even her own daughter, whose existence she ignores for the most part, not even when she causes Berthe to stumble and cut her cheek. Emma looks for something more "solid" upon which to base her love for Charles and settles upon something as insubstantial as public recognition. She encourages Charles to increase his renown through the operation on Hippolyte's club foot, and when things seem to be going well, Emma notices that Charles' teeth are really not that bad-looking. After the amputation, however, Emma comes to repent of her prior virtue and is filled with self-reproach for trusting Charles' ability and anger over the loss of their good name. Thus, she has none of the compassion, altruism, wisdom, or skill of Dr. Larivière, while he has none of her pride or selfishness.

Nevertheless, critics still find room for sympathizing with Emma. Louise Kaplan in her *Female Perversions: The Temptations of Emma Bovary* proposes, for instance, that "[a]dmire her or not, we sympathize with Emma's desire to give voice to her illusions" because Emma "is willing to risk all to breathe life into her illusions" (202, 206). Elizabeth Sabiston argues in *The Prison of Womanhood* that Emma's romanticism is "infinitely preferable to the materialistic philosophy of M. Homais, to the materialistic business of M. Lheureux, and the materialistic religion of the curé Bournisien" (77). According to Sabiston, Emma's idealistic pursuit of love is admirable in a milieu "given over to animalism and avarice" (72)—though she is careful to distinguish between Emma's plight, with which she believes Flaubert does sympathize, and the manner of her revolt, with which Flaubert does not (Sabiston 77). Is it love, then, that Emma pursues with Léon? Does she not, in fact, give herself over to animalism and pervert a noble ideal while enjoying her spiritual corruption? Can she be exculpated from avarice? She does not set about amassing a fortune, but she cannot accept love without all the decadent, material pleasures of a love nest. She has an undying passion in Charles, but what completes her pursuit of the ideal are the accoutrements—she replaces the essential with the accidental. For these reasons Flaubert's sympathy with his protagonist is limited. We must be careful not to transform Emma into some sort of quixotic figure. Not every dreamer is worthy of our sympathy because not every dream is worthy of attaining. Emma does deserve our sympathy for the way in which gender limits what she can become. As a woman Emma is fated to have her dreams and ambitions thwarted, for a woman, as she herself notes when Berthe is born, is not free to do anything, while a man is: "[U]ne femme est empêchée continuellement. Inerte et flexible à la fois, elle a contre elle les mollesses de la chair avec les dépendances de la loi. . . . [I]l y a toujours quelque désir qui entraîne, quelque convenance qui retient" (A woman is thwarted continually. Inert and flexible at the same time, she is up against the weakness of the flesh and her subordination to the law. . . . [T]here is always some desire that carries her forward, some convention that holds her back) (122–123). Emma flaunts convention, like Edna Pontellier, Anna Karenin, and Luísa; however, she is no more successful than these others at carving out a place for herself in society. Moreover, Emma is less adventuresome than these others, for her forays into scandalous behavior are done in anonymity in Rouen or in secret.

Emma's very last illusion is that Fr. Bournisien can offer her salvation. She has dabbled in religious conversion before, after Rodolphe's departure, but the feeling soon wore off, which is only natural, according to Balzac's *The Physiology of Marriage*, wherein he states that 79% of the women who experience "renewed religious fervor" are either about to be "indiscreet" or have just been so (100). On her deathbed she transfers all her lascivious passion for her lovers to Jesus, to the "God-Man." But the narrator undermines Emma's deathbed conversion by reminding us, as Fr. Bournisien anoints each of the parts of her body, that these same body parts have been the instruments of her sin: "*d'abord sur les yeux, qui avaient tant convoité toutes les somptuosités terrestres; puis sur les narines, friandes de brises tiédes et de senteurs amoureuses;*

puis sur la bouche, qui s'était ouverte pour le mensonge, qui avait gémi d'orgueil et crié dans la luxure" (her eyes, which had so fiercely coveted all earthly luxury; then her nostrils, so avid for warm breezes and amorous scents; then her mouth, which had opened to speak lies, cry out in pride and moan in lust) (343). Thus, this solemn religious rite is subverted by the narrator's reminding us of Emma's sinful passions, which she transfers in a passionate kiss to the crucifix.

Emma's death is not romanticized, nor does it elicit the reader's sympathy. It is an agonizing end, and the effects continue even as they prepare to bury her, with black bile spilling out of the corner of her mouth; moreover, she corrupts Charles from beyond the grave. He begins to express his passion and grief in typical, romantic manifestations of melancholy: he spares no expense and has Emma buried in her wedding gown, in three coffins (the material of which he specifies), which must be covered with a green velvet cloth. These material considerations of his wife's burial obscure the spiritual ones of prayers for the soul of the dead or the physical, moral, and spiritual provisions for his daughter's welfare. Charles' materialism and Berthe's neglect are additional effects of Emma's corruption. Sabiston identifies a judgment of Emma in the recurrent motif of her muddy boots, which she contrasts with Emma's desire for wings: "[I]t reminds the reader of her earthly, or earthy, ties, until we see Emma making her final descent into the earth: '*Elle descendait toujours*' ['She was still descending']—all the way to hell, is perhaps the implication" (50). Thus, Emma's final vision of her salvation by the "God-Man" is nothing more than an illusion—at least for her.

Thus, Tolstoy, Clarín, Fontane, Chopin, Queirós, and Flaubert offer their readers particular stories about wives who stumble into adultery that are meant to reflect the whole problem of adultery while at the same time giving us the discourse of their age. These adulteresses are, in the words of Henry James, "ounces of example," for Emma and Luísa, Anna and Ana, Effi and Edna are all meant to reflect, by their examples, the societal ill of adultery or, looked at another way, the way in which marriage has become sick. The adultery is really a manifestation of two related problems: the insufficient education of women and the socioeconomic contract of marriage. Since the actual act of adultery is shown to be an effect of the problem and not the cause or root of it, those who commit it are not thoroughly criminal or immoral in any of the cases. Nowhere in these six novels of adultery are the adulteresses explicitly condemned by the narrator, focalized through his or her eyes as a "criminal" or sinner," nor is their adultery a "crime" or "sin" in the discourse focalized through the same. On the contrary, when the adulteress' society is most severe in its judgment of her, the narrator is most wont to engage in vituperative attacks on the hypocrisy of such a society. When the words "crime" and "criminal" are mentioned in these novels, they apply to Vronsky in *Anna Karenin* and Don Fermín and Petra in *La Regenta*. Edna Pontellier in *The Awakening* acknowledges that she is a very wicked woman by all the *codes* with which she is familiar, but the narrator never says that she is wicked, nor is the code reified by any incident in the novel.

Chopin and Fontane are the most reticent to judge—not only the adulteresses but the husbands, lovers, and even society. Both recognized the interdependence between the individual and society. There are always bound to be pressures that come to bear upon our individual desires and needs, but we should not, for that reason, abolish all social mores. The needs of society must be balanced against the needs of the individual. On the far side of the spectrum of judgments fall Queirós and Flaubert, who though the most subtle in their judgments (the terms "crime," "criminal," "sin," and "sinner" never appear in *O primo Basílio* or *Madame Bovary*), criticize nearly everyone and every social institution in these novels without offering the reader anything to replace the current values of religion, science, love, money, and social status. Tolstoy and Clarín are the most explicit, particularly Tolstoy, for his judgment of Anna suggests that there is an absolute law of right and wrong that is revealed to all by God. Anna is certainly admirable for not heeding worldly wisdom that would have her mask her affair from her husband and live a life of deceit; however, she tragically ignores the wisdom of God, as well. In censuring so many of the people and institutions around Ana Ozores, Clarín exculpates his protagonist from much of the blame; his technique of psychological realism paints a sympathetic portrait of a woman at the mercy of biology and her surroundings. There is nothing "unnatural" about Ana's desires, only something "criminal" by the social code and "sinful" by the religious—both of which Clarín suggests with the speech of Don Víctor before the duel should be more closely aligned with the laws of Nature.

Although there is never an explicit condemnation of the adulteress in these six novels of adultery, the four novels that involve progeny (*Madame Bovary, Anna Karenin, Effi Briest*, and *The Awakening*) complicate the issue of judgment and justification of adultery by representing the plight of the innocent offspring of an unsuccessful marriage. The children engage our sympathies in these cases more than the husbands or wives since, even today, we tend to imagine childhood as it is described by Jean Jaque Rousseau: a time of highly impressionable, wide-eyed innocence and natural goodness. The children never play a central role in the novels, and yet they naturally impact the adulteresses' decisions in significant ways, particularly in *Anna Karenin*, where the ideal of motherhood is sanctified. We have only glimpses of Edna Pontellier's two boys, and yet, in many ways, they are more present to Edna than Seriozha and Berthe are to Anna and Edna (not to mention Anna's lovechild Ani). Seriozha, the product of the morallly acceptable, albeit loveless, marriage, continues to adore his mother even after she has abandoned him, and to her credit, Anna does agonize over her ability to replace her son with her lover. Effi's meeting with her daughter Annie after the former's banishment and divorce wounds Effi momentarily but not profoundly. Like the other mothers in the novel of adultery, she does not define herself in the role of mother, which alienates her from the women of her day who could see themselves only as such. Emma, alone, transgresses from neglect of her daughter to abuse, which induces a more severe criticism of her character. The children are the truly innocent victims in the novel of adultery; they have done nothing to warrant their mother's abuse, neglect, and/or dishonor or the stain that will mark them, as well as their whole line, in perpetuity.

NOTES

1. Booth, *The Rhetoric of Fiction*, 177.
2. Correspondence to Louise Colet, 9 December 1852: "The author, in his book, must be like God in the universe, everywhere present and nowhere visible."
3. Tolstoy significantly modified his characterization of Anna from the first to the final draft of the novel, making her far more noble and sympathetic to the reader than the original, spiteful, physically unattractive earlier version of Anna.
4. Tolstoy writes in *What Is Art?* that art is a means of communication between men, and it must be accessible to all men. It cannot be explained, only caught like a contagious disease, for "words convey thoughts; art conveys *feelings*" (49).
5. Anna says to Doily at Vozdvizhenskoe, "'But I was not to blame. And who is to blame? What does being to blame mean? Could things have been otherwise?'" (667).
6. She points to his eating oysters, womanizing, hunting, and overall "*bonhomie.*"
7. Meyer identifies a number of similarities between *Anna Karenin* and *Madame Bovary*, one of which is the authors' analogous use of horses to characterize the affairs of each of the heroines. Meyer also analyzes the ball scenes in both novels, the opera, and emblems, such as "adulteress, conveyance and grotesque peasant."
8. This idea is discussed in Meyer, 256.
9. "*Hermafrodita*" in modern usage, that is, "hermaphrodite."
10. Noel Valis claims, "Here [in the description of the town] the ironic opposition between a noble past, left chronologically imprecise, and a base present interested only in digestion and sleep is quite clear" (26).
11. The Marqués is in collusion with Don Álvaro, whom he permits to rule the Casino.
12. I am indebted to Paciencia Ontañón for her suggestion that Fermín is also a victim in *La Regenta*. Ontañón asserts that Fermín is as much a victim of his environment as is Ana since his dreams are likewise unachievable. He and Ana "*luchan por sobrevivir pero inútilmente...están condenados a un mal fin*" (fight to survive but futilely . . . they are condemned to a bad end) (130). Though his very office as a priest frustrates Fermín and obviates his dreams, he nevertheless wields such power in the novel that his victimization cannot be equivalent to Ana's.
13. There are corresponding central theater scenes in *Anna Karenin* and *Madame Bovary*. Anna is humbled by her venture in the public eye, and Emma, though she seems to appreciate the opera as does Ana Zorrilla's play, is seduced by the actors and the sentiment; thus, her appreciation of the opera does not raise her in our esteem as Ana's appreciation for the theater does her.
14. I am indebted to George Fenwick Jones' study *Honor in German Literature* for this discussion.
15. Radcliffe, 38.
16. Valerie Greenberg asserts that Effi "maintains the consistency of her spirited character to the end: resisting rather than, as is commonly supposed, submitting" (770). Greenberg questions the seeming contrition in Effi's final conversation with her mother and claims that each of the points "can be read in opposition to the usual interpretations" (777).
17. Margaret Culley, 226.
18. Margaret Culley argues that Edna's solitude drives her to her death. She acknowledges that Edna does have "brave moments of delight . . . in her solitary self," but that in the end she is not able to sustain these brave moments and thus, "when her two deliverers, the imagination (Robert) and the flesh (Arobin), have failed her, she begins to

Judgment Day

understand something of what Mademoiselle Reisz's presence and words have told her about the price of solitude, and . . . she swims out alone" (228). Carol Christ, on the other hand, suggests that we cannot even be sure that Edna's suicide is deliberate. Perhaps she "simply drifted into it," as she does into so many situations in the novel (36).

19. Emmitt, 315–333. The following citations from Emmitt are taken from this same article.

20. "From the Pittsburgh *Leader*," reprinted in the Norton critical edition of *The Awakening*, 153.

21. Moniz suggests that Queirós' women do not deserve their punishment of death but that Queirós could not free himself from the tradition of punishment for wrongdoing: "*Seus atos [de Amélia, Luísa, e Genoveva] não justificavam a pena de morte imposta pelo romancista, que seguia a tradição clássica de punir os faltosos sem se lbertar dos velhos preconceitos*" (Their acts [of Amelia, Luísa and Genoveva] did not justify the death penalty imposed by the novelist, who was following the classic tradition of punishing the guilty ones without liberating himself from the old preconceptions) (*As mulheres proibidas*, 43).

22. See Sabinston's *The Prison of Womanhood* for her discussion of this metaphor.

23. Furst, *Approaches to Teaching Madame Bovary*.

Conclusion

> It is not poverty which makes us poor, but desire.
> —Antisthenes, fifth century B.C.

The novel of adultery, unlike fabliaux of cuckolds and Spanish Golden Age drama of men of honor, is principally concerned with the inner passions of the wife and adulteress. No longer is the husband or lover of tantamount importance, nor does the tale of adultery serve to ridicule (the cuckold) or extol (the man of honor). The novel of adultery, which reached its golden age in the late nineteenth century, calls for compassion and social change; it reflects the author's attempt to realistically confront a societal ill and effect a change in the hearts and minds of his readers. In four cases, in *Madame Bovary*, *Anna Karenin*, *Effi Briest*, and *The Awakening*, the problem of an unhappy, stagnant marriage is complicated by offspring, and in these cases the protagonists choose death.[1] Whereas once we may have felt that the husband of an adulteress deserved his wife's infidelity because of his age, blindness, and passivity, with the novel of adultery, even when the husband is ridiculed, we are forced to see his humanity and the effects deception has upon the entire family. The children are innocent victims in the novel of adultery who must live with the consequences and stigma of their mother's act; moreover, the husbands in these novels do not fit neatly into the mold of cuckold or man of honor, for the traits of both are mingled with very vivid expressions of their humanity.

Charles, the most ridiculed of all, suffers more than any other husband. His naked emotion may not have been typical or admirable in a man of the nineteenth century; nevertheless, the sympathy that it elicits from the reader softens the ridicule. The fact that we do not often see with or through the eyes of Charles or any of the husbands, however, precludes more than a passing sympathetic response. While not villainous, the husbands in the novel of adultery are not overly sympathetic either. Karenin, Don Víctor, and Innstetten all forgive their wives but are too weak to go against the expectations of society. Because of their length and psychological realism, *Anna Karenin* and *La Regenta* offer us a greater understanding of the motivation of the figure of the husband and, therefore, greater identification, but even in these two novels, the focalization is principally through the eyes of the adulteress, if not the narrator. Thus, we see the wives, and not the husbands, as victims, victims of their minds and bodies and victims of the hypocritical punishment of society. As products of the milieu of the nineteenth century, the women have few life options, little education, and no suitable role models or confidantes. They are voyeurs as opposed to actors in the drama of life, and their vision is obscured by the colored glass through which they view the world.

In the texts where the naturalistic tenets of heredity, milieu, and the pressure of the moment are invoked to excuse the adulteress, most notably in *La Regenta*, the women's illicit passions are represented as their fate and not their fault.[2] Thus, environment and biology replace the character of the husband to justify the act of adultery or, at least, mitigate our judgment of it. In five of the texts, the wife's reading creates a longing for change and excitement; Effi does not require the stimulus of books, as she already has what some might call an overactive imagination: "She was strongly affected by all that was mysterious and forbidden" (Fontane 157). Her craving for excitement stems from her youth and immaturity and assuredly induces her to engage in the short-lived, illicit relations with Crampas. With little experience of the world, these protagonists cannot know that life does not imitate romance; according to Willa Cather in her review of *The Awakening*, women such as Emma Bovary and Edna Pontellier demand "more romance out of life than God put into it" (154). When they learn, as they all do, that their dreams of everlasting passion and excitement in adulterous love are unattainable, they cannot live with the reality of mundane existence. They cannot live outside society while at the same time they are stifled by it. Anna Karenin, Emma Bovary, and Edna Pontellier all commit suicide, a choice that is ironically in keeping with their romantic tendencies since none of them wonders what the reality of death will be like, thinking only that it will provide a release from the corruption of this life, the solitude, and the responsibilities of motherhood. Anna Karenin further imagines that her suicide will be her vengeance and victory over Vronsky, which it is, but it is also a decision made in the obscurity of candlelight and not by the clear light of day.

From a literary standpoint, the most extenuating circumstance that precludes our judgment of the adulteresses is that the novel of adultery is typically focalized through the eyes of the adulteress; hence, we have a very clear understanding of the wife's motivations for the act of deception. We reach that state of "fellow-feeling" described by Max Scheler in *The Nature of Sympathy* where, by identifying with the point of view of the protagonist (in this case, the adulteress) and without experiencing any of the pain of ecstasy ourselves, we phenomenologically intuit her feelings; thus, we are less apt to judge because of this intuition, which leads to understanding. Furthermore, where judgment is explicitly expressed in the text by an intrusive narrator, it falls upon the lovers and husbands and especially upon society. The wives are at best foolish for believing that their ideals could be realized; they are ignorant of the ways of the world and thus are easy prey to seduction. They are taken advantage of by hypocritical, envious confidantes and worldly donjuanesque types. When they seek help, their efforts are frustrated by self-interested or obtuse advisers, such as Fr. Bournisien in *Madame Bovary* and Don Fermín in *La Regenta*. Those who resist, most notably Anna and Ana, stretch their nerves to the breaking point before, during, and after the affair. Even those who do not, notably Emma, Edna, and Luísa, question, compare, and evaluate their experiences based upon what they expect and what they discover about the reality of love and adultery. Since Fontane chooses not to deal with the affair between Crampas and Effi in story time, merely sketching the course of it in a few snippets from their correspondence six and one-half years later, with only the merest suggestion of the deception in the time that it is occurring, we do not see into Effi's mind to see the effect that the adultery has upon her psyche while she is engaged in it. We only know that the deception bothered her much more than the act of adultery—a fact that causes her to lament her lack of principles. Effi's act of adultery has a maturing effect upon her, and only after her affair is she able to assume her role as the wife of a civil servant with pleasure, grace, and satisfaction. Edna, alone, questions her very identity as a woman in the universe and is defeated by the very solitude that initially fosters her development.

All the lovers here are seducers, but only one becomes seduced himself. Vronsky sets out to make a conquest of Anna and does so, but Anna, in turn, makes one of him. Vronsky and Anna are partners in crime, for although only Vronsky is labeled a "murderer" by the narrator, the effects of the crime of passion can be seen in the impoverishment of Anna's character. Tolstoy alone of the six novelists holds his characters responsible to "eternal values,"[3] to Christian precepts. *Anna Karenin*, thus, is more than a novel of adultery; it is a novel of marriage, family, men and emotion, and forgiveness. This novel gives us the clearest basis of judgment, both in the Christian precepts that inform its creation and in the explicit commentaries of the narrator, and yet it is particularly in this novel that we are called to put judgment aside. We are meant to feel for all the characters, note the cautionary tale of Anna and Vronsky, and follow the model of Kitty and Levin.

In the other novels, judgment is not unequivocally assigned to any one character or group of characters. The authors are too committed to a realistic representation of life to simplistically and wholeheartedly blame the husband, wife, lover, or society for the adultery. All, to varying degrees, have their share of the blame, though the adulteresses, with the exception of Emma Bovary, bear the least censure. Sinclair notes that it is characteristic of the novels of adultery that "they do not provide any false catharsis, any illusion that the problem has been solved, dealt with, made to go away" (185). Flaubert and Queirós, in particular, do not portray any solutions in the form of successful marriages or noble characters. Sinclair argues that Flaubert, for one, forces his reader "to an appreciation that love is not ideal, nor marriages likely to be happy" (185–186). An acceptance of this "truth" may induce readers (particularly female ones) to *work* toward a successful marriage, to abandon their idealizations of love and marriage, motherhood and high society, and see what is there to be seen. In the cases of Emma and Luísa, in *Madame Bovary* and *O primo Basílio*, the very love that they seek in adultery is harbored in the breasts of their unambitious, boring husbands. Even though the nineteenth-century novel of adultery is not didactic at heart, it nevertheless serves a cautionary purpose. As Peter Gay asserts, "For all its flirting with illicit experiences, much nineteenth-century fiction functioned as a prudent warning against the perils of precipitous infatuations, unsuitable alliances, marital irregularities."[4] He mentions as examples Tolstoy's *Anna Karenin*, George Eliot's *Middlemarch*, and Thackeray's *Vanity Fair*. Certainly, *Anna Karenin*, *La Regenta*, *O primo Basílio*, and *Madame Bovary* all serve to warn their readers against "precipitous infatuations," for not one celebrates adultery, not even as a means of revolt and free expression. In all, adultery is shown to cause suffering and disgrace to the husband, wife, and children. Only the lovers, already dear members of society proper, escape, as do the judge and jury in these novels: society itself.

The wives' preoccupation with adultery comes from their reading material and the theater that they attend—from fictionalized accounts; however, the further attraction of adultery for some (most notably Emma and Luísa) is that it is an activity associated with the upper class. Thus, it gains impetus and desirability from Emma and Luísa's materialism and imitation of their "betters." According to a *ressentiment* theory of ethics, the bourgeois established virtues of thriftiness and chastity out of repressed envy of the aristocracy. Emma and Luísa manifest the secret cravings, purportedly of all bourgeois housewives, for the wealth, status, and lack of restraint of the upper class, values that dehumanize them because of their slavish devotion to conform to high fashion—even to the extent of deceit and infidelity. In contrast, the other wives, Anna Karenin, Ana Ozores, Effi Briest, and Edna Pontellier, already enjoy the life of a wealthy, more privileged upper class. They have all they want materially and circulate among the elite of their respective societies; hence, materialism is not portrayed as one of their failings. Anna Karenin, Ana Ozores, and Edna Pontellier are stronger figures than the puppet-like Luísa, the passive-aggressive Emma Bovary, and the childlike Effi Briest because they are respected women with artistic and transcendental urges and lead rather than follow and, most importantly, because they struggle against their impulses to deviate from accepted codes of behavior. Effi likewise has the artistic sensibility of the others, but she is more earthy than transcendental, and she never struggles against her desires. As her mother notes, "She's [Effi's] fond of letting herself drift and if the current is going right, then so is she, too. She's not one for struggling or resisting" (198). In the end, she does not resist her fate; she is as resigned to it as her creator is to his at the ripe age of 75, the age at which he wrote *Effi Briest*. Anna, Ana, Effi, and Edna all long for emotional fulfillment, yet their consciences will not let them fully enjoy it when they think they have found it. They are nobler, thus, not solely on the basis of their more elevated class, but because of the effect that deception has upon their characters. They cannot completely disregard their responsibility to their children, their husbands, themselves, and/or divine precepts.

As late as the nineteenth century, society still judged a woman's honor in terms of her chastity. There can be no justification in the eyes of society for the woman's crime of infidelity. The lover, consequently, is never punished, only the woman, for the lover remains a scintillating addition to any soirée. The power of society is in its exclusiveness; thus, when an adulteress is identified in bourgeois society or refuses to play the game of secrecy in the aristocracy, the punishment of society is ostracization. We see this punishment best in *Anna Karenin, La Regenta,* and *Effi Briest,* for only in these cases do the women live the exposure of their crime. Emma Bovary commits suicide before her household mismanagement (a failing almost as grave as adultery in bourgeois society) becomes public knowledge; thus, she is never excluded from Yonville society, yet her daughter receives her mother's punishment, for Homais no longer allows his children to play with Berthe. Ana Ozores in *La Regenta* knows very well what it is like to suffer for the ill repute of one's mother. Her mother was a seamstress and purported dancer, and so Ana is born with her mother's class, occupation, and reputation as stigma of her own. The children of Anna Karenin, Emma Bovary, Effi Briest, and Edna Pontellier will bear similar stains upon their honor because of the sins of their mothers. The presence of such innocent victims in the nineteenth-century novel of adultery complicates a justification of the wife's adultery by asserting that the woman's adultery is a sign of her revolt, a cry for freedom and personal fulfillment, for such personal fulfillment is gained only at the expense of trampling the little lives. In addition, the wives of the nineteenth century would not have had the discourse for rebellion. As Martin Swales asserts with regard to Fontane's characters, they "are ill equipped to be rebels: and this is because they lack the alternative cognition—and discourse—that could make such rebellion possible. The inner life—and this is part of Fontane's shattering modesty—is not, and cannot be, insulated from the corporate realm in which it lives, moves, and has its being" (78). The "woman question," as it is termed, was certainly circulating throughout Europe in the nineteenth century, given impetus by John Stuart Mill's essay "The Subjection of Women" (1869), which was widely translated; however, our protagonists in these novels of adultery are not educated in the discourse of the woman question. They have received the typically paltry education in domestic chores, performative arts, and religion, nor do they attend fashionable soirées where progressive ideas on the right to equality with their husbands or protection from the law might have been discussed, nor do any of their confidantes demonstrate that they have been versed in these seminal ideas. The Napoleonic Code and its like prevailed over most of Europe until the very twilight of the century. The discourse of rebellion was simply not available to our protagonists, but it has affected the discourse of the nineteenth-century novel of adultery in that the adulteresses are not to blame for the immoral and hypocritical climate of their milieu or their ignorance in the ways of the world.

Virginia Woolf in *A Room of One's Own* concedes that it would have been impossible for a woman of Shakespeare's day to have written as Shakespeare, yet she later goes on to say that Jane Austen shares a very remarkable attribute with Shakespeare, which is that "it was the nature of Jane Austen not to want what she had not" (68). Both the novelist and the poet/playwright have left us compositions "without hate, without bitterness, without fear, without protest, without preaching" (68). They let the stories tell themselves; any personal agenda from their own life experiences is notably absent. With the exception of Fontane, whose outstanding characteristics are his tolerance and resignation, the same cannot be said of our writers here. Tolstoy preaches, and Clarín, Chopin, Flaubert, and Queirós protest, with varying degrees of bitterness, against the ills of adultery, materialism, religion, positivist science, and the nature of society. The attack upon society is most bitter, while the adulterous wives who do want what they do not have are excused their failings because of the prevalent naturalist philosophy, a philosophy criticized by Scheler since it defends a person by pointing out his "humanity," the lowest, most animal-like aspects of the species, common to all (*Ressentiment* 123). According to Scheler, Naturalists "stoop" to man as a natural being out of *ressentiment* towards God and more positive, spiritual values that are not inherent in the species (*Ressentiment* 122–123). It is typical of men laboring under some form of *ressentiment* to tear down without replacing, which is what we find in the works of Clarín, Flaubert, and Queirós, who tear down society and all it holds dear and their protagonists, to some extent, without establishing positive values in their stead. As particularly Fontane suggests, we must somehow find a way to balance the needs of society against the needs of the individual. The realist novel of adultery captures the problem; it is for the readers to find the solution. An answer is suggested by the realist method itself, which is to see through clear glass what is there to be seen and represent it precisely as one sees it, without embellishment. Do not demand more romance than God has put into life and desire only what you already have.

NOTES

1. Effi ostensibly dies of tuberculosis, according to her symptoms; however, her death reflects the point that she has reached in life—resignation, a quieting of the will-to-live.

2. Peter Gay in *The Tender Passion* identifies this as the naturalists' "doctrine of Fatalism," that one's "illicit passions are one's fate and not one's fault" (167).

3. The term is Max Scheler's, which he uses to denote feelings and emotions that have objective validity for all people in every age. See his *Ressentiment* for a further discussion of eternal values.

4. *The Tender Passion*, 151.

Bibliography

LITERARY TEXTS, CRITICISM, AND THEORY

Adelman, Gary. Anna Karenina: *The Bitterness of Ecstasy*. Boston: Twayne, 1990.

Alas, Leopoldo. *La Regenta*. Intro. Sergio Beser. Ed. José Luis Gómez. Barcelona: Planeta, 1989.

Armstrong, Judith. *The Novel of Adultery*. London: Macmillan, 1976.

Bambrough, Renford. "Ounces of Example: Henry James, Philosopher." In *Realism in European Literature*. Ed. Nicholas Boyle and Martin Swales. Cambridge: Cambridge University Press, 1986.

Bance, Alan. *Theodor Fontane: The Major Novels*. Cambridge: Cambridge University Press, 1982.

Bécarud, Jean. "*La Regenta* de 'Clarín' y la Restauración." *De La Regenta al 'Opus Dei.'* Madrid: Taurus, 1977. 11–30.

Bloom, Harold, ed. *Leo Tolstoy's* Anna Karenina. New York: Chelsea House, 1987.

Boccaccio, Giovanni. *The Decameron*. Trans. G. H. McWilliam. 2nd ed. New York: Penguin Books, 1995.

Booth, Wayne C. *The Rhetoric of Fiction*. 2nd ed. Chicago: University of Chicago Press, 1983.

Boyle, Nicholas and Martin Swales, eds. *Realism in European Literature: Essays in Honour of J. P. Stern*. Cambridge: Cambridge University Press, 1986.

Cather, Willa. "From the Pittsburgh *Leader*." In *The Awakening*. By Kate Chopin. Ed. Margaret Culley. New York: Norton, 1976. 153–155.

Chopin, Kate. *The Awakening*. Ed. Margaret Culley. New York: Norton, 1976.

Christ, Carol P. *Diving Deep and Surfacing: Women Writers on Spiritual Quest*. 2nd ed. Boston: Beacon Press, 1986.

Ciplijauskaité, Biruté. *La mujer insatisfecha: El adulterio en la novela realista*. Barlona: Edhasa, 1984.

Coffey, Mary Louise. *Feminine Resistance in the Nineteenth-Century Novel of Adultery*. Chapel Hill: University of North Carolina Press, 1989.

Cohn, Dorrit. *Transparent Minds: Narrative Modes for Presenting Consciousness in Fiction*. Princeton, New Jersey: Princeton University Press, 1978.

Coleman, Alexander. *Eça de Queirós and European Realism*. New York: New York University Press, 1980.
Collas, Ion K. Madame Bovary: *A Psychoanalytical Reading*. Geneva: Librairie Droz, 1985.
Culley, Maragaret. "Edna Pontellier: 'A Solitary Soul.'" In *The Awakening*. By Kate Chopin. Ed. Margaret Culley. New York: Norton, 1976. 224–228.
Dorsett, Heide K. "Fontane's Development of the New Woman in the Novels *Frau Jenny Treibel* and *Effi Briest*." M.A. Thesis, University of Wyoming Laramie, 1990.
Durand, Frank. "Characterization in *La Regenta* de Clarín: Point of View and Theme." *Bulletin of Hispanic Studies* 41 (1964): 86–100.
Emmitt, Helen V. "Drowned in a Willing Sea: Freedom and Drowning in Eliot, Chopin, and Drabble." *Tulsa Studies in Women's Literature* 12.2 (1993): 315–333.
Flaubert, Gustave. *Madame Bovary*. Intro. Bernard Ajac. Paris: Flammarion, 1986.
Fontane, Theodor. *Effi Briest*. Trans. Douglas Parmée. New York: Penguin, 1967.
Forster, E. M. *Aspects of the Novel*. New York: Harcourt Brace Jovanovich, 1985 (1927).
Friedman, Norman. *Form and Meaning in Fiction*. Athens: University of Georgia Press, 1975.
Furst, Lillian R. *Fictions of Romantic Irony*. Cambridge: Harvard University Press, 1984.
———. *Realism*. New York: Longman, 1992.
———. Lecture. University of North Carolina. Chapel Hill, North Carolina. Spring 1992.
Garland, Henry. *The Berlin Novels of Theodor Fontane*. Oxford: Clarendon Press, 1980.
Gaultier, Jules de. *Bovarysm*. Trans. Gerald M. Spring. New York: Philosophical Library, 1970.
Genette, Gerard. *Narrative Discourse: An Essay in Method*. Trans. Jane E. Lewin. Ithaca, New York: Cornell University Press, 1980.
Greenberg, Valerie D. "Resistance of *Effi Briest*: An (Un)told Tale." *PMLA* 103 (1988): 770–782.
Haig, Stirling. *The Madame Bovary Blues: The Pursuit of Illusion in Nineteenth-Century French Fiction*. Baton Rouge: Lousiana State University Press, 1987.
Hess, Josefina Acosta de. *Galdós y la novela de adulterio*. Madrid: Editorial Pliegos, 1988.
James, Henry. *The Art of the Novel*. Intro. Richard P. Blackmur. New York: Scribner's, 1962.
Jones, George Fenwick. *Honor in German Literature*. University of Chapel Hill Studies in the Germanic Languages No. 25. Chapel Hill, North Carolina: Chapel Hill University Press, 1959.
Kaplan, Louise J. *Female Perversions: The Temptations of Emma Bovary*. New York: Doubleday, 1991.
La Capra, Dominick. *Madame Bovary on Trial*. Ithaca, NY: Cornell University Press, 1992.
Lubbock, Percy. *The Craft of Fiction*. New York: The Viking Press, 1957 (1921).
Martin, Ronald E. *American Literature and the Universe of Force*. Durham, North Carolina: Duke University Press, 1981.
Melón Ruiz de Gordejuela, Santiago. "'Clarín' y el bovarysmo." *Archivum* 2 (1952): 69–87.
Mendonça, Antônio Sérgio. *Bovarysmo & Paixão*. Porto Alegre: Centro de Estudos Lacaneanos, 1992.
Meyer, Priscilla. "*Anna Karenina*: Tolstoy's Polemic with *Madame Bovary*." *The Russian Review* 54.2 (1995): 243–260.
Miller, D. A. *Narrative and Its Discontents: Problems of Closure in the Traditional Novel*. Princeton, New Jersey: Princeton University Press, 1981.

Bibliography

Miller, Leslie L. "Fontane's *Effi Briest*: Innstetten's Decision: In Defense of the Gentleman." *German Studies Review*. 4 Oct. 3 (1981): 383–402.

Miller, Phillip B., ed. *An Abyss Deep Enough: Letters of Heinrich von Kleist*. New York: Dutton, 1982.

Moniz, Edmundo. *As mulheres proibidas: O incesto em Eça de Queirós*. Rio de Janeiro: José Olympio, 1993.

Ontañón de Lope, Paciencia. *Ana Ozores,* La Regenta*: Estudio Psicoanalítico*. Mexico City: Universidad Nacional Autónoma de México, 1987.

Pattison, Walter T. *El naturalismo español: Historia externa de un movimiento literario*. Madrid: Editorial Gredos, S.A., 1965.

Prince, Gerald. *Narratology: The Form and Functioning of Narrative*. Berlin: Mouton, 1982.

Queirós, Eça de. *O primo Basílio*. Lisboa: Publicações Dom Quixote, 1990.

Radcliffe, Stanley. *Fontane: Effi Briest. Critical Guides to German Texts*. Ed. Martin Swales. Wolfeboro, NH: Grant and Cutler, 1986.

Ramazani, Vaheed K. *The Free Indirect Mode: Flaubert and the Poetics of Irony*. Charlottesville: University Press of Virginia, 1988.

Robinson, A. R. *Theodor Fontane: An Introduction to the Man and His Work*. Cardiff: University of Wales Press, 1976.

Sabiston, Elizabeth Jean. *The Prison of Womanhood: Four Provincial Heroines in Nineteenth Century Fiction*. Houndmills, Bassingstoke, Hampshire: Macmillan, 1987.

Schyfter, Sara E. "La loca, la tonta, la literata: Woman's Destiny in Clarín's *La Regenta*." *Theory and Practice of Feminist Criticism*. Ed. Gabriela Mora & Karen S. Van Hooft. Ypsilanti, MI: Bilingual Press, 1982. 229–241.

Sherrington, R. J. *Three Novels by Flaubert: A Study of Techniques*. Oxford: Clarendon Press, 1970.

Sinclair, Alison. *The Deceived Husbands: A Kleinian Approach to the Literature of Infidelity*. Oxford: Clarendon, 1993.

Sobejano, Gonzalo. "Leopoldo Alas, la novela naturalista y la imaginación moral de *La Regenta*. In *La Regenta*. By Leopoldo Alas. Barcelona: Noguer, 1976. 11–58.

Sontag, Susan. *Illness as Metaphor*. New York: Vintage, 1979.

Stern, J. P. "Realism and Tolerance: Theodor Fontane." In *Re-interpretations*. London: Thames and Hudson, 1964. 301–347.

Swales, Martin. "The Problem of Nineteenth-Century German Realism." In *Realism in European Literature*. Cambridge: Cambridge University Press, 1986. 68-84.

Tanner, Tony. *Adultery in the Novel: Contract and Transgression*. Baltimore: Johns Hopkins University Press, 1979.

Tolstoy, Leon Ilich. *Anna Karenin*. Trans. Rosemary Edmonds. New York: Penguin Books, 1978 [1954].

Ullman, Stephen. "Reported Speech and Internal Monologue in Flaubert." In *Style in the French Novel*. Oxford: Basil Blackwell, 1964.

Valis, Noel Maureen. *The Decadent Vision in Leopoldo Alas: A Study of* La Regenta *and* Su Único Hijo. Baton Rouge: Lousiana State University Press, 1981.

Wansink, Susan. *Female Victims and Oppressors in Novels by Theodor Fontane and François Mauriac*. New York: Peter Lang, 1998.

Whitcomb, Curt. "Tolstoy's *Anna Karenina*." *The Explicator* 53 (1994): 50–54.

White, Nicholas and Naomi Segal, eds. *Scarlet Letters: Fictions of Adultery from Antiquity to the 1990s*. New York: St. Martin's Press, 1997.

Woolf, Virginia. *A Room of One's Own*. New York: Harcourt, 1989.

Zavala, Iris M. *Ideología y Política en la novela española del siglo XIX*. Salamanca: Anaya, 1971.

Zimmermann, Gisela. "The Civil Servant as Educator: *Effi Briest* and *Anna Karenina*." *The Modern Language Review* 90.4 October (1995): 817–829.
Zorrilla, Don José. *Don Juan Tenorio: Drama Religioso fantástico en dos partes*. Intro. N. B. Adams. New York: Alfred A. Knopf, 1929.

PHILOSOPHICAL WORKS

Bentham, Jeremy. *An Introduction to the Principles of Morals and Legislation*. Ed. J. H. Burns and H. L. A. Hart. London: Athlone Press, 1970.
Berdiaev, Nikolai. *The Destiny of Man*. Trans. Natalie Duddington. London: Geoffrey Bles, 1954.
———. *Solitude and Society*. Trans. George Reavey. Glasglow: Robert Maclehose, 1938.
Fuller, Margaret. *Woman in the Nineteenth Century and Other Writings*. Ed. Donna Dickenson. New York: Oxford University Press, 1994.
Kierkegaard, Søren. *Either/Or*. Ed. and trans. Howard V. Hong and Edna H. Hong. Princeton, New Jersey: Princeton University Press, 1987.
———. *Fear and Trembling*. Trans. Alastair Hannay. New York: Penguin Books, 1985.
Mill, John Stuart. *Auguste Comte and Positivism*. Ann Arbor: University of Michigan Press, 1961.
Nietzsche, Friedrich. *The Birth of Tragedy and The Genealogy of Morals*. Trans. Francis Golffing. New York: Doubleday Anchor Books, 1956.
———. *The Portable Nietzsche*. Trans. Walter Kaufmann. New York: Penguin, 1976.
———. *The Will to Power*. Trans. Walter Kaufmann and R. J. Hollingdale. Ed. Walter Kaufmann. New York: Vintage, 1968.
Scheler, Max. *The Nature of Sympathy*. Trans. Peter Heath. Intro. W. Stark. Hamden, CT: Archon Books, 1970.
———. *Ressentiment*. Trans. William W. Holdheim. Ed. Lewis Coser. New York: Schocken Books, 1972.
Schopenhauer, Arthur. *The World as Will and Representation*. Trans. E. F. J. Payne. Vols. 1 and 2. New York: Dover, 1969.
Tolstoy, Leo N. *What Is Art?* Trans. Aylmer Maude. Intro. Vincent Tomas. New York: Liberal Arts Press, 1960.

HISTORICAL AND SOCIOLOGICAL TEXTS

Acton, William. *Functions and Disorders of the Reproductive Organs*. London:Lindsay and Blakiston, 1984.
Álvarez, A. *The Savage God: A Study of Suicide*. New York: Random House, 1972.
Badinter, Elisabeth. *Mother Love: Myth and Reality*. Foreword Francine Du Plessix Gray. New York: Macmillan, 1981.
Balzac, Honoré. *The Physiology of Marriage*. Intro. Sharon Marcus. Baltimore: Johns Hopkins University Press, 1997.
Berdiaev, Nikolai. *The Bourgeois Mind and Other Essays*. Freeport, NY: Book for Libraries Press, 1966.
Bill, Valentine Tschebotarioff. *The Forgotten Class: The Russian Bourgeoisie from the Earliest Beginnings to 1900*. New York: Praeger, 1959.
Blackbourn, David and Geoff Eley. *The Peculiarities of German History: Bourgeois Society and Politics in Nineteenth-Century Germany*. New York: Oxford University Press, 1984.

Bibliography

Craig, Gordon A. *The Germans*. New York: Meridian, 1991.
da Costa, D. Antonio. *A mulher em Portugal*. Lisboa: Companhia Nacional Editora, 1892.
Cunningham, C. Willett. *Feminine Attitudes in the Nineteenth Century*. New York: Haskell House, 1973.
Ellis, Sarah Stickney. *The Daughters of England: Their Position in Society, Character, and Responsibilities*. London: J. and H. G. Langley, 1843.
———. *The Wives of England, Their Relative Duties, Domestic Influence, and Social Obligations*. London: J. and H. G. Langley, 1843.
Engels, Friedrich. "The Origins of the Family, Private Property, and the State." In *Karl Marx and Frederich Engels Selected Works in One Volume*. London: Lawrence and Wishart, 1968. 461–583.
Gay, Peter. *Education of the Senses*. Vol. 1 of *The Bourgeois Experience: Victoria to Freud*. New York: Oxford University Press, 1984.
———. *The Naked Heart*. New York: Norton, 1995.
———. *The Tender Passion*. New York: Oxford University Press, 1986.
Gilman, Charlotte Perkins. *Women and Economics: A Study of the Economic Relation between Men and Women as a Factor in Social Evolution*. Ed. Carl Degler. New York: Harper and Row, 1966.
Hartcup, Adeline. *Love and Marriage in the Great Country Houses*. London: Sidgwick and Jackson, 1984.
Hume, Leslie Parker, ed. *Victorian Women: A Documentary Account of Women's Lives in Nineteenth-Century England, France, and the United States*. Stanford, CA: Stanford University Press, 1981.
Langland, Elizabeth. *Nobody's Angels: Middle-Class Women and Domestic Ideology in Victorian Culture*. Ithaca, NY: Cornell University Press, 1995.
Marcus, Stephen. *The Other Victorians: A Study of Sexuality and Pornography in Mid-Nineteenth Century England*. NY: Basic Books, 1966.
Nash, Mary. *Mujer, familia y trabajo en España, 1875–1936*. Barcelona: Anthropos, Ed. del Hombre, 1983.
Ossowska, Maria. *Bourgeois Morality*. Trans. G. L. Campbell. New York: Routledge and Kegan Paul, 1986.
Payne, Stanley G. *A History of Spain and Portugal*. Madison: University of Wisconsin Press, 1973.
Pearsall, Ronald. *Public Purity, Private Shame: Victorian Sexual Hypocrisy Exposed*. Weidenfeld and Nicolson, 1976.
Pilbeam, Pamela M. *The Middle Classes in Europe: 1789–1914 France, Germany, Italy and Russia*. Chicago: Lyceum Books, 1990.
Pons, Anaclet y Justo Serna. *La ciudad extense: la burguesía comercial-financiera en la Valencia de mediados del XIX*. Valencia: Diputación de Valencia, 1992.
Ranulf, Svend. *Moral Indignation and Middle Class Psychology: A Sociological Study*. New York: Schocken Books, 1964.
Robertson, Priscilla. *An Experience of Women: Pattern and Change in Nineteenth Century Europe*. Philadelphia: Temple University Press, 1982.
Sheehan, James J. *German Liberalism in the Nineteenth Century*. Chicago: University of Chicago Press, 1978.
Smith, T. R., ed. *The Woman Question*. New York: Boni and Liveright, 1918.
Stanton, T. R., ed. *The Woman Question in Europe. A Series of Original Essays*. Source Book Press, 1970.
Treitschke, Heinrich. *History of Germany in the Nineteenth Century*. Ed. Gordon A. Craig. Chicago: University of Chicago Press, 1975.

Trudgill, Eric. *Madonnas and Magdalens: The Origins and Development of Victorian Sexual Attitudes.* New York: Holmes and Meier, 1976.

Walters, Ronald G. *Primers for Prudery: Sexual Advice to Victorian America.* Englewood Cliffs, NJ: Prentice-Hall, 1974.

Ziff, Larzer. *The American 1890s: Life and Times of a Lost Generation.* New York: Viking, 1966.

Index

Abyss, 45, 54, 69, 99
Álvaro, Don, 73–74
Ana: as artist, 52, 55n; false mysticisim, 96, 99; and reading, 51–52, 92–93; romantic imagination, 53–54, 92–93, 96. *See also* Class; Women
Anna: and the imagination, 31; milieu, 84–85; and motherhood, 33–34; and reading, 30; and suicide, 34. *See also* Class; Women
Anna Karenin, 6; focalization in, 18; judgment in, 82–91; milieu, 88; and voice, 12–14
Arobin, 76
Awakening, The: focalization in, 17; Nature, 107; society, 108; and solitude, 109–110; and voice 14–16, 109

Basílio, 72–73, 119
Booth, Wayne, xvii, 81
Bourgeoisie. *See* Middle class; *Ressentiment* ethics
Bovarism, 48, 49, 55n
Bovary, Charles, 58–62; education of, 58–59
Bovary, Emma: death of, 28, 125–126; education of, 2; and materialism, 25–27, 123–124; as mother, 28; reading, 122; romantic imagination, 23–25, 26, 125. *See also* Class; Women
Briest, Effi: and ambition, 37, 101; and death, 38–39; disobedience, 5; and reading, 38; resignation, 132; romantic imagination, 35; and suicide, 34; youth, 36, 101. *See also* Class; Women
Briest, Frau von, 101–102

Children, as touchstones, 32, 89, 127
Class, of adulteresses, xii, 3, 5, 29, 50–51
Cohn, Dorritt, xv–xvi
Crampas, 76–77, 105

Determinism, 84–86, 90, 91, 92, 99, 127, 130
Dueling, 67, 103

Edna: childlike behaviors, 110–111; defiance, 39; motherhood, 44–45; and music, 39–40; and the sea, 40–41, 107, 111; sensuality, 110; sentimentalism, 39, 112; and suicide, 41, 44–45, 107, 109, 111–113; transformation, 42–43. *See also* Class; Women
Effi. *See* Briest, Effi
Effi Briest, 6; chance, 106; focalization in, 18; honor, 67, 104, 105; modal terms, 103; and voice, 9–11. *See also* Tuberculosis
Eternal values, 131, 134n

Fermín, Don, 78, 94. *See also Ressentiment* ethics
Flaubert, Gustave, style, 81, 119–120, 131
Focalization, xvii, 16, 130
Free, indirect discourse, 113, 119–120. *See also* Narrated monologue

Gay, Peter, xi, xix, 132
Genette, Gerard, xv, xvi–xvii, 16

Honor, 100, 106, 118, 132–133; in *Anna Karenin*, 83; in *Effi Briest*, 67, 100, 104, 105; in *La Regenta*, 95–96; in Spanish literature, 65–66

Innstetten, 67–68, 100–101, 102–103

Jorge, 62–64

Karenin, 68–70; and forgiveness, 83

Landadel, 36
Lebrun, Robert, 77
Luisa: bovarism, 48; death of, 118; education of, 46; impulses, 114, 116; insights, 116–117; milieu, 113, 114; reading, 115; romantic imagination, 48, 116; sensuousness and materialism, 115; townspeople, 118–119. *See also* Class; Women

Madame Bovary: dramatized narrator, 7; excised episode, 22; and voice, 6, 7–8
Middle class, xii; in Portugal, 3; in Russia, 4; in Germany, 4
Miller, D. A., xi, 100
Modal terms, xvi, 81, 103
Motherhood, 23, 127; ideal of, 83–84; Dolly Oblonsky, 82–83

Narrated monologue, xv–xvi
Narrative, iterative, 15
Narrators: dramatized/undramatized, xvii; in *Madame Bovary*, 120–121, 123
Nietzsche, Friedrich, and *ressentiment* ethics, xii–xiii
Nonnarratable, xi, 100

Ossowska, Maria, xiv

Pontellier, Mr., 70–71
Positivist law, 106
Primo Basílio, O: focalization in, 17, 72; and voice, 8–9
Prince, Gerald, xvi
Psychonarration, xv–xvi

Quoted monologue, xv

Ranulf, Svend, xiv
Regenta, La, 6, 93–94; and the church, 95, 99; and *Don Juan Tenorio*, 96–98; focalization in, 18; judgment in, 91–100; natural law, 91, 95–96; and voice, 11–12. *See also* Determinism
Ressentiment ethics, xii–xiii, 88, 114, 132, 134; of Don Fermín, xiii, xv, 51, 67, 78; in *O primo Basílio*, 118
Restoration, 2
Rodolphe, 71–72

Scheler, Max, xiii, 134; eternal values, 131, 134n

Tanner, Tony, xi
Tenorio, el, 94, 98
Tuberculosis, disease metaphor, 35, 104–105

Vetusta, critique of, 93–94
Víctor, Don, 64–67; and Golden Age drama, 95–96
Vronsky, 74–76, 131; suicide, 86; as young Werther, 86

Will-to-live, 29, 31, 32, 69, 84, 86, 87
Woman question, 133
Women: class, xii; education of, 1–2, 4, 5; life options, xii, 130; in Portugal, 3; in Spain, 2; status of, in France, 1, 125; status of, in Germany, 5

About the Author

MARIA R. RIPPON is Visiting Assistant Professor of Spanish at the Citadel, the Military College of South Carolina.